GET SET FOR SCHOOL®

Readiness & Writing

Pre-K Teacher's Guide

GET SET FOR SCHOOL®

NAME ___________________

My First School Book

Coloring, Drawing, Counting, Writing, and School Readiness

COW BOOT FISH CAT DUCK

8001 MacArthur Blvd
Cabin John, MD 20818
301.263.2700
getsetforschool.com

Authors: Jan Z. Olsen, OTR and Emily F. Knapton, M.Ed., OTR/L
Illustrator: Jan Z. Olsen, OTR

Fifth Edition

ISBN: 978-1-934825-54-9

123456789Webcrafters161514

Printed in the U.S.A

The Get Set for School® program and teacher's guides are intuitive and packed with resources and information. Nevertheless, we are constantly developing new ideas and content that make the program easier to teach and to learn.

To make this information available to you, we created a password-protected section of our website exclusively for users of this teacher's guide. Here you'll find new tips, in-depth information about topics described in this guide, other instructional resources, and material you can share with students, parents, and other educators.

Just go to **getsetforschool.com/click** and enter your passcode: **TGRW12**

Enjoy the online resources, and send us any input that you think would be helpful to others: janolsen@getsetforschool.com

WELCOME

Welcome to the Get Set for School® Readiness & Writing program, created for you and your Pre-K children.

The program suits a wide range of children and adapts to their changing needs as they grow. The Readiness & Writing program acknowledges what all great educators know and research supports: that learning needs to be joyful, child-friendly, and active. We believe in meeting children where they are and giving them the experiences that will enable them to blossom.

We build skills in delightful ways, but also carefully, deliberately, and one step at a time. We've analyzed the skills that children need for kindergarten, and then planned a curriculum that builds those skills developmentally, through play, music, activities, and hands-on materials.

This Pre-K teacher's guide will help you select just the right tools and teaching strategies. We created activities so that children of different ability levels may participate successfully. We know that you want children to have a positive, play filled early school experience even as they prepare for kindergarten.

We support teacher guided learning. Children need teachers who model, sing, and teach the skills and habits needed for school. We believe you'll enjoy using our program to help children develop important foundation skills.

Get Set for School is an award-winning curriculum, but it needs you to bring it to life. You choose the activities, and set the pace that's just right for your children. We hope you'll take advantage of this guide, our training workshops, and our free online resources. We are delighted to share this curriculum with you.

Emily F. Knapton   Jan Z. Olsen

Emily F. Knapton, M.Ed., OTR/L   Jan Z. Olsen, OTR

P.S. As you get further along and see this icon for A Click Away, be sure to visit **www.getsetforschool.com/click** for more program information. You'll also enjoy viewing our online video lessons. When you see this ▶ in a lesson, be sure to visit our virtual classroom.

(The Children's Curriculum Winner from the Association of Educational Publishers and The Teacher's Choice™ Award from *Learning® Magazine*)

A	B	C	D	E	F	G	H	I	J	K	L	M	N
153	147	133	145	123	121	139	125	127	143	151	119	157	159

1 - Introduction

21 - Readiness

33 - Drawing

47 - Alphabet Knowledge

63 - Colors & Coloring

83 - Pre-Writing

WOOD PIECE PLAY

HANDS-ON LETTER PLAY

109 - Writing

173 - Counting & Numbers

199 - Resources

Get to Know Get Set for School®

Get Set for School Pre-K Philosophies and Principles

We understand that Pre-K children learn through movement and participation. They need explicit modeled instruction. They also need playful learning opportunities to explore and internalize new ideas. Our playful approach is at the heart of our success. Young children are not ready to sit still and focus for long periods of time. They learn best when they move, manipulate objects, build, sing, draw, and participate in dramatic play. Pre-K children need instruction tailored to their different styles of learning. You need tools to meet these needs. Our unique Pre-K programs make teaching easy and rewarding for you in many ways:

- Research based approach that addresses different learning styles
- Developmental progression that builds on what children already know
- Friendly voice that connects with children
- Developmentally appropriate lessons that break difficult concepts into simple tasks
- Hands-on multisensory materials that entice children to learn

What and How We Teach

Pre-K is a time of rapid growth and development. It is a time of preparation for kindergarten and for future success in school and in life. To achieve, children need to be eager, able, and social in their learning.

Eager – Children learn naturally through everyday experiences with people, places, and things. They are eager to learn, explore, and experiment. They are born imitators and scientists who thrive on active hands-on interaction with the physical world. They learn through play and through physical and sensory experiences. The materials throughout the learning space affect how children feel, what they do, and how they learn.

Able – Children need to learn the core competencies of the culture – how to read, write, and do math. We actively and deliberately fill the day with what we want children to learn. They build familiarity and competency with music, play, vocabulary, and with hands-on materials and lessons. Materials and lessons are flexible so that you can teach in a developmental sequence from the simplest to the more complex tasks. This approach ensures that children develop basic readiness skills so that they are prepared for school success.

Social – Pre-K is social and challenging. Children are learning how to work and play with others. We use music and hands-on materials to encourage inclusive participation and the development of social, physical, language, math, and early readiness skills. We read, draw, sing, build, and dance with children, enticing them to join us on a learning adventure. Our materials also encourage family involvement to continue learning at home. Many activities have take-home components to encourage children to form connections between learning in school and home situations.

A Developmental Curriculum

Pre-K children will enter your classroom with different and continually evolving abilities. To meet the needs of Pre-K children, a curriculum must be accessible at all points within this wide spectrum of needs and skills. It should invite participation, build a base of understanding, and challenge children to grow. This curriculum supports you in meeting the wide ranging needs of children throughout the year.

We teach in developmental order by starting at the level that does not assume prior knowledge or competency. We also enable children to excel by respecting their present level of development and building from there. Children need to learn certain skills explicitly. In Pre-K, we focus on developing social and school behaviors—how to play and participate in a school environment. We also focus on preparing children for school. The school world is the world of symbols, where letter and numbers take on meaning and are used for reading, writing, and math. As they enter that world, we teach them letters and numbers, what they are and how we use them. They learn that we read and write from top to bottom and left to right. They learn how to hold crayons and form letters and numbers that are right-side up and made correctly. We give them their first tools for learning.

Supporting Parents and Teachers

Parents are a child's first and most important teachers. Our materials encourage family involvement to continue learning activities at home. Lessons sometimes ask families to lend items from home to personalize activities. Many of the activities have take-home components to encourage children to form connections between home and school.

Some of our materials are also designed to be taken home and shared with families as children practice skills learned in school. This is a great opportunity for children to show their families what they are learning and ask for help and participation.

Get Set for School makes a seamless transition between home and school. We recognize that Pre-K often is a child's first experience away from home. Our curriculum encourages children to share family experiences, while acknowledging and celebrating cultural differences.

Three Core Learning Areas

Get Set for School® is a curriculum that prepares young learners for school with three complete programs: Readiness & Writing, Language & Literacy, and Numbers & Math. These programs complement and expand your existing Pre-K program. You engage children with the following strategies:

- Creative lessons that enable children of different abilities to achieve
- Child friendly language and activities
- Developmentally based teaching that works at every level
- Hands-on approach that promotes active participation

Readiness & Writing

This program is the core of Get Set for School. The handwriting component is based on more than 25 years of success with Handwriting Without Tears®. Writing requires many skills that are essential for school: physical, language, cognitive, social, and perceptual. Our Readiness & Writing program uses music, movement, and multisensory manipulatives to teach all the core readiness skills including crayon grip, letter and number recognition, number and capital letter formation, and body awareness.

Language & Literacy

This program is a wonderful complement to our Get Set for School Readiness & Writing program. We use dramatic play, singing, finger plays, manipulatives, and movement to teach children to rhyme, clap syllables, make and break compound words, and identify sounds. We expose children to rich literature to foster a love of reading, build vocabulary, and learn how books work. Children learn facts from informational text. They learn to use new words and develop oral language skills by listening, retelling, and narrating stories. They also learn that there is meaning in the words they say as they watch teachers write what they say.

Numbers & Math

This program is a natural extension of our Get Set for School readiness program and helps children build number sense right from the start. We use manipulatives, music, and rhymes, to teach counting, comparisons, spatial awareness, patterning, sequencing, matching, sorting, problem solving, and even Pre-K geometry skills. Lessons give children time to play with real objects and test their ideas so that math becomes real and meaningful. Children also develop oral language that helps them learn about and express math concepts.

Using Your Teacher's Guide

Are you concerned about how you keep Pre-K playful and fun as you meet Pre-K standards? Did you know that seat work and worksheets can be detrimental to young children? We believe that Pre-K children can meet high expectations with the right balance of exposure, play experiences, and explicit teaching. This guide will help you do just that for your children.

You may already be familiar with our award-winning *Pre-K Teacher's Guide* and *Get Set for School,* our child friendly activity book. In 2011, we added two new programs: Language & Literacy and Numbers & Math to our Pre-K curriculum. These new programs have the same high quality you expect from us. (One of the math products is already an award winner.) The third program is the one you may know: our Readiness & Writing program. We've created new editions for that.

This the 2012 *Readiness & Writing Pre-K Teacher's Guide* (formerly, *Pre-K Teacher's Guide*). It's been updated and reorganized. The student book is also a new edition. The changes are fewer, but it has a new name, *My First School Book.*

We'd like to tell you about this guide, what you'll find, and how to use it. The guide begins with an Introduction that tells you about Get Set for School®, our curriculum, philosophy, products, and lessons plans. At the back of the book are important resources, including an informal assessment "Check Readiness," as well as benchmarks, Scope & Sequence, teaching guidelines, and index.

At the core is our developmentally based program, a guide to developing key readiness skills or domains. Although the program progresses, you can use Favorite Activities all year long to meet children's needs wherever they are.

1. Readiness
2. Drawing
3. Alphabet Knowledge
4. Colors & Coloring
5. Pre-Writing
6. Writing
7. Counting & Numbers

Readiness

Read this first. Here is the information you need about child development. Our backgrounds and years of experience in occupational therapy and teaching inform the work we do and the way we teach. We consider the social aspect of learning and encourage those skills. We help children develop motor skills, learn to hold a crayon for drawing, to color, and write.

Drawing

Children are artists. They're wild and joyful expressionists. They're also deliberate realists. They can do it all. Learn how drawing skills develop. Then learn about Mat Man®, a storybook character that children build on the floor. This activity is wildly popular and effective. It's known for enabling children of all abilities to draw Mat Man and anyone else. *My First School Book* and *My Book* are two books that also invite and encourage drawing.

Alphabet Knowledge

This is everything about letters that isn't writing. It's singing, speaking, matching, sorting, and naming. These activities are not dependent on the child's ability to hold or manage a writing tool. They're still active and hands-on. Many have a social component, as children notice letters in their names and in their friends' names. You'll build your children's letter naming repertoire, so that they'll go to kindergarten recognizing and naming all the letters: capital and lowercase.

Colors & Coloring

We have developed coloring pages and crayons that captivate children and make coloring fun. Our Flip Crayons® have two colors, one at each end. Flipping or turning the crayons is fun and promotes fine motor skills. *My First School Book* begins with basic crayon skills, just aim and scribble, and moves to fill-in coloring. Children learn 10 colors and have opportunities to try them all with simple pictures and shapes. *My Book,* a personal book, encourages coloring too.

Pre-Writing

We're known for preparing children for writing success. We use Wood Piece Play to develop vocabulary, concepts, motor and social skills. It's fun to trade Big Lines and Little Curves, to sing the "Wood Piece Pokey" and to reach into a box to find...a Big Curve—and other pieces. These activities have a strong social and class behavior component. They're fun and inclusive, but they also teach children to attend to and respond to your teaching. Hands-On Letter Play is next, and children are taught letter formation with Wood Pieces, dough, magnetic stamps, and the Wet–Dry–Try slate activity. You have a wide range of multisensory ways to teach and review letter formation.

Writing

My First School Book helps you teach good habits from the very beginning. The book is organized developmentally so that children progress successfully. Teachers carefully guide children in the most important habits, holding the crayon correctly, using the helping hand, and starting letters at the top. Every kindergarten teacher is pleased when children arrive with good habits, especially starting letters at the top. Every lesson in the guide will show you how to teach, and how to support or challenge children according to their current stage. You also help children learn to write their names, first in all capitals and then in title case.

Counting & Numbers

The engaging pre-writing activities also work for numbers. Children learn counting and number concepts in so many ways with music, nursery rhymes, on bodies, with animals, and with many hands-on products. Read about *I Know My Numbers,* a set of 10 number booklets that children use at school and then take home to continue learning.

You'll easily find just what you're looking for in this newly organized edition. The information you need about each domain is presented first, and then the activities and lessons follow in the suggested teaching sequence.

Activity Design

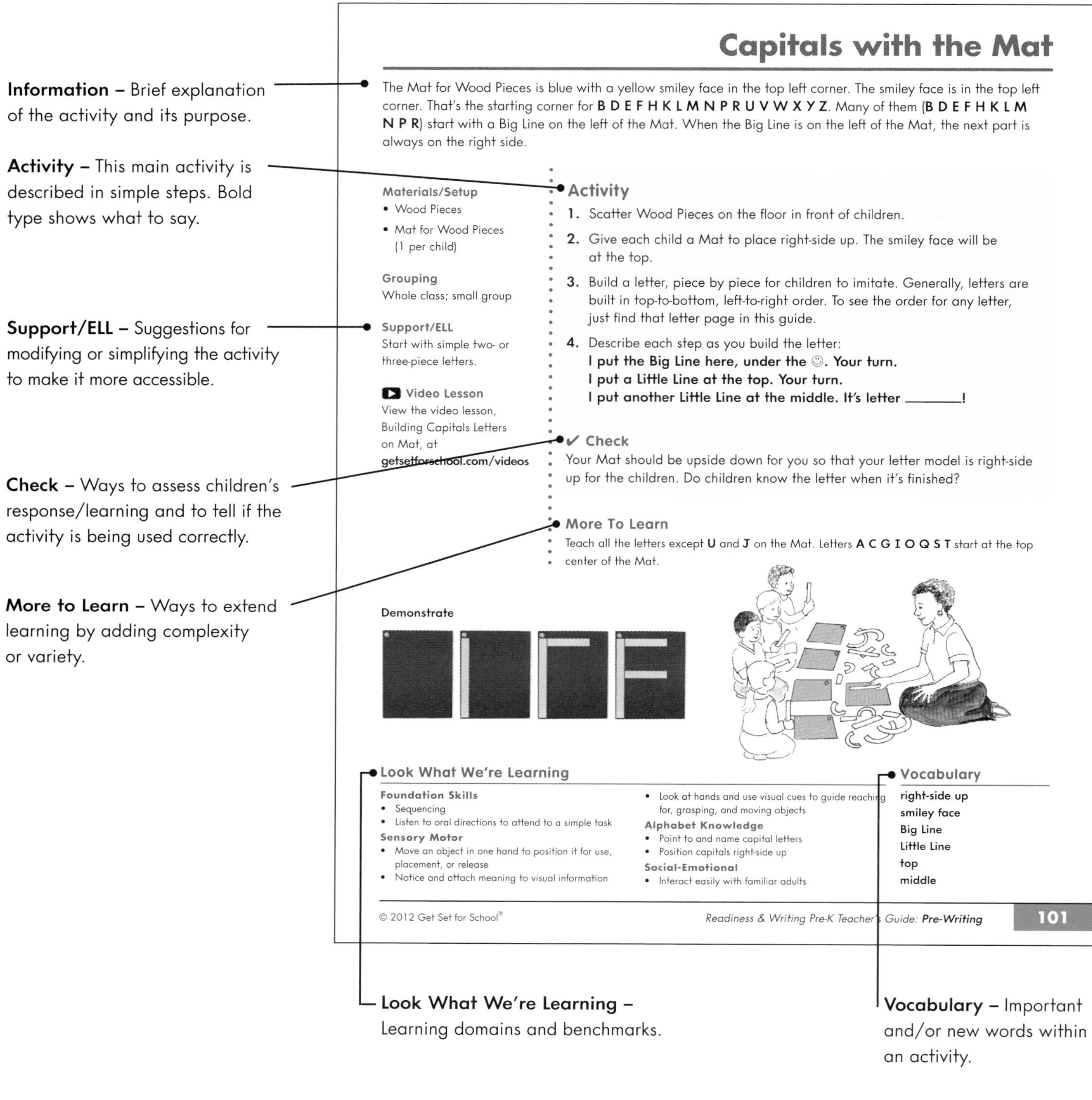

Information – Brief explanation of the activity and its purpose.

Activity – This main activity is described in simple steps. Bold type shows what to say.

Support/ELL – Suggestions for modifying or simplifying the activity to make it more accessible.

Check – Ways to assess children's response/learning and to tell if the activity is being used correctly.

More to Learn – Ways to extend learning by adding complexity or variety.

Look What We're Learning – Learning domains and benchmarks.

Vocabulary – Important and/or new words within an activity.

Capitals with the Mat

The Mat for Wood Pieces is blue with a yellow smiley face in the top left corner. The smiley face is in the top left corner. That's the starting corner for **B D E F H K L M N P R U V W X Y Z**. Many of them (**B D E F H K L M N P R**) start with a Big Line on the left of the Mat. When the Big Line is on the left of the Mat, the next part is always on the right side.

Materials/Setup
- Wood Pieces
- Mat for Wood Pieces (1 per child)

Grouping
Whole class; small group

Support/ELL
Start with simple two- or three-piece letters.

Video Lesson
View the video lesson, Building Capitals Letters on Mat, at **getsetforschool.com/videos**

Activity
1. Scatter Wood Pieces on the floor in front of children.
2. Give each child a Mat to place right-side up. The smiley face will be at the top.
3. Build a letter, piece by piece for children to imitate. Generally, letters are built in top-to-bottom, left-to-right order. To see the order for any letter, just find that letter page in this guide.
4. Describe each step as you build the letter:
   I put the Big Line here, under the ☺. Your turn.
   I put a Little Line at the top. Your turn.
   I put another Little Line at the middle. It's letter ______!

✔ Check
Your Mat should be upside down for you so that your letter model is right-side up for the children. Do children know the letter when it's finished?

More To Learn
Teach all the letters except **U** and **J** on the Mat. Letters **A C G I O Q S T** start at the top center of the Mat.

Demonstrate

Look What We're Learning

Foundation Skills
- Sequencing
- Listen to oral directions to attend to a simple task

Sensory Motor
- Move an object in one hand to position it for use, placement, or release
- Notice and attach meaning to visual information
- Look at hands and use visual cues to guide reaching for, grasping, and moving objects

Alphabet Knowledge
- Point to and name capital letters
- Position capitals right-side up

Social-Emotional
- Interact easily with familiar adults

Vocabulary
right-side up
smiley face
Big Line
Little Line
top
middle

Letter Lesson Heading – Letter is shown prominently at the top. Key words for teaching the letter are centered.

Activity – The letter lesson follows these steps:

Introduce the letter and the page.

Look and Learn – Find letter on page. Associate letter with word and picture.

Color and Draw – Color the pictures and add drawings.

Trace and Write – Crayon trace the letter with teacher direction.

Check – Ways to tell if correct writing habits are being developed.

Support/ELL – Suggestions for modifying or simplifying the activity to make it more accessible.

More to Learn – Ways to extend learning by adding complexity or variety.

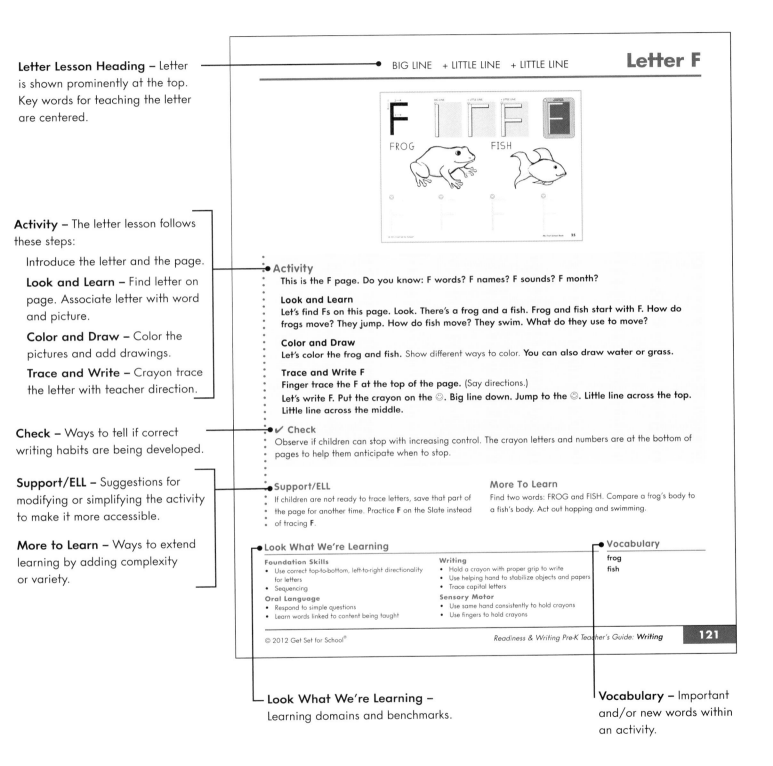

BIG LINE + LITTLE LINE + LITTLE LINE **Letter F**

Activity

This is the F page. Do you know: F words? F names? F sounds? F month?

Look and Learn

Let's find Fs on this page. Look. There's a frog and a fish. Frog and fish start with F. How do frogs move? They jump. How do fish move? They swim. What do they use to move?

Color and Draw

Let's color the frog and fish. Show different ways to color. **You can also draw water or grass.**

Trace and Write F

Finger trace the F at the top of the page. (Say directions.)

Let's write F. Put the crayon on the ☺. Big line down. Jump to the ☺. Little line across the top. Little line across the middle.

✓ **Check**

Observe if children can stop with increasing control. The crayon letters and numbers are at the bottom of pages to help them anticipate when to stop.

Support/ELL

If children are not ready to trace letters, save that part of the page for another time. Practice **F** on the Slate instead of tracing **F**.

More To Learn

Find two words: FROG and FISH. Compare a frog's body to a fish's body. Act out hopping and swimming.

Look What We're Learning

Foundation Skills
- Use correct top-to-bottom, left-to-right directionality for letters
- Sequencing

Oral Language
- Respond to simple questions
- Learn words linked to content being taught

Writing
- Hold a crayon with proper grip to write
- Use helping hand to stabilize objects and papers
- Trace capital letters

Sensory Motor
- Use same hand consistently to hold crayons
- Use fingers to hold crayons

Vocabulary

frog
fish

© 2012 Get Set for School® *Readiness & Writing Pre-K Teacher's Guide: **Writing*** 121

Look What We're Learning – Learning domains and benchmarks.

Vocabulary – Important and/or new words within an activity.

Hands-On Products for Readiness & Writing

Adding the Readiness & Writing Curriculum

This curriculum fits easily into your daily Pre-K routine. As you become familiar with the program, you will gradually incorporate new activities and choose those that suit your children's readiness. Here's how:

Building

You are already using sturdy wood blocks because they invite children to a world of imagination and self-directed play where they actively move, turn, and place objects.

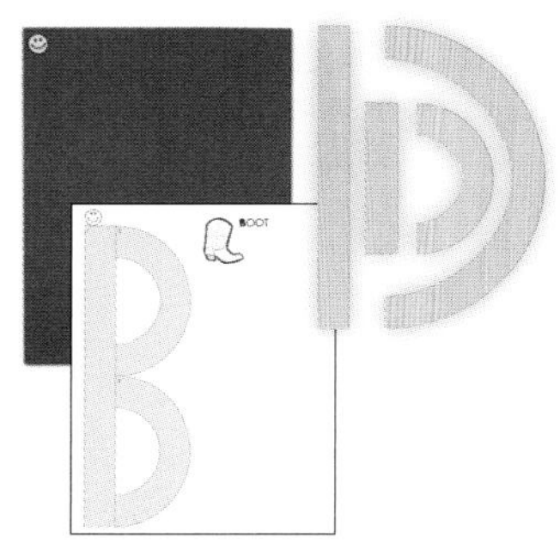

ADD THE WOOD PIECES SET FOR CAPITAL LETTERS

Included are the four basic shapes used to build capital letters: eight Big Lines, six Little Lines, six Big Curves, six Little Curves.

As children polish, sort, and stack, they learn the names of the Wood Pieces. When they use Wood Pieces in teacher directed play, they learn size, shape, and position concepts. When they're ready for letters, they use the Wood Pieces to build letters. For example: they make **B** with a Big Line + Little Curve + Little Curve.

Music, Circle Time, and Finger Plays

You sing to and with children. There are songs for starting tasks, for saying good-bye, and for picking up toys. Children love to participate and play simple instruments. For some, it is music that unlocks language. That's why we created the *Sing Along* and *Sing, Sound & Count With Me* CDs.

ADD *SING ALONG* AND *SING, SOUND & COUNT WITH ME*

At first, just play the CDs during free play time until you and the children become familiar with the tunes and words. You'll soon find favorite songs and finger plays to use during circle time and throughout the day.

Playing With Dough

Children like to play with dough. All that pinching, squeezing, rolling, and pressing helps develop small muscles in their hands. They feel and see size and shape differences.

ADD ROLL-A-DOUGH LETTERS®

With Roll-A-Dough Letters, children roll balls into snakes, and use snakes to make letters. Letter and Number Cards model a dough letter. Children simply roll out the dough and place it on the card. For example: build **A** by rolling two big lines and one little line.

Stamp and See Screen®

Now you see it, now you don't! It's fun to stamp letters and erase them. Children use four different magnetic stamps (they correspond to the four Wood Pieces) to stamp letters. They can also use the magnetic chalk to trace or write letters. You can guide children as they make magnetic letters. This is an excellent pre and post writing activity. Use it to teach and to review.

A-B-C Touch & Flip® Cards

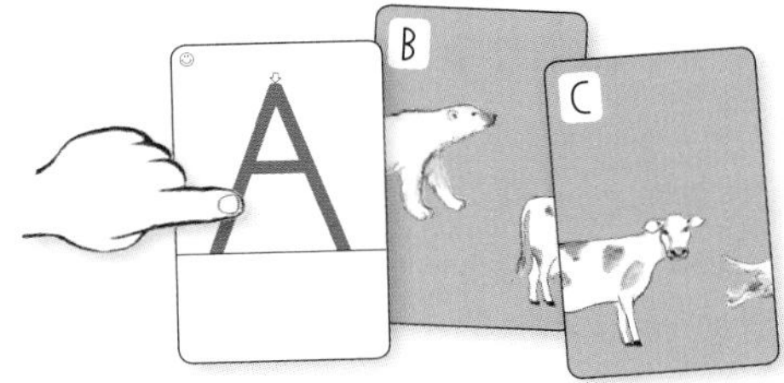

Children can do ABC order before they know the letters. It's easy with these cards. Children simply put the fronts and backs of animals together, and the cards and letters are in order. **A** for alligator, **B** for bear, **C** for cow, and so forth. The animals cards reverse to tactile letter cards with a large capital to finger trace. That's just one deck. The other deck has double-sided cards: capitals on one side, lowercase on the other. These versatile cards are engaging for children of all abilities. The 1-2-3 Touch & Flip® Cards have equally compelling features for counting and tracing numbers.

Colors and Coloring

Children know, or soon will know, the primary and secondary colors. They can find, match, and name them. Give them opportunities to color on the floor, on the table, or at the easel. Provide small bits of colored chalk or crayon because small pieces promote a good grip and finger strength naturally.

ADD "CRAYON SONG" AND FLIP CRAYONS®

Use the song to teach your children how to place their fingers and hold a crayon correctly. That's the best start for handwriting because a good crayon grip leads to a good pencil grip. The Flip Crayons delight children and encourage them to move their fingers to flip the crayon to a new color.

Language and Letters

You read to, talk to, and sing with children. Classrooms have a rich language and letter environment with words and the alphabet on display. Children's names are on cubbies and charts.

ADD LETTER PLAY ACTIVITIES AND *MY FIRST SCHOOL BOOK*

Show children how to build letters with the Wood Pieces and how to write letters on the Slate with Wet–Dry–Try. Then use *My First School Book* to teach letter strokes and how to write letters correctly, starting at the top and making them in the correct sequence.

Counting and Numbers

Children can count out loud. You have taught them to notice the number of fingers on your hand, legs on a dog, and wheels on a car. You have taught them one-to-one correspondence.

ADD THE *SING ALONG* CD AND THE SLATE CHALKBOARD

At first, children learn to count on their own bodies. Songs such as "Count on Me," "Five Fingers Play," and "Toe Song" teach an awareness of numbers. Use the Wet–Dry–Try activity with the Slate to teach students how to write numbers 1 through 10 correctly and without reversals.

ADD ANY ACTIVITY

Pick and choose activities, not just for their stated purpose, but for how they foster social skills. During the day and during the year, you're helping children develop in many ways.

Using *My First School Book*

A Workbook for Scribbling, Coloring, Drawing, Writing, and Counting

Tell children to aim the crayon and put it on the fireworks. The little finger side of the crayon hand should rest on the paper. Remember the helping hand–it has to be flat and resting on the paper. Now it's time to scribble. Children don't lift the crayon or hand. They just wiggle and scribble. This step helps them develop their crayon grip and finger control without any concern for what it looks like. Children can use their newly acquired crayon grip on the coloring pages. Each coloring page teaches color and shape recognition and language skills.

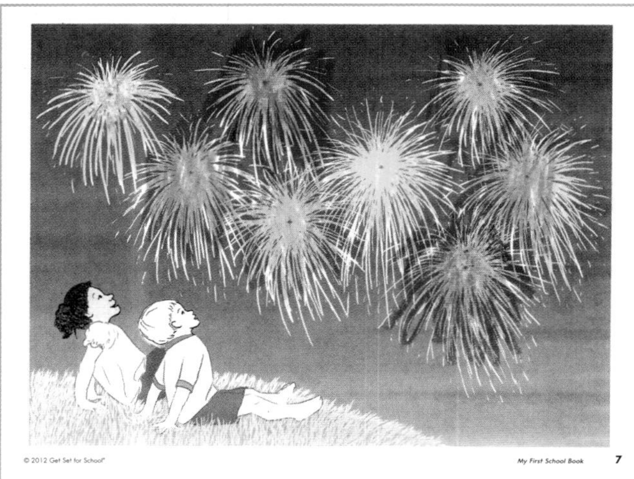

Aim and Scribble Page

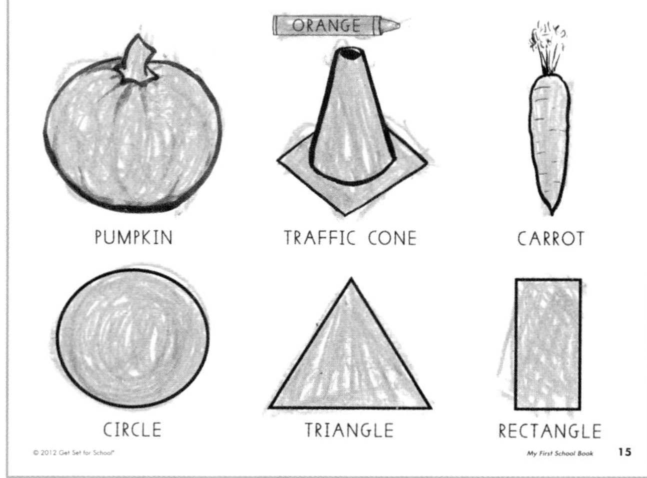

Coloring Page

Children prepare for letter pages with pre-stroke pages. They practice steering the crayon, starting and stopping. Children may trace the crayon lines over and over as they learn to make vertical, horizontal, curved, or diagonal lines. These appealing pages prepare children to trace correctly and learn how to make shapes, letters, and numbers. Crayon skills continue to be refined with coloring, and children develop more control to start and stop strokes. Children are encouraged to add their own finishing touches and extra drawings to all the workbook pages.

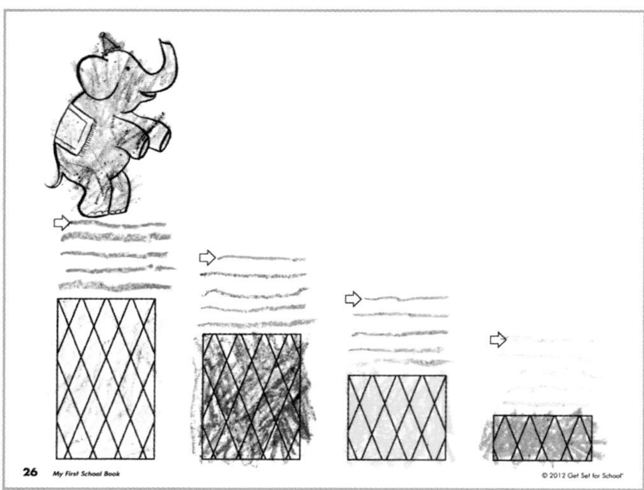

Pre-Stroke Page for Letter E

Letter E

Tracing and Writing in *My First School Book*

Our workbook pages are designed with a unique gray crayon stroke. After trying various tracing methods, we found that this is the easiest stroke for children to trace. Our letters are also easy to start. That's because we show children where to start with a starting symbol. It may be a ☺ or an ⇨. To prepare, the children simply place the crayon by the starting icon and then follow the gray crayon stroke. All letters and numbers begin at the top, which makes it easy to start. It's also easy to stop. The page stops! Notice how the letters and numbers are placed at the bottom. Children know that they aren't supposed to write on the table. They see the page ending and get ready to slow down and stop.

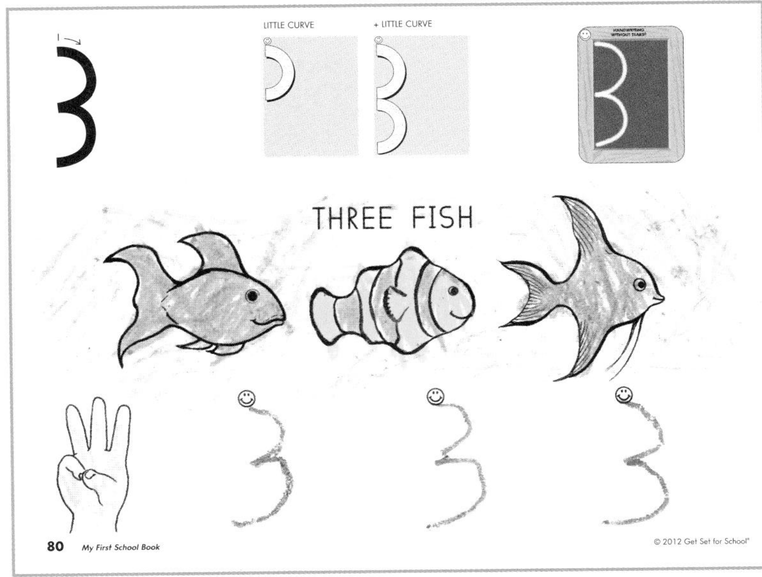

Pre-K Classroom & Children

An environment where children know where to locate items, what comes next in the day, and why they are participating in various activities provides structure and builds security. A cheerful, well-organized classroom helps you to teach effectively and allows your students easy access to the toys and materials that will help them grow and learn.

Social Environment

Provide a welcome environment where all children feel accepted and part of the classroom community. Teach and model ways to share, resolve conflict, and speak kindly to help children learn and get along with others. Doing so builds self-confidence. Your young English language learners will need extra support to feel secure in an environment they may not readily understand.

Physical Setup

A good classroom setup promotes desired learning and behavior. Make sure the setup of your room offers a range of play and learning places:

1. Dramatic play centers: for play kitchen, stores, puppet theaters
2. Manipulatives area: for blocks and building materials, model cars, people, and animals
3. Large indoor play and exercise area: to run, jump, hop, and dance
4. Gathering place and circle time: for stories, singing, finger plays, and sharing
5. Quiet places: for books and a retreat
6. Tables and chairs: for drawing, coloring, and writing
7. Sensory and art centers: for a community easel, sand, and/or water tables

Materials

There is a wide range of developmentally appropriate materials for you to choose from. Every now and then, replace the materials in your room to offer new experiences. As you add things to your classroom, discuss the additions with your students.

Walls

Walls can work for you because they can define spaces and support learning. They can also work against you if you display every good picture because you'll have chaos and disorder. Use your walls actively and selectively. Choose signs and labels to help children understand the purpose of print and to recognize letters and numbers.

Audio

Every Pre-K classroom needs music. Music encourages movement, which promotes learning. We use music to teach a number of skills including social, motor, and letters and language. In consideration of children who are sensitive to noise, use a low volume when you are asking them to focus on other work. Consider the wealth of our musical heritage. Include classical, jazz, country, and other genres as well as children's music. Music is an important part of culture because the language, rhythms, and instruments introduce children to other times and places.

Multisensory Instruction

Pre-K teachers are teaching four-year-olds, but that's a wide range. There are the almost fours and nearly fives, girls and boys, early and late bloomers, advantaged and challenged, English speakers and those just learning.

As a Pre-K teacher, you know the importance of self-directed play and multisensory, active learning. You teach with finger paint, sand tables, dough, and dress up. Research is on your side, supporting multisensory teaching to address children's diverse learning styles: visual, tactile, auditory, and kinesthetic.

This Readiness & Writing Program includes multisensory products that are also designed to help you teach and children to excel. For example: We don't have children build letters by themselves in any random place because that often leads to upside down, backward, incorrect letters. Instead, you build the letter step by step on your Mat and the children imitate on theirs. They follow your lead and learn to build/write letters correctly and easily. The ☺ on the Mat orients them.

Visual

- Illustrations of letter formation give clear, step by step, visual direction.
- Pages are black and white, simple, and uncluttered for clarity.
- Illustrations in workbooks help children make strokes in the correct direction.

Tactile

- Wet–Dry–Try on a Slate or blackboard gives children touch and repetition without boredom.
- Workbook models are big enough for finger tracing.
- The frame of the Slate helps children make lines and keep letters and numbers well proportioned.

Auditory

- Language is consistent and child friendly to help children learn and remember easily.
- Our two CDs use the power of music to facilitate participation, memory, and joyful learning.
- Rhythm and rhyme are used in *My Book* and *I Know My Numbers* to develop language and phonological awareness.

Kinesthetic

- Music and movement teach letter formation.
- Door Tracing and Imaginary Writing teach use of large arm movements and provide visual cues.

You can facilitate multisensory experiences if you:

- Prepare ahead
- Use the ☺ to orient children to the top
- Follow the lesson plans
- Are dynamic and joyful
- Vary the types of multisensory lessons you use
- Share techniques with parents

Handwriting in Pre-K and Kindergarten

Pre-K children are not ready for either formal paper/pencil lessons or for kindergarten workbooks. They need an informal readiness program that suits their developmental needs and abilities. Here's the difference between informal readiness and formal instruction:

PRE-K

Informal Readiness & Writing

Structured, teacher selected activities

When

Pre-K and kindergarten

Readiness Materials - For Instruction

Wood Pieces, Mat, Slate, Roll-A-Dough Letters®, Stamp and See Screen®, *Sing Along* CD, *Sing, Sound & Count With Me* CD

Writing Materials

- Crayons
- *My First School Book* (a crayon book)
- *My Book*
- *I Know My Numbers* (a crayon book)
- Unlined paper, paper strips for name

Writing Readiness Skills

- Fine motor skills, behavior, participation and imitation, stop/start
- Holding crayon correctly
- Building letters and numbers step by step
- Writing capitals, numbers, name
- Play writing

KINDERGARTEN

Formal Handwriting Instruction

Structured, teacher directed lessons

When

Kindergarten

Readiness Materials - Before Instruction

Wood Pieces, Mat, Slate, *Rock, Rap, Tap & Learn* CD

Writing Materials

- Pencils, crayons
- *Letters and Numbers for Me* workbook (a pencil book)
- Lined paper

Handwriting Skills

- Holding pencil correctly
- Forming capitals, lowercase letters, and numbers
- Writing simple words and sentences
- Developing habits for reading/writing

Informal or Formal?

Pre-K and kindergarten should all be able to participate in readiness because the activities promote effective learning. Readiness activities appeal to children's varied learning styles. The hands-on letter play also offers social and motor skill benefits. This informal curriculum prepares children to do well in a formal handwriting program. Even in kindergarten, formal instruction should not begin until children can demonstrate the following:

1. Hand dominance
2. Knowledge of simple size and shape concepts for big line/little line, big curve/little curve
3. Ability to hold a crayon with the fingers placed correctly
4. Satisfactory level of attention, cognitive skills, and cooperation
5. Imitation of a vertical line, a horizontal line, a circle, and a cross

Next Step: *Letters and Numbers for Me*

Typically, children are ready to start writing their lowercase letters the summer before kindergarten. By this time, they have had an opportunity to gain experience writing capitals and learning to recognize lowercase letters. Many Pre-K children will write lowercase letters in their names. With careful demonstration, they can learn to imitate those letters and form them correctly.

Our *Letters and Numbers For Me* workbook is used to teach handwriting in kindergarten. It features capital letters in gray blocks to help children with letter size and placement. It also teaches children lowercase letters, words, sentences, and numbers.

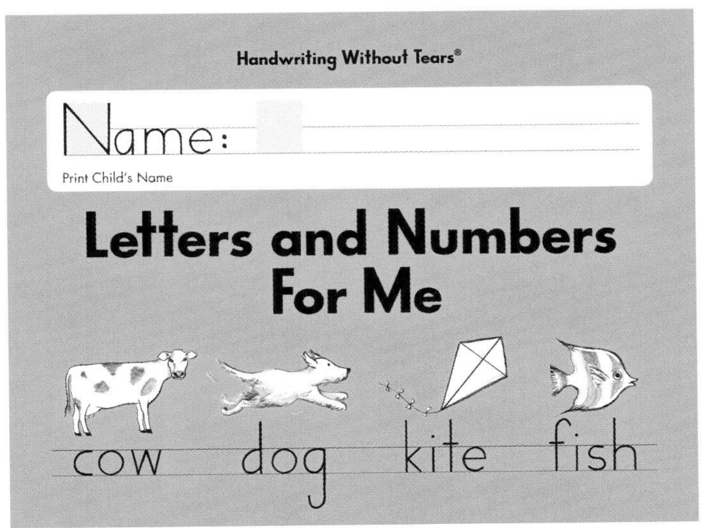

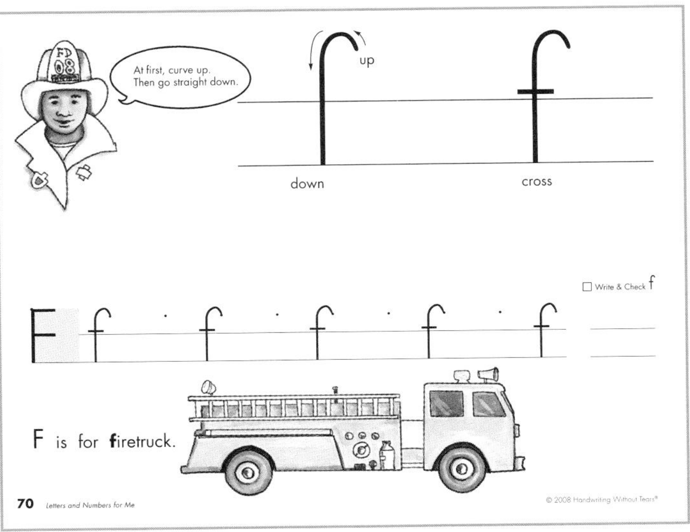

Readiness

Have you ever played ball with a baby? You hand the ball back and forth, roll it, and then gently lob it into waiting arms. You begin slowly and enjoy what a child can do as you let that child's abilities guide what and how you teach. That's how you teach developmentally.

This is a developmentally based program. Research shows us the predictable order in which children develop skills. However, these skills do not just happen at certain ages. They develop through human interaction and emotional connection (Boyd, Barnett, Bodrova, Leong, & Gomby 2005). Fine motor skills and the ability to color, draw, and write develop over time in a social environment with encouragement and instruction (NAEYC & IRA 1998).

The Get Set for School® Readiness & Writing Program:

- Recognizes the social-emotional component in learning, and considers this aspect in activities and in teaching strategies.
- Uses task analysis to guide the order of instruction for fine motor skills, alphabet knowledge, drawing, coloring, pre-writing, writing, number and counting skills.
- Is child friendly, teaching in the ways young children learn most naturally with movement, music, play, and multisensory activities. (This is a time for very limited seat work because young children need social, active, hands-on learning experiences.)
- Supports dynamic instruction, adapting the curriculum to children's changing needs and skills. (Without rushing children, teachers carefully use a mix of play and teacher directed activities to prepare them for school success.)
- Provides ongoing support for educators with teacher's guides, activity booklets, teaching tools, training opportunities, and free online resources.

Objectives

- Develop social-emotional skills with modeling and a variety of school experiences
- Develop fine motor skills with both unilateral and bilateral activities
- Develop strength and postural stability through indoor/outdoor play
- Decide on handedness
- Develop writing readiness
- Learn how to hold crayon with mature grasp (thumb and one or two fingers)
- Use helping hand to stabilize paper when coloring, drawing, or writing
- Imitate and copy strokes and shapes (age appropriate)

Here is some of the significant research for readiness. For additional readiness research, see the reference section at the end of this teacher's guide.

Boyd, J., W.S. Barnett, E. Bordova, D. J. Leong, and D. Gomby. 2005. "Promoting Children's Social and Emotional Development Through Preschool Education." New Brunswick, NJ: National Institute for Early Education Research.

National Assocation for the Education of Young Children & International Reading Association. 1998. "Learning to Read and Write: Developmentally Appropriate Practices for Young Children." *Young Children* 53(4):30-46. Accessed August 2011. http://www.naeyc.org/files/naeyc/file/positions/PSREAD98.pdf

Developing Social Skills

Social skills are like other readiness skills. Some develop quite naturally through play and daily activities. Many need to be modeled or taught. Preschoolers have the wonderful advantage of learning social skills from a teacher who likes young children. They have ready-made playmates and a safe place to play and learn. You as the teacher guide social skills, welcome children, keep them safe, teach them routines, and help them make transitions. You show them how to care for themselves, help each other, pass and share, take things out and put them away—all important life and social skills.

Try more readiness and writing activities to foster social skills:

Skill: Pass, share, play beside others **Try:** Wood Piece Play, page 84

This is an ideal entry level social activity. Children simply sit and polish Wood Pieces. Even non-verbal or shy children can fit in easily. There are natural opportunities to exchange or pass the pieces and talk. You can join in the activity, trade pieces, and discuss them with the class.

Skill: Be in front of others **Try:** Animal Legs, page 184; *Sing Along* CD, track 13

Public speaking is said to be the number one fear we all have. Yet we expect Pre-K children to Show and Tell. Some children take to it quite eagerly, but others don't. This activity eases children into being in front of others and does not require talking. Children simply show a stuffed animal as you and classmates sing a song to count legs. Play the CD during free play a few days before the activity. This familiarity helps all children participate fully.

Skill: Follow directions, imitate teacher **Try:** Hands-On Letter Play, pages 96-99

This activity teaches children to build **B D E F P R** perfectly with the letters right-side up and without reversals. (The Mat and the smiley face are the secret.) The social part is in learning to follow a teacher step by step. Because these are Wood Pieces, it's easy to fix any mistakes (wrong piece or place). Every child follows every step correctly.

Skill: Wait and take turns **Try:** Build & Sing Mat Man®, pages 36-37; *Sing Along* CD, Track 8

Pass out Mat Man® part by part. Each child gets a part: an eye or ear, an arm, a leg, and so forth. Then you and the children rebuild him from his head to his feet. Children know what they're holding and when it's time for that part. The children do their parts and return to their place. They anticipate and participate as they take turns in a group project.

Music is important to the development of social skills. The familiarity of a tune or a song puts children at ease and lets them know what's expected. Children often help pick up at school because of the way you ask them with a song and a smile. The next page has another social skill with music.

Shake Hands

This is an important social skill. Little children can easily wave good-bye, but they need to learn how to meet people. This activity teaches that important social skill and right discrimination.

Materials/Setup

- *Sing Along* CD, "Hello Song," Track 7

Grouping

Whole class

Support/ELL

Talk about greetings in other cultures. Be aware of the students in your room and observe their traditions for greetings.

Activity

Each day, choose a different sensory stimulus (touch, scent, visual, auditory).

1. Greeting—Shake hands with each child. Smile and make eye contact.
2. Say, **Hello–This is your right hand. I'm going to do something to your right hand.**
   - Lotion—Put a dab on the right thumb. **Rub your fingers together.**
   - Rubber Stamp—Stamp the right hand. **Look at your right hand now.**
   - Flavor—Dab a flavor on the right hand to smell.
   - Water—Dip child's right fingertips in a cup. Have them shake fingers.
3. Direct students to raise their right hands and say with you: **This is my right hand. I shake hands with my right hand.**

✔ Check

Observe students shaking hands. Are they using their right hand?

More To Learn

In the USA, children can practice putting right hands over hearts for the Pledge of Allegiance.

Hello Song

Little kids can wave bye, bye
But only big kids know
How to stand perfectly still
And say, "Hello"

Give 'em your right hand
Look 'em in the eye
Put a smile on your face
Then you say, "Hi"
Repeat 1X

"It's nice to meet you
How do you do?"
They'll be so happy
To be meeting you
Greetings are a way to say
"I hope you have a wonderful day"

Give 'em your right hand,
Look 'em in the eye
Put a smile on your face
Then you say, "Hi"
Repeat 1X

I'm a big kid and I know
To use my right hand when I say hello
To put my right hand for you to take
We meet each other and we shake
Shake, shake, so

Give 'em your right hand
Look 'em in the eye
Put a smile on your face
Then you say, "Hi"
Repeat 3X

Look What We're Learning

Foundation Skills

- Exhibit appropriate social skills
- Listen to oral directions to attend to a simple task
- Participate in school routines
- Imitate teacher's body movements

Oral Language

- Learn new words linked to content being taught

Vocabulary

right

Developmental Stages in Writing

The correct use of a writing tool requires instruction. Correct grip needs to be taught. Awkward grips just happen. The way in which children hold a crayon, chalk, or pencil depends on their developmental stage, the writing tool they use, and the instruction they receive. Here is a general guide of how children develop with proper instruction and practice.

2-year-old

scribble mark, vertical line, horizontal line

Writing hand/arm – Child uses all fingers to hold crayon in palm of hand. Arm is in the air expressing anticipation

Helping hand/arm – Has no purposeful use

Present skill – Child makes random contact with paper

Next skill – Child learns how to make scribbles, lines down, and lines across

3-year-old

circle, cross

Writing hand/arm – Child uses all fingers to hold crayon in palm of hand, while arm is down on the table, but not well planted

Helping hand/arm – Child is just starting to use the helping hand

Present skill – Copies lines down and lines across

Next skill – Child learns how to make a circle and cross

Developing Motor Skills for Twos and Threes

Outside – Use playground equipment, swings, slides, big push and riding toys, sandbox play, and balls to help children develop gross motor skills.

Inside – Use building blocks to teach controlled release, nesting toys to engage both sides of the body, and toy trains, animals, and cars to teach manipulation skills. Use puzzles to teach visual discrimination and placement skills and pictures to encourage pointing.

Daily Life – Encourage children to put on and remove shoes and jackets, button and unbutton, wash hands, and brush teeth. Also encourage them to eat small food pieces to practice picking up very little things. Have children help with simple take-out and put-away tasks.

4-year-old

square, triangle

Writing hand/arm – Mature grasp begins to emerge (thumb with one or two fingers). Notice the elbow. It's up. This is arm writing. The hand moves freely in the air

Helping hand/arm – Child starts to hold the paper deliberately

Present skill – Child copies line down, line across, circle, and cross

Next skill – Child learns to make a square and a triangle, trace letters and numbers, hold a crayon, use a stencil to develop the helping hand, and then continues with free exploration

5-year-old

diamond

Writing hand/arm – Uses mature grasp as hand rests on the paper. This is handwriting

Helping hand/arm – Child purposely uses the hand to hold and place the paper

Present skill – Child copies a cross, circle, square, and triangle

Next skill – Child begins to draw circle, square, and triangle independently, draws a diamond, learns to write letters and numbers (holding a crayon if needed), and draws

Developing Motor Skills for Fours and Fives

Outside – Continue previous activities. Add simple games and building projects.

Inside – Continue previous activities. Finger painting, easel work, and drawing with little pieces of chalk or crayon promote coordination and holding habits. Finger plays, music, and imitation build body awareness. Play dough, toys with small pieces, and simple crafts like bead stringing help children develop fine motor skills.

Daily Life – Continue previous activities. Add more helping tasks (pouring, spreading, setting table) that use precise fine motor control.

Children's Hand Skills

Many preschool activities incorporate fine motor experiences. Often, Pre-K children (especially boys) need some additional fine motor support. For more tips and ideas you can send home to parents, visit, **getsetforschool.com/click**

- Do finger plays. Find them in *Sing Along* CD (tracks 10 and 16), in *I Know My Numbers* booklets, and in finger play books.
- Cut pictures out of newspapers or magazines. Take a large black marker and draw a line around the pictures to give a guideline.
- Hide small objects in the dough and have children find them.

Use familiar and new finger plays from the *Sing Along* CD. Here is a popular one for you to try.

Ten Little Fingers

I have ten little fingers and they all belong to me
I can make them do things, just you wait and see
I can wiggle them high, and wiggle them low
I can push them on the floor, and stretch them just so
They can make little Os, if I touch them together
They can even make a cup, to catch rain in rainy weather
I can stretch them out wide, or close them real tight
I might just fold them quietly, when I sleep at night

Other things to consider when you are trying to develop hand skills include:

Toys

We live in a world of technology. Toys are different today than they were several years ago. They light up, talk, and play music at the push of a button. Even many educational toys do not give the child anything to do beyond pushing buttons. Be picky and select toys that require children to use hand skills to move pieces, manipulate parts, or snap things together.

Easel Activities

Vertical or slanted surfaces are great for developing hand skills. Other vertical surfaces include mirrors, windows, walls (tub walls too), and refrigerators. Vertical surfaces enable children to create their own working space at just the right height! When a child's arms and hands are positioned upward, working against gravity, they are building strength in the shoulders and arms. Also, a child's wrist is forced into a neutral position, which is the position that is used later, when the child begins to write. For more ideas on easel activities, turn to page 35.

Playground Play

Most children's upper body strength and motor coordination develop through play. Playground equipment helps children develop the strength and coordination required for fine motor skills. Some children may never have the opportunity to use playground equipment, so allow time in your day for them to experience the benefits of monkey bars, swings, and other great playground equipment.

Educating Parents

Parents are a child's most important teachers and love to help their children learn. Educate parents about preschool activities by sending home the parent articles in the back of this guide.

The Dominant Hand

Children decide their dominant hand. However, if a child is truly undecided by the time handwriting training begins, choose the hand that is more skilled to be the writing hand. Without a dominant hand, experience and training is divided between two hands and children develop nearly equal hand skills. However, those children are not as skilled with one hand as their peers who have established a dominant hand. A teacher, parent, and occupational therapist (if available) should observe the child. Watch how the child colors, draws, writes, zips a jacket, eats, and so forth to determine which hand is more skilled.

To determine handedness, watch children as they do one-handed (unilateral) and two-handed (bilateral) activities. Unilateral activities show preference. Bilateral activities that use a skilled hand and a holding hand show the hand that is more skilled. You can look for handedness by observing children holding:

- Bubbles and dipping wand
- Boxes for removing objects
- Beads and stringing thread
- Flowers for picking petals
- Funnels in which to spoon sand
- Wood Pieces for polishing

The Helper Hand

1. We suggest activities that require use of the helping hand:
    - Wood Pieces – Hold a Wood Piece and rub it with the non-dominant hand.
    - Slate – Hold a slate steady on the table and write on it with chalk.
    - Stencils, shapes, and rulers – Hold them steady with one hand while marking with the other.
    - Hand tracing – Hold one hand flat as the other hand traces around it.
2. As you prepare children to write, tell them to hold their paper with a flat helping hand so they can stay relaxed as they write.
3. If children ignore the helping hand when they color or start to write, try this:
    Give the helping hand a name. Ask a child to choose a name, one that starts with the same letter as the child's name. Then talk directly to the hand (not the child), and call the hand by the new name. Tell the helping hand to help the child and hold the paper. Children think it's funny when you talk to the hand. They don't get embarrassed because it's the helping hand, not them, that's being reminded.

Use Your Oven Rack

You can help children learn vertical and horizontal lines by using your oven rack. Place the rack on a large sheet of paper and give children a crayon to make lines back and forth. When they hold the rack with the other hand, they get stabilization practice with the helping hand.

Teaching Crayon Grip

Close to 50 percent of three-year-olds have the fine motor ability to hold a small crayon correctly (Schneck & Henderson 1990). But the correct grip has to be taught. You can end awkward or even fisted pencil grips with direct teaching of specific strategies. Young children are pliable and can learn good habits. Here are strategies to teach correct crayon grip.

Demonstrate Grip - Standard or Alternate

The standard grip, also called the "tripod grip," uses three fingers to hold the crayon or pencil. The thumb is bent, the index finger points to the tip of the crayon, and the crayon rests on the side of the middle finger. The last two fingers are curled in the palm and give the hand stability.

An alternative grip called the "quadropod grip" (four fingers) is another way children may hold the crayon. The thumb is bent, the index and middle finger point to the tip of the crayon, and the crayon rests on the ring finger. This grip is efficient and does not need to be corrected.

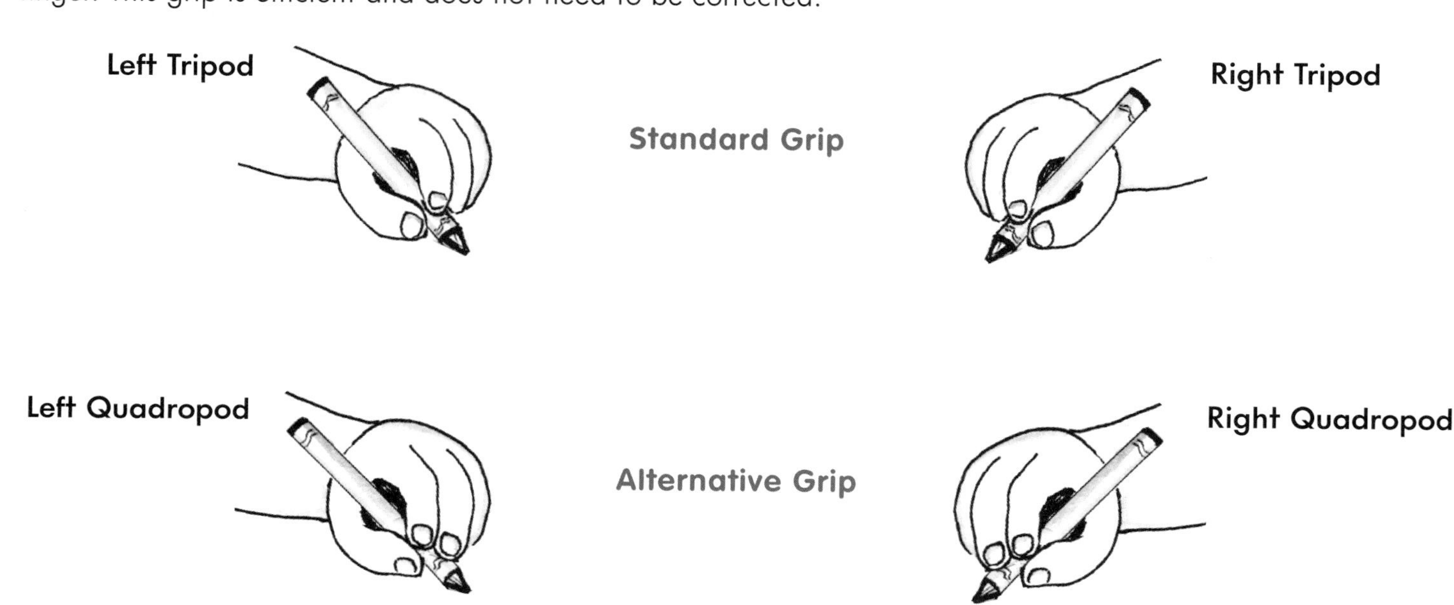

Little Crayons/Little Pencils

FLIP Crayon
301.263.2700 WWW.HWTEARS.COM

The best tool for Pre-K children is the crayon. Crayons create a natural resistance and build strength in the hand. They prepare the hand for using a good pencil grip. Our Flip Crayons® are ideal for little hands. They are designed with dual colors and dual tips to encourage fine motor development: when children flip the crayons, they use in-hand manipulation skills, which lead to improved coordination. If you do move a child to pencils, use a golf-size pencil. Avoid fat primary pencils because those are too heavy and long for little hands. Children will do better with a short pencil that's in proportion to their hands. You can use markers in moderation.

Pencil Grips

Avoid using pencil grips or any other type of adaptive writing device for Pre-K children. Pencil grips are for older children who find them helpful. Young children are motivated to learn new skills. If they are holding a crayon or small pencil incorrectly, demonstrate the proper grip and try the techniques described above or on page 29.

Crayon Song

The time to teach proper grip is when children become interested in coloring. Show them how to hold their crayons correctly: demonstrate finger placement and model a correct grip.

Materials/Setup

- *Sing Along* CD, track 5, "Crayon Song"
- Crayons (1 per child)

Grouping

Whole class

Support/ELL

Drop and pick up crayons a few times throughout the day to give children a chance to practice positioning their fingers. This practice also allows you more opportunities to model a correct grip.

Video Lesson

View the video lesson, Teaching Crayon Grip, at **getsetforschool.com/videos**

Activity

1. Introduce and name the fingers that hold the crayon:

   Thumb – **Everyone, hold up your thumb. Say "Hi" to your thumb.**

   Pointer – **Hold up your pointer finger. Wiggle it around. Say "Hi" to pointer fingers.**

   Middle – **Hold up middle finger next to pointer. Middle finger is taller than the pointer finger. We call him "Tall Man." Your fingers have important jobs. I'm going to teach you a song so you can remember their jobs.**

2. Sing "Crayon Song" and show children how you hold a crayon.
3. Continue to sing the song as you slowly check the children's grips.

✔ Check

Observe children and check for correct grip. You may need to physically position fingers on the crayon. Can children drop it and pick it up correctly?

More To Learn

Observe children as they hold a pencil or a crayon. Are they holding the wrong end? In a silly way, have children tell you what is wrong with your grip.

Crayon Song

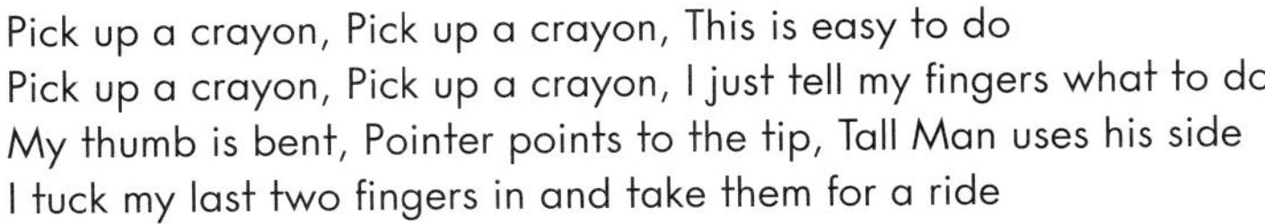

Pick up a crayon, Pick up a crayon, This is easy to do
Pick up a crayon, Pick up a crayon, I just tell my fingers what to do
My thumb is bent, Pointer points to the tip, Tall Man uses his side
I tuck my last two fingers in and take them for a ride

Now I'm holding it just right, But not too tight, Every finger knows what to do
And now I have a big surprise, A big surprise for you
Let's drop it and do it again!

NOTE: Use the CD just to learn the tune. Then, as you teach, use the song without the CD. As you sing the song, walk around the room and position children's fingers for them correctly on the crayon. It will take several repetitions before children will pick up the habit naturally.

Look What We're Learning

Writing
- Hold a crayon with proper grip to write

Foundation Skills
- Listen to oral directions to attend to a simple task
- Imitate teacher's body movements
- Listen to and repeat songs and finger plays

Sensory Motor Skills
- Use same hand consistently to hold crayons
- Move fingers for finger plays

Vocabulary

thumb
pointer
middle

Stages of Learning

Pre-Instructional Stages

Readiness includes all the many activities that develop skills. Pre-instructional readiness activities promote fine motor skills, drawing, coloring, alphabet knowledge, pre-writing, writing, number, and counting skills.

Share, Play, Socialize
Participate, take turns, and communicate with materials, music, and teacher modeling.

Make Mat Man®
Take turns. Learn body parts and how to draw with Mat Man.

Sing & Imitate
Join the class to sing about shapes, letters, numbers, and even how to say hello!

Instructional Stages Now & Ahead

Readiness continues into kindergarten, but it is in kindergarten where we begin formal handwriting instruction. Instruction follows three steps: 1. Imitate the teacher, 2. Copy from a model, 3. Write independently. Even emergent writers follow these three stages as they learn to trace letters and start to write their names.

Stage 1 - Imitation
The child sees the motions as you write step by step. Child hears the directions.

Stage 2 - Tracing
Children look at the model of a letter and trace over it.

Build Letters
Know how to pick and place Wood Pieces to build letters. (1 Big Line + 1 Big Curve = D)

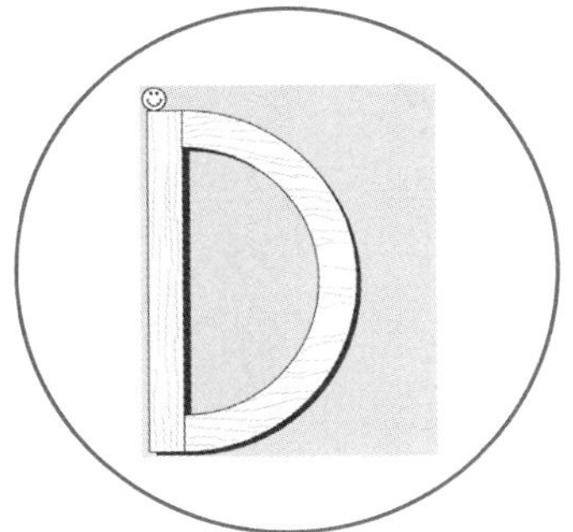

Trace on a Slate
Make capitals and numbers on a reversal-proof slate! Do it with multisensory Wet-Dry-Try.

Color and Write
Practice in a child friendly workbook, with pictures and models to promote good habits.

Stage 3 - Emergent Writing
Children write without a model and typically take interest in writing the letters in their names.

Drawing

Drawing begins early. Babies run their fingers through pudding on highchair trays. Pre-K children use finger paint. Drawing begins with movement as very young children make marks in food or finger paint (Bailer 2003).

Movement is the key to drawing. At first, children just like to move and see the marks they make. Gradually they see the relationship between the two (National Center for Infants, Toddlers, and Families 2011). That's when they start moving a crayon deliberately. They'll pull a crayon down or across or diagonally to make the kind of line they want. They'll plan to move the crayon round and round to make a circular shape. That's the beginning of intentional drawing. Encourage the continuation of experimental, abstract art with finger paints and movement to music for free expression in art.

Children want to produce figurative, representational art with recognizable pictures, and they love to talk about their drawings (Robertson 2007). In this way, they express themselves on paper, and drawing becomes a part of written expression in kindergarten and in the early grades.

This program will help you develop young artists: children who like to draw and who draw with creativity and skill. It's easy when children draw with music, Mat Man®, shapes, and you.

Objectives

- Draw expressively, experimenting with various ways to move and produce marks
- Draw figuratively, making a recognizable face/person
- Draw recognizable shapes and simple pictures
- Add personal elements to shapes or picture

Below is some of the significant research for drawing. For additional drawing research, see the reference section at the end of this teacher's guide.

Bailer, Kathleen. 2003. "Developmental Stages of Scribbling." Accessed August 2011. http://www.k-play.com/pdf/The%20Developmental%20Sta.pdf

Robertson, Rachel. 2007. "The Meaning of Marks: Understanding and Nurturing Young Children's Writing Development." *Child Care Exchange* 176:40-44.

National Center for Infants, Toddlers, and Families. 2011. "Learning to Write and Draw." *Zero To Three* Accessed August 2011. http://www.zerotothree.org/early-care-education/early-language-literacy/writing-and-art-skills.html

Developing Drawing Skills

Drawing Development

Just as there is a developmental order for imitating and copying shapes, there is also an order in which children develop drawing skills. Children typically move in stages.

2-year-old: scribbles, traces of movement, circular and linear strokes

3-year-old: intentional figure–generic circle for face, lines for arms/legs

4-year-old: recognizable figure–more parts, accuracy in placing parts, may resemble subject

5-year-old: figure in scene–dimensional figure with familiar objects at base of paper

That order is fairly consistent, but children can develop excellent skills at every stage with simple teaching strategies and opportunities. When children like what they draw, they like to draw, so their skills and creativity blossom. Here are the teaching strategies that enable children to draw well.

Strategies for Developing Drawing Skills

1. Help children use drawing materials. Provide small bits of crayon or chalk to promote finger strength and crayon grip. Show children how to hold crayons.
2. Put music, movement, and marks together. Start with just streamers to let children see the effect of moving different ways. (Rotate, move side to side, up and down, wiggle...) Continue to experiment with expressive easel art.
3. Bring Mat Man® to school. He helps children transition from abstract, expressive drawing into figurative drawing. Mat Man building is a hands-on social activity that teaches children how to draw people.
4. Introduce shapes and strokes in developmental order. See pages 24-25. Also, take advantage of another developmental fact: Children can imitate strokes/shapes weeks or months before they can copy them. So draw for children and inspire them to explore and learn.

Support

The strategies above are for all children, including those with special needs. At this age, not all needs are identified and even a later birthday can make a huge difference in skills. Happily, the strategies you'll be learning work well for all children. For proof, see the before and after samples on page 38. Notice that even children on the autism spectrum, who may not like to look at faces or respond to spoken words, learn to draw with music and Mat Man.

Expressive Easel Art

Unleash children's creativity while developing their fine motor skills. Consider turning an old bi-fold door into a big community easel. Play instrumental music because music encourages moving and drawing is the trace of movement. Let Beethoven and Louis Armstrong come to school! When children stand up and work against gravity, they build strength in their shoulders and arms. Children learn through imitation, so in Pre-K and kindergarten, put the less experienced children by the more experienced. Place small baskets of Flip Crayons® or small bits of crayons around the easel.

Materials/Setup
- Community easel
- Flip Crayons
- Instrumental music

Grouping
Small groups (self chosen)

Support/ELL
Model moving to music and expressive drawing on the easel for children who are unfamiliar with the activity.

Activity

1. Play music that encourages children to move.
2. Lead children to dance, move arms to the music.
3. Children go to easel and draw.

Note about crayons and crayon grip:
When children use large arm movements to draw, they may use a palmar grip, the grip that Picasso would use to draw a mural. The crayon is in the palm, but still held by the thumb and index/middle finger tips. Use Flip Crayons or small bits of broken crayons for this.

✔ Check

Notice effect of music tempo. Look for large, whole arm strokes. Do children talk as they draw?

More To Learn

Give children some starting strokes to break the ice—scribbles, zigzags, and anything that allows them to experiment with strokes.

Look What We're Learning

Foundation Skills
- Imitate teacher's body movements

Sensory Motor
- Use same hand consistently to hold crayons and perform skilled tasks
- Use fingers to hold crayons
- Use large muscle groups to maintain posture/position and mobility
- Use both sides of the body in activities
- Handle art materials without an avoidance response
- Move naturally and place body to perform tasks

Build & Sing Mat Man®

Young children are often asked to draw pictures of themselves or of other people. Bring Mat Man to school to teach drawing with building and singing. First, the teacher builds Mat Man on the floor, and then she gives him away, piece by piece: "You have the nose." Mat Man is gone, but he comes back to life with the "Mat Man" song. Children sing about each part, stopping to put it in place. They learn about body parts, where they go, and what they do. When children know how to build Mat Man, they can easily approach drawing the same way. Look at this little girl's drawing of Mat Man. See how she went from Mat Man to drawing other people and personalizing them.

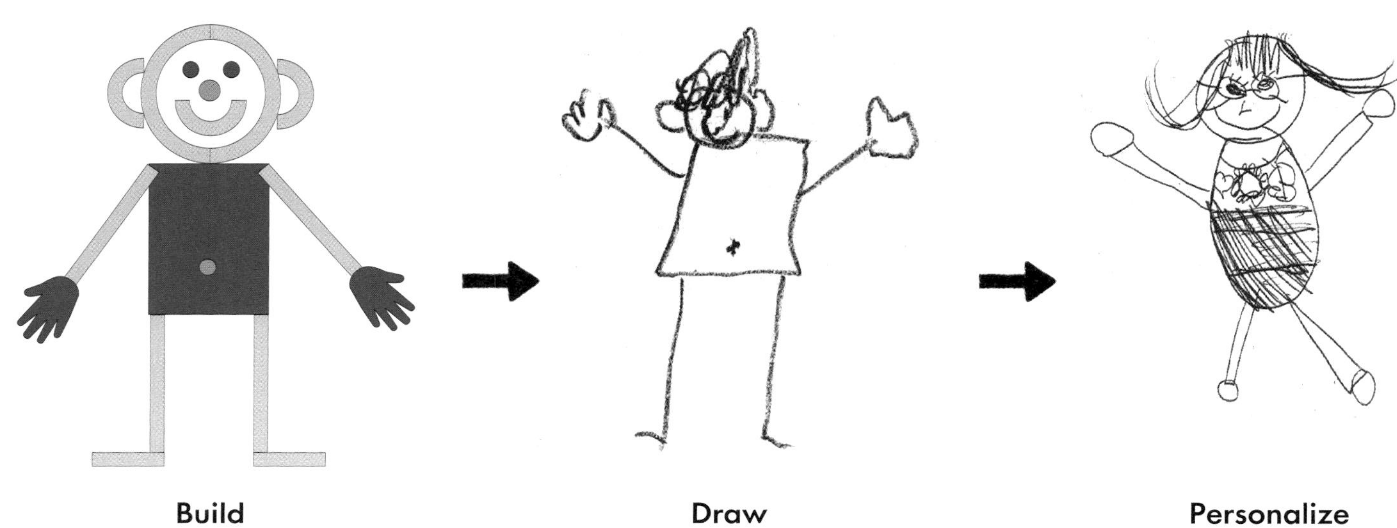

Mat Man

from the *Sing Along* CD, track 8

Tune: The Bear Went Over the Mountain

Mat Man has	**1** head,	**1** head,	**1** head	Mat Man has *(repeat)*	**1** head	So that he can* *(repeat)*	think
Mat Man has	**2** eyes,	**2** eyes,	**2** eyes		**2** eyes		see
Mat Man has	**1** nose,	**1** nose,	**1** nose		**1** nose		smell
Mat Man has	**1** mouth,	**1** mouth,	**1** mouth		**1** mouth		eat
Mat Man has	**2** ears,	**2** ears,	**2** ears		**2** ears		hear
Mat Man has	**1** body,	**1** body,	**1** body		**1** body	To hold what is inside*	heart, lungs, stomach
Mat Man has	**2** arms,	**2** arms,	**2** arms		**2** arms	So that he can* *(repeat)*	reach
Mat Man has	**2** hands,	**2** hands,	**2** hands		**2** hands		clap
Mat Man has	**2** legs,	**2** legs,	**2** legs		**2** legs		stand
Mat Man has	**2** feet,	**2** feet,	**2** feet		**2** feet		walk

*Wait for children to respond. Your children may call out other responses (i.e. feet = run) than listed. Add extra verses when you add new accessories.

Materials

- Mat
- Wood Pieces:
  - 2 Big Curves (head)
  - 3 Little Curves (ears, mouth)
  - 4 Big Lines (arms, legs)
  - 2 Little Lines (feet)
- Accessories:
  - 2 Hands
  - 2 Eyes (water bottle caps)
  - 1 Nose (juice cap)
  - Other items as desired
- *Sing Along* CD, "Mat Man," track 8

Grouping

Whole class, or modify

Support/ELL

Preview activity or build a smaller part—perhaps just Mat Man's head.

Video Lesson

View the video lesson, Building and Drawing Mat Man, at **getsetforschool.com/videos**

Activity

1. Children sit on the floor in a circle.
2. Teacher builds Mat Man on the floor.
3. Teacher gives Mat Man's parts to the children.
4. Children build Mat Man with you as they sing the "Mat Man" song, *Sing Along* CD, track 8.
5. Extra accessories (belly button, hair, clothing, seasonal items) make Mat Man more interesting or change him into a different Mat person.

✔ Check

Observe if children are anticipating each part. Check how parts are placed. Listen for vocabulary and knowledge of body functions.

More To Learn

Discuss what is inside the body. Print Mat Man's insides. Learn about the beating heart, the lungs, and the stomach.

Look What We're Learning

Foundation Skills

- Name parts of the body
- Listen to oral directions to attend to a simple task
- Imitate teacher's body movements
- Sequencing

Social-Emotional

- Take turns with peers

Oral Language

- Demonstrate active listening by attending to instruction

Sensory Motor

- Move an object in one hand to position it for use, placement, or release
- Notice and attach meaning to visual information

Vocabulary

head	arms
eyes	hands
nose	legs
mouth	feet
ears	
body	

Draw Mat Man®

Here are children's drawings before and after Mat Man, which were done on the same day. That means that neither time nor maturity caused the improvement. Mat Man did! Drawings done even weeks later show that the improvement remains. Children's drawings will consistently be more complex (number of body parts) and accurate (parts placed correctly) than before. What does change over time is the personality of the drawings.

Mat Man Before and After

Before After
4-Year-Old: Same Day

Before After
4-Year-Old: Same Day

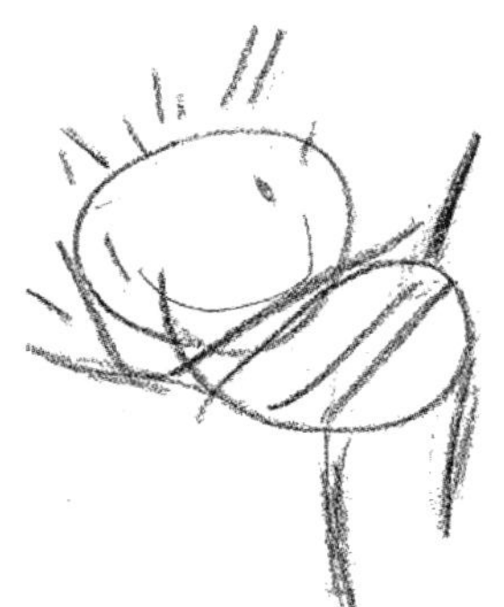

Before After
5-Year-Old: 9 Days After Activity

Before After
5-Year-Old (with autism): Same Day

Materials/Setup

- Blank paper (1 per child)
- Crayons
- Easel
- Markers
- *Sing Along* CD, "Mat Man," track 8

Grouping

Any size

Support/ELL

For extra exposure, you may draw Mat Man for children who simply sing and talk. On another day, children will also draw.

Video Lesson

View the video lesson, Building and Drawing Mat Man, at **getsetforschool.com/videos**

Activity

1. Children sit at tables/desks facing you. You draw a large Mat Man at the board or easel.
2. Draw each part in order. Sing/say: **Mat Man has one head. Watch me draw the head. Now it's your turn!** (*Sing Along* CD, track 8, page 36)
3. Encourage children to add other details to their drawings.

✔ Check

Observe how children hold crayon and paper. Do children join in as parts are repeated?

More To Learn

Children add more body parts or accessories when they repeat the activity. They change Mat Man into another person.

Look What We're Learning

Foundation Skills
- Name parts of the body
- Listen to oral directions to attend to a simple task
- Imitate teacher's body movements
- Describe self in terms of physical traits

Oral Language
- Demonstrate active listening by attending to instruction

Writing
- Use helping hand to stabilize papers

Sensory Motor
- Use same hand consistently to hold crayons and perform tasks
- Use fingers to hold crayons

Social-Emotional
- Show desire for independence

Mat Man® Pattern

Instructions:

- Use these patterns to make body parts with colorful paper. Laminate for durability.
- Use a juice cap for nose and water bottle caps for eyes.
- Use thick yarn or fringe for hair.

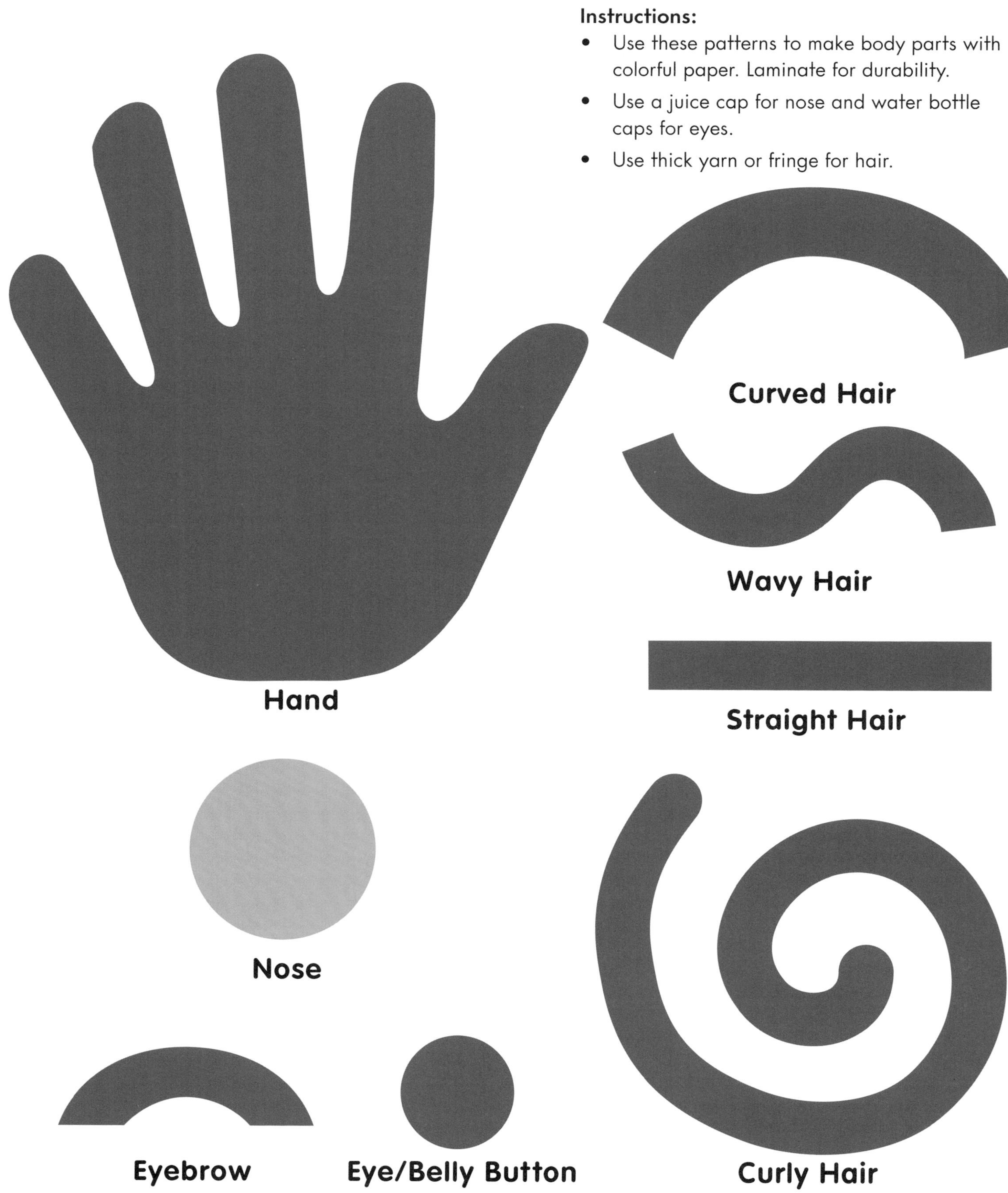

Mat Man Shapes Book

In the *Mat Man Shapes* book, Mat Man® gets new Mats of different shapes and then does different things. With an oval, he sits by Humpty Dumpty. This is a shape naming and coloring page. Shapes are important for developing observation and drawing skills. *My First School Book* features shapes on coloring pages, and also on this Mat Man shape page.

Materials
- *My First School Book*, page 63
- *Mat Man Shapes*
- Crayons

Grouping
Any size

Support/ELL
Build Mat Man with other shapes. You can find shape patterns in the back of the *Mat Man Shapes* book.

Activity

1. You and children read the shapes from top to bottom, left to right as if they are a page: rectangle, oval, triangle, star, circle, square, heart, and diamond.
2. Children point to each shape as it is named.
3. You name a shape randomly for children to find.
4. Children trace and color the page and try to draw shapes on another piece of paper.

✔ Check
Observe the class as you point to and name shapes. Do children join in and name the shapes correctly?

More To Learn
Ask children to name and find the oval, and name the shape that comes after oval.

Look What We're Learning

Foundation Skills
- Recognize familiar two-dimensional shapes

Concepts About Print
- Understand that print can be read and has meaning

Comprehension
- Listen to perform a task

Oral Language
- Repeat teacher's words
- Demonstrate active listening by attending to stories
- Learn words linked to content being taught

Sensory Motor
- Use same hand consistently to hold crayons and perform skilled tasks

Vocabulary

rectangle
oval
triangle
star
circle
square
heart
diamond

Draw Shapes in *My First School Book*

Children enjoy learning about shapes–especially when their shape turns into a picture. They are proud of their work and will show it to others. Our shape pages in *My First School Book* teach children their shapes and then how to draw those shapes. Children will enjoy making choices and turning their shapes throughout the book into special pictures.

Materials/Setup

- *My First School Book*
- *Sing Along* CD, "My Teacher Draws," track 17
- Crayons

Grouping

Whole class

Support/ELL

Some children may ask for assistance with their drawing. You can provide hand-over-hand assistance or model ideas to get them started.

Activity

1. Choose any one of the shape pages in *My First School Book*.
2. You may choose to model shapes for children. Consider using *Sing Along* CD, track 17, "My Teacher Draws" as a fun way to bring shapes to life.
3. After you have modeled the shape, have the children take a turn.
4. In the final box, they can choose what to turn their shape into.

✔ Check

Observe formation of the shapes. Can children draw them without a visual model?

More To Learn

Find different shapes in the classroom. Have children see if they can find squares in windows, rectangles in doors, and so forth.

Look What We're Learning

Foundation Skills

- Recognize familiar two-dimensional shapes
- Use correct top-to-bottom, left-to-right directionality for symbols
- Listen to oral directions to attend to a simple task
- Imitate teacher's body movements

Oral Language

- Demonstrate active listening by attending to instruction

Writing

- Hold a crayon with proper grip to write

Sensory Motor

- Use same hand consistently to hold crayons and perform skilled tasks
- Use fingers to hold crayons

Draw in *My First School Book*

In *My First School Book,* we purposely left the coloring and drawing up to the children. You'll notice on the pages that there are very few details because we want the children to add them–just like the example below. The child added clouds, grass, a tree, sunshine, window panes, and a door knob. Children take pride in their work, and develop important motor skills along the way.

Materials/Setup

- *My First School Book*
- Crayons

Grouping

Whole class

Support/ELL

Some children may ask for assistance with their drawings. You can provide hand-over-hand assistance or model ideas to get them started.

Activity

1. Each letter lesson includes a picture. Begin by discussing the pictures (see each individual letter lesson).
2. Children may first color their picture or draw to add detail.
3. Encourage children to add detail.
4. Allow children to share their pictures with others.

✔ Check

Observe what children are drawing, and see if they will tell you a story. Observe their crayon grip and attention to detail.

More To Learn

Challenge children to find the letter that comes after _____ or before _____.

Look What We're Learning

Foundation Skills

- Recognize and identify basic colors
- Recognize familiar two-dimensional and three-dimensional shapes
- Use correct top-to-bottom, left-to-right directionality for letters, numbers, and other symbols
- Listen to oral directions to attend to a simple task

Concepts About Print

- Turn pages from front to back, one at a time

Alphabet Knowledge

- Point to and name capital letters
- Point to and name lowercase letters

Sensory Motor

- Use same hand consistently to hold crayons and perform tasks
- Use fingers to hold crayons

Draw in *My Book*

Children will love to draw freely in *My Book*. This becomes children's personalized story book. They will enjoy drawing themselves, their friends, family members, and their favorite foods and things to do. Allow them to share their drawings with you. They will also want to share them with others.

Materials/Setup
- *My Book*
- Crayons

Grouping
Whole class; individual

Support/ELL
Children may ask you to help them draw. Demonstrate how to draw simple pictures with shapes.

Video Lesson
View the video lesson, Draw in *My Book*, at **getsetforschool.com/videos**

Activity

1. Open *My Book* to any one of the drawing pages.
2. Allow children to draw freely to create their own personalized story.
3. Walk around the room, and allow children to share their thoughts. Write what they say at the bottom of their books.
4. Allow students to share with others.

✔ Check
Observe drawing. Are children drawing in context with the theme of a given page?

More To Learn
Practice concepts about print. Help children identify the author, title, front, back, pages, text, and illustrations. These are the first steps to foster interest in reading.

I wake up and brush my teeth before school.
I wash up and get dressed. That's the rule.

Look What We're Learning

Foundation Skills
- Know name

Concepts About Print
- Understand that print can be read and has meaning
- Turn pages from front to back, one at a time
- Follow print from top to bottom and left to right on a page

Oral Language
- Communicate thoughts with words

Writing
- Share drawings and writing with others
- Hold a crayon with proper grip to write

Social-Emotional
- Demonstrate positive self esteem

Draw with Line It Up™

Experience the excitement of drawing as a class with Line It Up Picture Cards. Children will have many ideas about the pictures you discuss. They will know exactly what they will add. They will anticipate their turn. Along with drawing, children are also learning to participate, take turns, and share materials in the room.

Materials/Setup
- Line It Up Bar*
- Line It Up Picture Cards

Grouping
Whole class

Support/ELL
Some children may ask for assistance with their drawing. You can provide hand-over-hand assistance or model ideas to get them started.

*For more information about Line It Up, go to **www.getsetforschool.com**.

Activity
1. Choose a card to draw on.
2. Invite a child to hang it up in the bar.
3. Discuss the picture.
4. Allow children to discuss what they would like to add to the picture.
5. Encourage them to add a lot of detail.

✔ Check
Observe children as they take turns and use their crayon grip.

More To Learn
Plan ahead and read a book related to the picture you will color and draw. The story will inspire children to be artists.

Look What We're Learning

Oral Language
- Communicate thoughts with words
- Talk about experiences and observations

Writing
- Enjoy writing and engage in writing activities
- Share drawings with others
- Hold a crayon with proper grip to write
- Use helping hand to stabilize objects and papers

Sensory Motor
- Use same hand consistently to hold crayons
- Use fingers to hold crayon
- Use the right amount of pressure to hold and use tools
- Notice and attach meaning to visual information

Alphabet Knowledge

ABC blocks are classic toys because the ABCs are the building blocks for reading and writing. The ABCs are already in children's lives, but in Pre-K, their alphabet knowledge will blossom. Children will learn to name letters as you teach them how to build and write letters. They will learn the alphabet and to recognize letters with songs, wall cards, books, puzzles, letter cards, and other engaging activities.

Alphabet knowledge develops in stages. It starts with singing the ABCs correctly from A to Z. Then it's a matter of putting letter names and letter symbols together (Strickland & Schickedanz 2009). Most children know a few sight letters. But even children who don't can point to and say letters one by one when the letters are in ABC order. As alphabet knowledge grows, children expand their sight letter repertoire and learn to name letters in any order.

The capitals are the key to the development of letter recognition. They are the first letters children can recognize (NAEYC & IRA 1998). It helps that each capital is so distinctive. Even before children can name letters, they can recognize and find them. If you ask, "Where is **O**?" a child may point to **O** in STOP. But if you ask, "What is this letter?" the same child may not remember "**O**." Gradually, children learn to both recognize (know what a letter looks like) and name (remember and say the name) all the capitals.

The capitals make lowercase letters easy. Children who learn capitals first as a group can easily tell capitals from lowercase letters. They learn lowercase letters quickly because they already know all the lowercase letters that are the same as (**c o s v w x z**) or similar to (**j k p t u y**) the capitals. They already know other lowercase letters from their names. By kindergarten, they'll know them all.

Objectives

- Sing the "ABC Song"
- Say the alphabet from memory
- Say/sing and point to capitals in ABC order, one by one
- Orient capital letter cards right-side up
- Recognize and name capitals in random order
- Orient lowercase letter cards right-side up
- Recognize and name lowercase letters
- Distinguish capitals from lowercase letters

Below is some of the significant research for Alphabet Knowledge. For additional Alphabet Knowledge research, see the reference section at the end of this teacher's guide.

National Association for the Education of Young Children & International Reading Assocation. 1998. "Learning to Read and Write: Developmentally Appropriate Practices for Young Children." *Young Children* 53(4):30-46. Accessed August 2011. http://www.naeyc.org/files/naeyc/file/positions/PSREAD98.pdf

Strickland, D.S., and J.A. Schickedanz. 2009. *Learning About Print in Preschool,* 2nd ed. Newark, DE: International Reading Association.

ABC's on the *Sing Along* CD

Singing the ABCs is the easiest way to memorize all the letter names. It's the start of alphabet knowledge. Teachers asked us to slow the tempo so children will clearly hear **L M N O P** as individual letters. Take a slow pace for singing and pointing to letters in ABC order.

Materials/Setup

- *Sing Along* CD, "Alphabet Song," track 2
- Pre-K Color Wall Cards

Grouping

Whole class

Support/ELL

Sing without the CD to slow things down.

Activity

1. Sing the "Alphabet Song," track 2 on the *Sing Along* CD along with children as they sing every letter clearly.
2. Sing the "Alphabet Song" again. Point to letters on the Pre-K Color Wall Cards as you sing.

✔ Check

Check that children are looking at cards and listen as they sing together.

More To Learn

Sing the alphabet with inside and outside voices. Learn this song from the *Sing, Sound & Count With Me* CD, track 17.

Look What We're Learning

Foundation Skills

- Say the alphabet by rote
- Participate in school routines
- Listen to and repeat songs

Alphabet Knowledge

- Point to and name capital letter
- Point to and name lowercase letters

Comprehension

- Listen to perform a task

Sensory Motor

- Notice and attach meaning to visual information

ABC Sing & Point

Children learn even unfamiliar capitals by pointing to letters in ABC order. First, play and sing the "ABC Song" until it's familiar. Then slowly sing the song, pausing to help children begin each letter line correctly. Finally, sing and point with the CD.

Materials/Setup
- *My First School Book*, page 4
- *Sing Along* CD, "Alphabet Song," track 2 and "Alphabet Song (Instrumental)," track 3

Grouping
Whole class

Support/ELL
Instead of singing, just say letters slowly as children point. They will join in when they can.

Activity

1. Children open *My First School Book* to page 4 and get ready to point.
2. Sing and point to the letters one by one, without the CD. Pause to help children begin with the first letter on each line.
3. Sing and point with track 2, or sing and point with the instrumental version, track 3.

✔ Check

Check handedness and for accurate pointing to the letters. Listen for children singing together.

More To Learn

Sing "There's a Dog in School," track 4. Children can bark the alphabet, too!

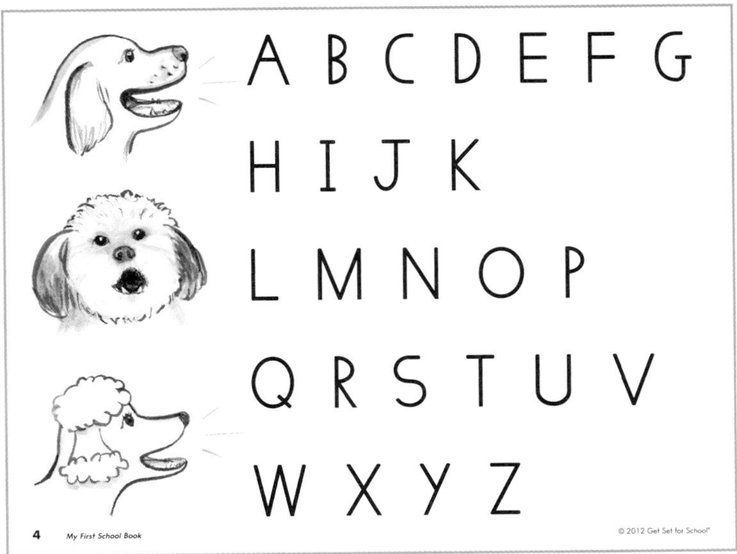

Look What We're Learning

Foundation Skills
- Use correct top-to-bottom, left-to-right directionality for letters

Alphabet Knowledge
- Point to and name capital letter
- Point to and name lowercase letters

Comprehension
- Listen to perform a task

Sensory Motor
- Notice and attach meaning to visual information

Alphabet Animals on Parade

The picture side of the A-B-C Touch & Flip® Cards has animal puzzles. Children put the animals together in three lines by color and the animals and letters are in alphabetical order. Flip the cards and the letter side is in alphabetical order too. Children don't even need to know letters to put animals and letters in ABC order.

Materials/Setup

- A-B-C Touch & Flip® Cards (Picture Set)

Grouping

Three groups of two children

Support/ELL

Instead of using all the cards/colors, work with one color or even a smaller set.

Activity

1. Put one green card on far left edge of the table, one yellow card in the middle, and one blue card on the right.
2. Children work in three pairs to sort the cards by color: green, yellow, blue.
3. Each color team puts the animals together on the edge of the table.
4. Marvel at the Alphabet Animals, and name them with children.
   Green: Alligator, bear, cow, etc.
   Yellow: Insects, jellyfish, kangaroo, etc.
   Blue: Rhinoceros, snakes, turtles, etc.
5. Children flip the cards in A to Z order and name each letter as it is turned.

✔ Check

Listen for children naming animals and letters correctly.

More To Learn

Read the animal cards saying, **A is the first letter in the word alligator.** Get out ABC animal books and look for animal/letter matches.

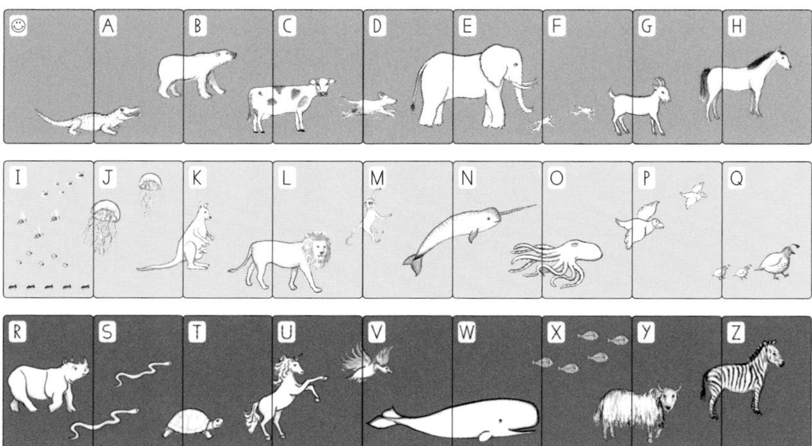

Look What We're Learning

Foundation Skills

- Recognize and identify basic colors
- Observe and sort

Alphabet Knowledge

- Point to and name capital letters

Sensory Motor

- Move an object in one hand to position it for use, placement, or release
- Notice and attach meaning to visual information

Social-Emotional

- Cooperate with other children
- Work with others to solve problems

Three a Day – Capitals to Say

Children learn three different capitals each day. Choose three children to put up the capital cards that begin their names. The class reads the capitals cards from left to right. Take them down and repeat. Children learn capitals, letter orientation, and the left-to-right reading with this fun activity.

Materials/Setup

- Line It Up™ Bar
- Three random Line It Up Letter Cards

Grouping

Whole class

Support/ELL

Help children to place letters right-side up. Name letters and have children repeat. Finger trace letters.

Activity

1. Three children put up their cards, beginning from left. E.g.: **J B L**
2. Teacher and children read the capitals chorally from left to right.
3. The children take them down and put them up again. A different child gets to be first, second, or third. Read again. E.g.: **L J B.**

✔ Check

Check orientation of letters. Are they placed right-side up? Do children start naming letters from the left?

More To Learn

Introduce beginning sounds. **This is Julie. Julie begins with the /j/ sound.**

Look What We're Learning

Alphabet Knowledge

- Point to and name capital letters
- Position capitals right-side up

Oral Language

- Demonstrate active listening by attending to instruction

Sensory Motor

- Notice and attach meaning to visual information
- Play with body awareness, balance, and regard for people and equipment
- Move naturally and place body to perform tasks

Social-Emotional

- Cooperate with other children
- Take turns with peers

CAPITALS on the Edge

Capital/lowercase confusion? Not when children play Capitals on the Edge. They pick up scattered letter cards, flip them over to the capital side, and line them up on the table edge. As they place them, they learn capitals from their friends. When the capitals are on the edge, you and children "read" them.

Materials/Setup

- A-B-C Touch & Flip® Cards (Letter Cards only)

Grouping

Small groups (2-3) standing at tables

Support/ELL

You may join in the activity until children can do it independently.

Activity

1. Scatter Letter Cards (six or more) any side up, any way on the table.
2. Demonstrate with one card to how to put a capital on the edge.
3. Children put all the capitals are on the edge.
4. You admire the capitals on the edge. You and children "read" them: Capital **B**, capital **K**, capital **M**, and so forth.
5. Mix up cards and repeat. Add more cards if desired.

✔ Check

Observe how children help their friends decide on capital or lowercase.

More To Learn

Encourage children to join as you "read" the letters from left to right. Let a child point as you say the letters.

Look What We're Learning

Foundation Skills

- Use correct top-to-bottom, left-to-right directionality for letters

Alphabet Knowledge

- Point to and name capital letters
- Position capitals right-side up

Sensory Motor

- Notice and attach meaning to visual information
- Play with body awareness, balance, and regard for people and equipment
- Move naturally and place body to perform tasks

Social-Emotional

- Cooperate with other children
- Work with others to solve problems

Name That Capital

Children watch you build a capital piece by piece. They watch, wondering which piece will be next and which letter it will be. The suspense draws their attention and participation. They learn how to build letters and name capitals.

Materials/Setup

- Sound Around Box™*
- Magnetic Pieces for Capitals

Grouping

Whole class

Support/ELL

Give children possible choices if they need them. I'm going to make an **F**, a **P** or a **D**. I wonder what it will be.

Video Lesson

View video lesson, Show Me Magnetic Wood Pieces, at **getsetforschool.com/videos**

*For more information about Sound Around Box, go to **getsetforschool.com**

Activity

1. Stand or sit in front of children.
2. You build a capital on the Sound Around Box™ piece by piece. **This capital starts with Big Line . . . then a Little Curve at the top. It's P and then I add a Little Line like this. Now it's . . .**
3. Children guess or name the letter as quickly as they can and help each other.

✔ Check

Notice and encourage guessing. Listen for better and better guessing or naming.

More To Learn

Ask children to tell how many pieces each letter uses. Say the pieces in the order used: **L has one Big Line and one Little Line.**

Look What We're Learning

Foundation Skills
- Sequencing
- Participate in school routines

Alphabet Knowledge
- Point to and name capital letters

Comprehension
- Listen to perform a task

Oral Language
- Demonstrate active listening by attending to instruction

Sensory Motor
- Notice and attach meaning to visual information
- Take turns with peers

Letter & Picture Match

Matching activities suit young children. They've known same and different since they were babies. Just try giving a baby the wrong sleepy toy. Children can indicate yes/match or no/match. You casually add the letter names and words they need.

Materials/Setup

- Capital Letter Cards for Wood Pieces

Grouping

One or two

Support/ELL

Show the reverse side of the card with the large letter. Have a child finger trace the large letter saying the name of the letter.

Activity

Row 1: Capitals made with Wood Pieces

- Name the first capital, ______ **Let's find a match.**
- Point to next capital, **Does this match ______?**
- If yes, say, **You are right. ______ matches ______.**
- If no, say, **You are right. ______ doesn't match ______.**

Row 2: Pictures/words that begin with the same capital letter (Do as Row 1).

Row 3: Capitals made with chalk on Slates (Do as Row 1).

Row 4: Capital and lowercase letters (Do as Row 1, but say capital ______ or lowercase ______).

✔ Check

Are children learning letters and pictures? When you ask, **Does this match?** Do they begin to say, **Yes, ______ matches ______,** or **No, ______ doesn't match ______.**

More To Learn

Instead of matching, try "reading" the whole card from top to bottom, left to right.

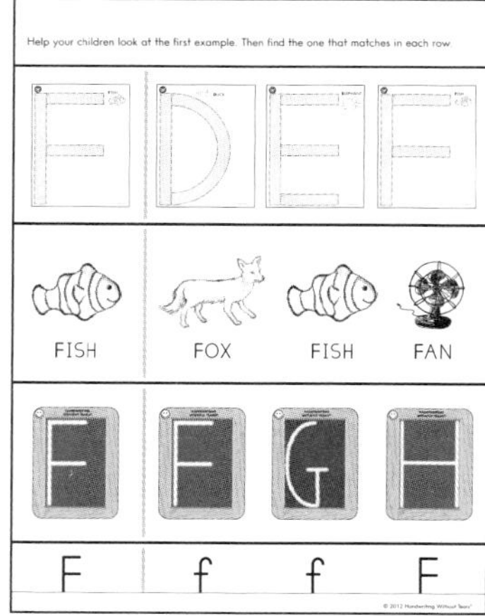

Look What We're Learning

Foundation Skills

- Listen to oral directions to attend to a simple task

Alphabet Knowledge

- Tell the difference between letters, pictures, and other symbols
- Point to and name capital letters
- Point to and name lowercase letters
- Match all capital and lowercase letters

Sensory Motor

- Notice and attach meaning to visual information

Oral Language

- Demonstrate active listening by attending to instruction

Social-Emotional

- Interact easily with familiar adults

Sign In Please!

This adaptation from an old TV show is still a crowd pleaser. Children enjoy the suspense (What letter will it be?) and the affirmation (I knew it would be **D.**). You keep the name of each new letter a secret until it is written. Children will be excited to keep doing this activity.

Materials/Setup

- White or blackboard with wide stop line near bottom
- Erasable crayon, marker, or chalk

Grouping

Whole class

Support/ELL

Help children start at the top. Make stopping easy by using a thick stopping line at first.

Activity

1. Write **A**, describing each step: **Big Line, Big Line, Little Line.**
2. Ask, **Whose name begins with A? Adam's name begins with A.**
3. Introduce Adam. Pause to let children finish your sentences.
   This is . . . Adam. Adam starts with letter . . . A.
   The first sound in Adam is . . . /a/.
4. Adam signs in with a big line down from **A**. He stops on the line. Continue writing letters for children to sign in alphabetically.

✔ Check

Observe handedness. Do children slow down to stop on the line?

More To Learn

This is math too. This chart shows how many children have the same letter. It shows the letters that don't correspond with children's names in the class.

Look What We're Learning

Foundation Skills
- Know name
- Listen to oral directions to attend to a simple task
- Participate in school routines

Alphabet Knowledge
- Recognize and name letters in own first name

Oral Language
- Demonstrate active listening by attending to instruction

Sensory Motor
- Use same hand consistently to hold crayons and perform skilled tasks
- Use fingers to hold crayons
- Use the right amount of pressure when holding and using tools
- Notice and attach meaning to visual information

Lowercase Letters on the Edge

When children can put capitals on edge, they're ready for lowercase. They pick up scattered cards, flip them to the lowercase side, and line them up on the table edge. As they place them, they learn lowercase letter **s** from their friends. When all the lowercase cards are on the edge, you and children "read" them.

Materials/Setup

- A-B-C Touch & Flip® Cards (Letter Cards only)

Grouping

Small groups (2-3) standing at tables

Support/ELL

Begin with lowercase letters that are same or similar to capitals (**c j k o p s t u v w x y z**).

Activity

1. Scatter Letter Cards (six or more) any side up, any way on the table.
2. Demonstrate how to put one lowercase letter on the edge.
3. Children put all the lowercase letters on the edge.
4. Admire all the lowercase letters on the edge. "Read" together: lowercase **m**, lowercase **r**, lowercase **b**, and so forth.
5. Mix up cards and repeat. Add more cards if desired.

✔ Check

Observe how children help their friends decide capital/lowercase. Look at their use of cues, the ☺ at the top, or the baseline. Listen for words: capital, lowercase, letter names.

More To Learn

Use more cards and "read" the letters quickly.

Look What We're Learning

Foundation Skills

- Use correct top-to-bottom, left-to-right directionality for letters

Alphabet Knowledge

- Point to and name lowercase letters
- Position lowercase letters right-side up

Sensory Motor

- Notice and attach meaning to visual information
- Play with body awareness, balance, and regard for people and equipment
- Move naturally and place body to perform tasks

Social-Emotional

- Cooperate with other children
- Work with others to solve problems

Name of the Day

Some children don't notice the alphabet on the wall. They will if you add their names under the Pre-K Color Wall Cards with this "Name of the Day" activity. Children will learn letters in the alphabet, letters in their names and in their friend's names.

Materials/Setup

- Pre-K Color Wall Cards
- Name Cards

Grouping

Whole class

Support/ELL

For the first few names, choose short names.

Activity

1. Choose a "Name of the Day" child.
2. Write the name slowly on a Name Card, saying each letter: **Capital F, lowercase i, o, n, a. Fiona! Fiona begins with F.**
3. Class slowly points to Pre-K Color Wall cards, saying the alphabet, but stopping at child's letter. **A, B, C, D, E, F Stop! Fiona begins with F.**
4. You tape Fiona's name under **F**.

Repeat activity another day until all names are displayed.

✔ Check

Notice sight reading some names. Notice poise.

More To Learn

Talk about where names are in the alphabet: beginning/middle/end. Discover whose names begin with the same letter.

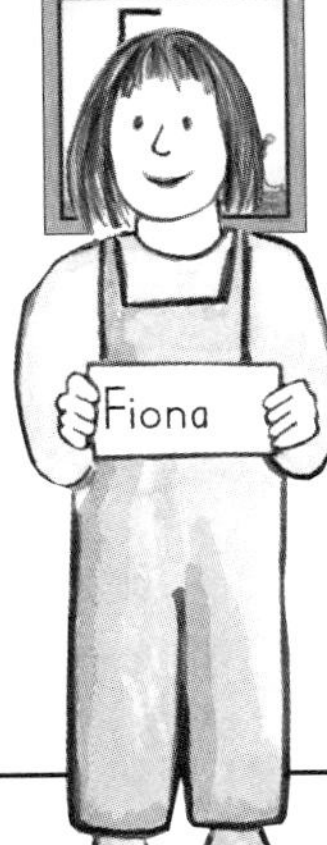

Look What We're Learning

Foundation Skills

- Know name

Alphabet Knowledge

- Recognize and name letters in own first name

Concepts About Print

- Recognize own name in print
- Recognize the names of friends and family in print

Oral Language

- Demonstrate active listening by attending to instruction

Sensory Motor

- Notice and attach meaning to visual information

ABC's on the *Rock, Rap, Tap & Learn* CD

Music makes learning memorable and joyful. Start by playing the CD in the background during free play. This builds familiarity. Then, when you sing in activities, children happily remember and are ready to participate.

Materials/Setup

- *Rock, Rap, Tap & Learn* CD, tracks 1, 19, 25

Grouping

Whole class

Support/ELL

Tap on the floor or tap the rhythm with paint sticks.

Activity

Choose an ABC song and an activity to go with it.

- "Alphabet Boogie," track 1: Do a simple boogie to the ABCs. This song helps naming the letters and gross motor skills.
- "Tapping to the ABCs," track 25: The name says it all!
- "Descending Letters," track 19: Make a baseline and write lowercase **g**, **j**, **y**, **p**, **q** to show children how the descending letters go below the line.

✔ Check

Observe children's gross motor skills. Are they showing rhythm as they tap and do the boogie to the ABCs?

More To Learn

With the "Descending Letters," track 19, line up descending letters randomly (from A-B-C Touch & Flip® Letter Cards). Children point to **g**, **j**, **y**, **p**, **q**.

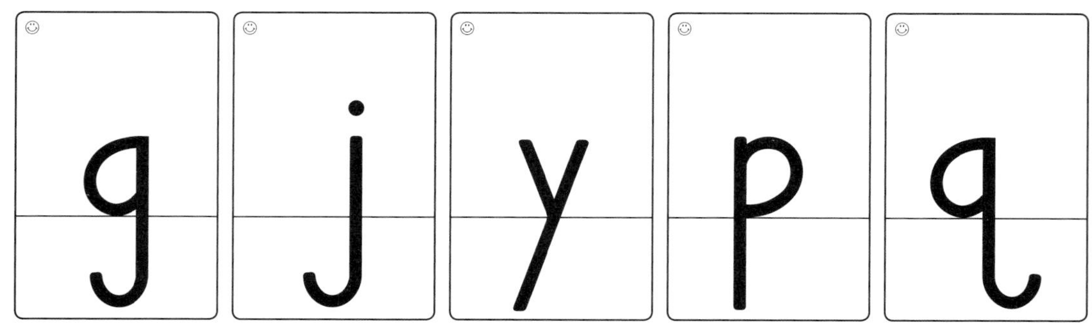

Look What We're Learning

Foundation Skills

- Listen to and repeat songs
- Participate in school routines

Alphabet Knowledge

- Point to and name capital letters
- Point to and name lowercase letters

Sensory Motor

- Use large muscle groups to maintain posture/position and mobility
- Use both sides of the body in activities
- Know where the body is in relation to space
- Tolerate motion in activities
- Play with body awareness, balance, and regard for people and equipment

Capital & Lowercase Letters

Here are the Pre-K Wall Cards in the child's book. This page is for school use now and for home use later. At home, children will remember them from school. Parents and children can point, think, and talk together about the alphabet and pictures. Parents may also use the activity suggestions in their child's book.

Materials/Setup

- *My First School Book*, pages 72–73

Grouping

Whole class

Support/ELL

Underline the sight letters children know. Keep them in review with random naming. Underline more letters as the child's knowledge of letters by sight grows.

Activity

1. Look for same and different: **Find capital A and lowercase a. Do they look alike? Find capital Z and lowercase z. Do they look alike?**
2. Talk about first letters and beginning sounds. **D is the first letter in the word duck. Listen to the first sound in d....uck. /d/ is the first sound.**
3. Point to letters in the beginning, middle, or end of the alphabet.
4. Help two children find the first letters in their names. Whose letter comes first in the alphabet?
5. Guess the letter. Hide the letters and just look at the picture. Which letter is hidden?

✔ Check

Check if children can find letters. Listen to them name letters.

More To Learn

Challenge children to find the letter that comes after _____ or before _____.

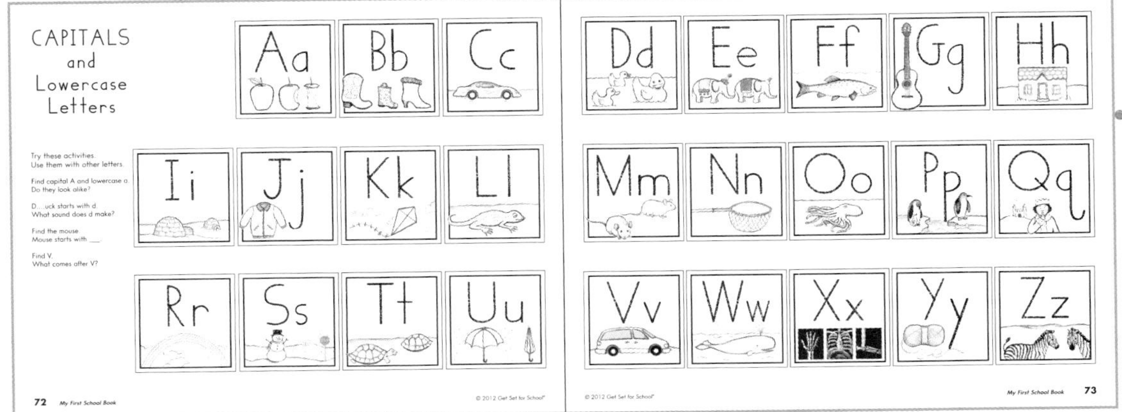
CAPITALS and Lowercase Letters

Try these activities.
Use them with other letters.

Find capital A and lowercase a.
Do they look alike?

D....uck starts with d.
What sound does d make?

Find the mouse.
Mouse starts with ___

Find V.
What comes after V?

Aa Bb Cc Dd Ee Ff Gg Hh Ii Jj Kk Ll Mm Nn Oo Pp Qq Rr Ss Tt Uu Vv Ww Xx Yy Zz

72 *My First School Book* © 2012 Get Set for School®

© 2012 Get Set for School® *My First School Book* 73

Look What We're Learning

Foundation Skills

- Use correct top-to-bottom, left-to-right directionality for letters
- Observe and sort
- Listen to oral directions to attend to a simple task

Alphabet Knowledge

- Point to and name capital letters
- Point to and name lowercase letters

Oral Language

- Demonstrate active listening by attending to instruction
- Ask and respond to simple questions

Sensory Motor

- Use same hand consistently to hold crayons and perform skilled tasks
- Use fingers to hold crayons
- Notice and attach meaning to visual information

Lowercase Matching

Some lowercase letters are harder to recognize, because they are so different from their capitals. We feature them here: **a i d r e n f h g m t l**. With matching, children continue to learn and build on what they already know.

Materials/Setup
- *My First School Book*, page 74-75
- Crayons

Grouping
Whole class

Support/ELL
Show children how to circle correctly: **Make a C for Circle. Turn C into a circle.**

Activity

1. **This is a matching page. See capital A and lowercase a. Let's look for matching lowercase a. Does lowercase g match? No. Does lowercase a match? Yes. That's why a is circled.**
2. **Look at capital I and lowercase i. Look for matching lowercase i. Does lowercase o match i? No. Does lowercase i match i? Yes. Circle lowercase i.**
3. Continue with capital **D** and lowercase **d**, and other letters.

✔ Check
Do children begin to use the word "lowercase"? Children locate the matching letter. See if they are circling using a Magic C stroke.

More To Learn
Find the letters that don't look like their capitals on the alphabet display on pages 74–75 of the workbook.

Lowercase Matching

Aa - ga   Rr - ri

Ii - oi   Ee - ae

Dd - da   Nn - nr

74 My First School Book   © 2012 Get Set for School®

Lowercase Matching

Ff - tf   Mm - mn

Hh - hn   Tt - ft

Gg - pg   Ll - kl

© 2012 Get Set for School®   My First School Book 75

Look What We're Learning

Foundation Skills
- Recognize and use common prepositions in speech
- Use correct top-to-bottom, left-to-right directionality for letters
- Participate in school routines
- Listen to oral directions to attend to a simple task

Alphabet Knowledge
- Recognize and name letters in own first and last name
- Point to and name capital letters
- Point to and name lowercase letters

Oral Language
- Demonstrate active listening by attending to instruction
- Ask and respond to simple questions

Sensory Motor
- Notice and attach meaning to visual information

Capital – Lowercase Matching

This is a fun matching activity that children do together. A simple puzzle puts capitals in alphabetical order. When capitals are in ABC order, it's easier to name them. Then children match capitals to capitals. Finally, they flip capitals to make a lowercase match.

Materials/Setup
- A-B-C Touch & Flip® Cards

Grouping
Three groups of two standing at three tables

Support/ELL
Plan pairs that can help each other and work together.

Activity
1. Three pairs put their animal puzzles together. **(A-H, I-Q, R-Z)**
2. Children flip cards over to show the capitals in alphabetical order.

   A B C D E F G H or **I J K L M N O P Q** or **R S T U V W X Y Z**
3. You give children out of order letter cards to match below the capitals.

A B C D E F G H	**I J K L M N O P Q**	**R S T U V W X Y Z**
A B C D E F G H	**I J K L M N O P Q**	**R S T U V W X Y Z**
4. Children flip the capitals to show lowercase matches.

A B C D E F G H	**I J K L M N O P Q**	**R S T U V W X Y Z**
a b c d e f g h	**i j k l m n o p q**	**r s t u v w x y z**

✔ Check
Observe how children help each other and name letters as they match letters.

More To Learn
Change groups to play again. Take away one letter (both capital and lowercase) and ask what's missing.

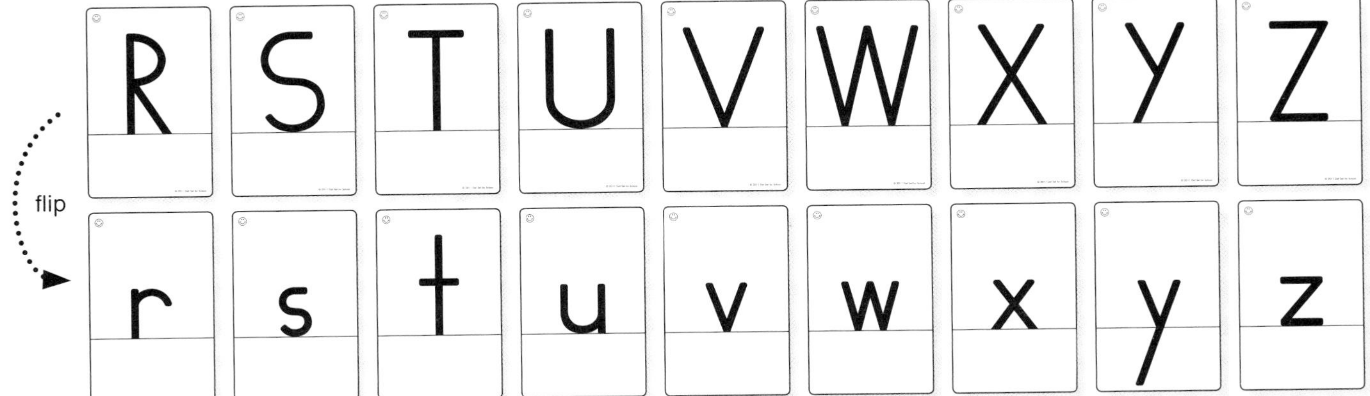

Look What We're Learning

Foundation Skills
- Use correct top-to-bottom, left-to-right directionality for letters
- Listen to oral directions to attend to a simple task

Alphabet Knowledge
- Point to and name capital letters
- Point to and name lowercase letters
- Match all capital and lowercase letters

Sensory Motor
- Notice and attach meaning to visual information

Social-Emotional
- Cooperate with other children
- Take turns with peers
- Work with others to solve problems

Colors & Coloring

Coloring plays an important role in Pre-K. People generally think of coloring as a choice between coloring books (too detailed and complex) or blank pages (not engaging or appealing). There's a better coloring option. Give young children simple coloring pages that invite and encourage coloring skill. At first, coloring is about learning to hold and move the crayon (Yakimishyn & Magill-Evans 2002). The Aim and Scribble pages (see pages 67-69) support those skills. Coloring is about recognizing and naming colors. Children learn about colors with 10 different color pages. For example, they use RED on the red page and think about RED for a STOP sign. Each color page features one color with pictures and related shapes to promote crayon/coloring control.

What about coloring in the lines? This skill develops gradually. When children color, they learn about form, size, shape, and direction. Fill in coloring on the color pages gives children experience with circular, diagonal, up and down, and side to side strokes. Staying in lines is easy when children follow the direction of a shape.

Coloring is also social. Children may want you to color with them or on their page. Seeing how you move the crayon helps them. When children have learned their colors, encourage creativity in coloring. There may be a gray elephant on the GRAY coloring page, but the elephant on the **E** page may be any color. Notice that the pictures always give space for free drawing and coloring. The pictures are there simply to interest children, to entice them to the page, to make them want to color and draw.

Objectives

- Use correct crayon grip
- Recognize and name 10 or more colors
- Notice colors and associate colors with familiar objects
- Develop fill-in coloring skill by adjusting coloring strokes to pictures being colored
- Color and draw creatively for pleasure

Below is some of the significant research for Colors and Coloring. For additional Colors and Coloring research, see the reference section at the end of this teacher's guide.

Yakimishyn, J.E., & J. Magill-Evans. 2002. "Comparisons Among Tools, Surface Orientation, and Pencil Grasp for Children 23 Months of Age." *American Journal of Occupational Therapy* 56:564-572.

Developing Crayon & Coloring Skills

Crayons

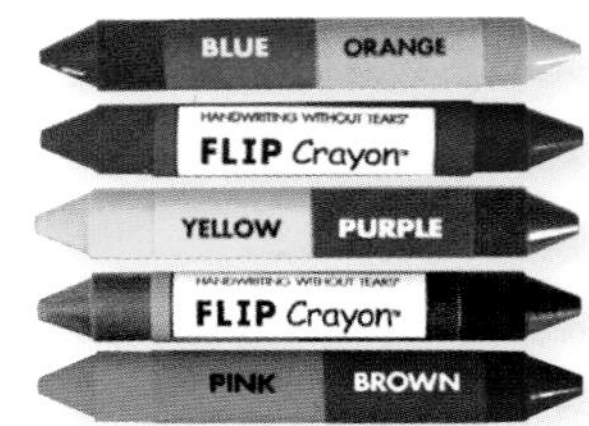

Even two-year-olds get crayons at restaurants. When parents give crayons, they should also teach children how to hold them. This is the year to help both your children and their parents. Give parents tips for helping with crayon grip. Give children small bits of broken crayon to make them use their fingertips (not a fisted or awkward grip). Flip Crayons® help children develop hand coordination and fine motor skills. Use "Crayon Song" on page 29 to teach correct crayon grip. Watch the video Crayon Song: Teaching Crayon Grip in our video library at **getsetforschool.com**. Picking-up and holding crayons correctly is the first step in learning a correct grip.

Crayon Skills

This step-by-step technique used in *My First School Book* is a great way to develop a correct crayon grip or to fix an awkward one. The trick is that you teach the grip in three separate stages. After children pick up a crayon and practice how to hold it correctly, you show them how to aim the crayon and scribble on paper. Then, you teach them how to make deliberate strokes.

The Aim and Scribble, Aim and Color, and Aim and Trace pages are uniquely designed to teach crayon skills: pick up, hold, aim and place, and move the crayon. Beginners love to land on a star or a firefly and make it shine when they wiggle and scribble.

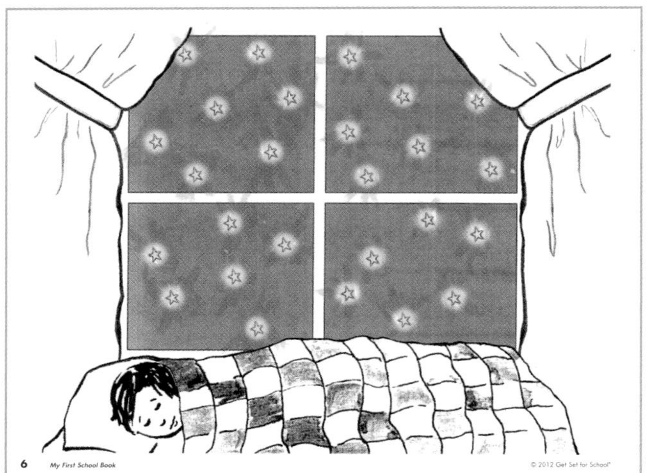

Aim and Scribble

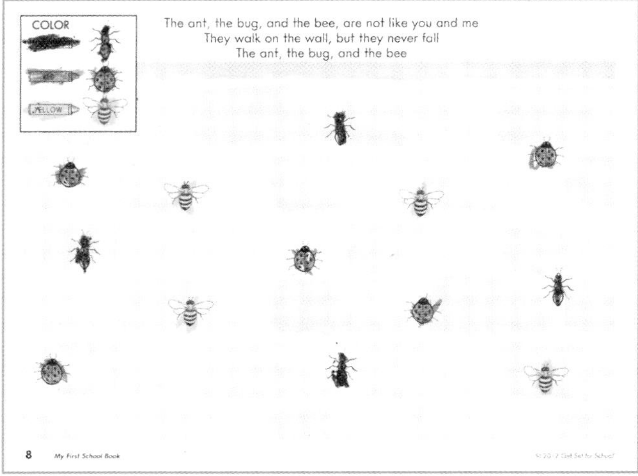

Aim and Color

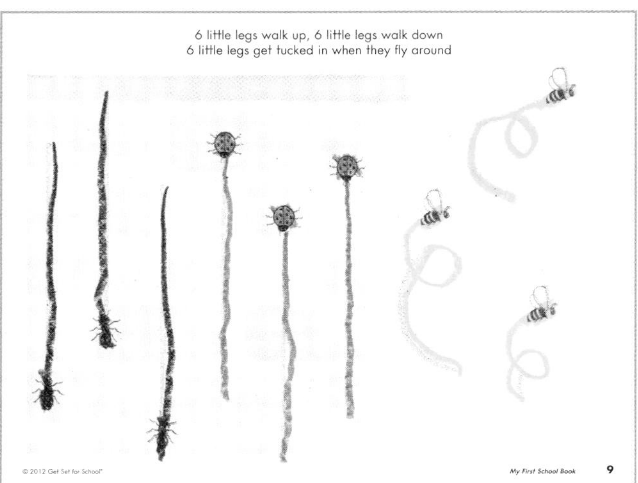

Aim and Trace

Coloring Skills

Fill-in coloring is next. On pages 10-19, children use just one color. They learn that one color and how to move the crayon for fill-in coloring. The pictures and shapes encourage children to stay within a certain area and use back and forth, up and down, side to side, or circular strokes.

The pictures and shapes are easy to color. They have bold outlines and plenty of uncluttered space. With these pages, you teach the names of all the pictures, colors, and shapes.

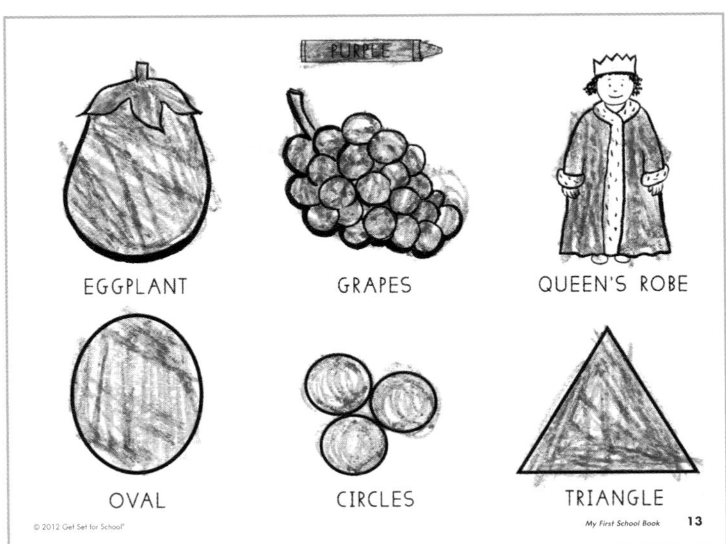

Coloring Page

Generally, the shape of the illustration will determine the stroke a child uses. See the crayon stroke pattern on the cow below. If a child is unable to organize his/her stroke to accommodate the shape of the illustration, encourage up and down strokes, which are easiest.

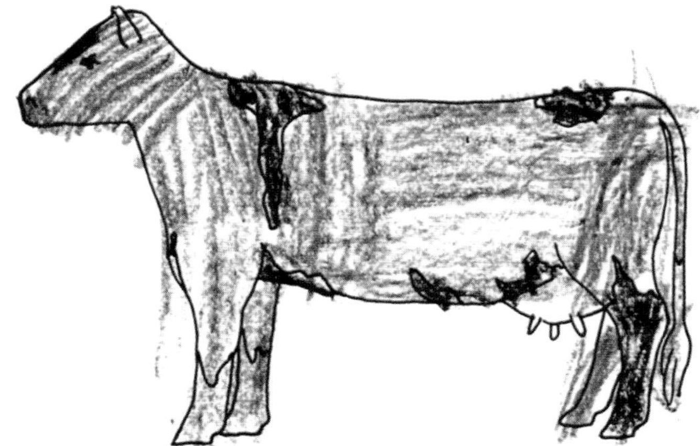

Child's Coloring Sample

This cow shows that the child has learned to move the crayon and color with different strokes and control:

- Up and down, vertical
- Side to side, horizontal
- Diagonal
- In the lines or along the direction of the lines

Coloring can give you clues about a child's readiness for formal handwriting instruction. When children color, observe their grip, focus, control, and use of their helper hand.

Teach Crayon Grip in Three Easy Steps

This step-by-step technique is a great way to develop or fix a correct crayon grip. The trick is to teach the grip in three separate stages. First, you help children pick up a crayon and hold it correctly. Second, you show them how to aim the crayon and scribble on paper. Third, you teach them how to make deliberate strokes.

1. **Pick Up** (Remember they don't write at this stage, so don't have paper on the table.)

   Tell children to pick up their crayons and hold them in the air! Help them place their fingers correctly. Then say, "Wow, that is just right! Let's take the crayons for a ride in the air." Now tell them to gently drop the crayons. Do it again. Sing the "Crayon Song", page 29, when you do this activity. Continue until children can automatically pick up and hold crayons correctly.

2. **Aim and Scribble** (Use blank paper with a dot like this • or start *My First School Book.*)

   Tell children to aim the crayon and put it on the dot or star. The little finger side of the crayon hand should rest on the paper. Some children will need help putting down the crayon hand. Remember the helping hand. It has to be flat and resting on the paper. Now it's time to scribble. Don't lift the crayon or hand, just wiggle and scribble. The beauty of this step is that children develop their crayon grip and finger control without being critical of how the writing or drawing looks.

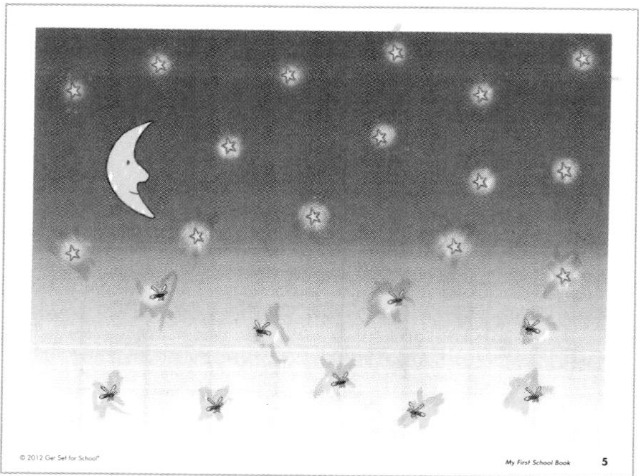

3. **Color/Trace/Draw** (Use *My First School Book.*)

   Have children pick up a crayon and use it for workbook pages or free drawing. Continue using previous steps as needed to reinforce the correct habits. This will get your students off to a wonderful start.

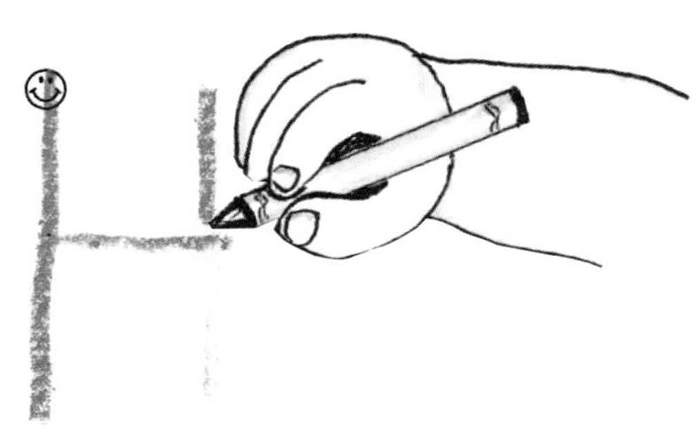

Night Sky — Aim & Scribble

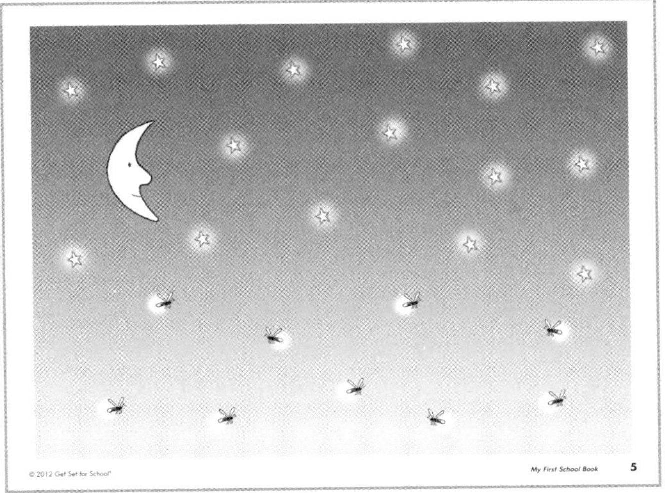

Activity

Have you ever seen stars in the sky? What color are they? What color is the moon? Have you ever seen a firefly? When do fireflies come out?

Look and Learn

Let's find fireflies. Point. **Let's find stars.** Point. **Let's find the moon.** Point.

Color and Draw

Let's sing the "Crayon Song" (See page 29). **Let's color the moon yellow.**

Trace and Write F

Let's scribble stars. Put the crayon on the star. Scribble. Let's scribble fireflies. Put the crayon on the firefly. Scribble.

✔ Check

Look at handedness. Children should use one hand consistently for holding crayon. Help children place helping hands.

Support/ELL

Help children with crayon grip. If necessary, use small bits of yellow crayon that must be held with fingertips.

More To Learn

Talk about the moon and how it changes. The C-shaped moon in the picture is a waning moon.

Look What We're Learning

Foundation Skills

- Listen to oral directions to attend to a simple task

Oral Language

- Demonstrate active listening by attending to instruction
- Respond to simple questions
- Learn words linked to content being taught

Writing

- Use helping hand to stabilize objects and papers

Sensory Motor

- Use same hand consistently to hold crayons
- Use fingers to hold crayons
- Use the right amount of pressure to hold and use tools

Vocabulary

stars
moon
fireflies

Twinkle – Aim & Scribble

Activity

Do you sleep under a quilt? What color is it? Have you ever seen stars in the sky? What color are they?

Look and Learn

Let's find the quilt. Point. **Let's find stars.** Point.

Color

Let's color the quilt. Let's color the curtains.

Scribble

Let's scribble stars. Put the crayon on the star. Scribble.

✔ Check

Observe handedness. Children should use one hand consistently to hold a crayon. Help them place their helping hand.

Support/ELL

Bring in a real quilt and show curtains to students for an opportunity to touch the curtains, feel a quilt, and have a discussion.

More To Learn

Sing "Twinkle, Twinkle Little Star."

Look What We're Learning

Foundation Skills
- Listen to oral directions to attend to a simple task

Oral Language
- Demonstrate active listening by attending to instruction
- Respond to simple questions
- Learn words linked to content being taught

Writing
- Use helping hand to stabilize objects and papers

Sensory Motor
- Use same hand consistently to hold crayons
- Use fingers to hold crayons
- Use the right amount of pressure to hold and use tools

Vocabulary

star
quilt
curtains
moon
night
girl

Fireworks — Aim & Scribble

Activity

Have you ever seen fireworks? What color are they? Do we see fireworks during the day or at night?

Look and Learn

Let's find fireworks. Point. **Let's find the children.** Point.

Color

Let's color the children.

Scribble

Let's scribble fireworks. Put the crayon on the center of the firework. Scribble.

✔ Check

Observe handedness. Children should use one hand consistently to hold a crayon. Help children place helping hands.

Support/ELL

Children may be unfamiliar with fireworks. Read a book to your class about fireworks.

More To Learn

In the USA, discuss the Fourth of July. In other countries, discuss other celebrations. Perhaps children have been to fireworks displays.

Look What We're Learning

Foundation Skills

- Listen to oral directions to attend to a simple task

Oral Language

- Respond to simple questions
- Learn words linked to content being taught

Writing

- Use helping hand to stabilize objects and papers

Sensory Motor

- Use same hand consistently to hold crayons
- Use fingers to hold crayons
- Use the right amount of pressure to hold and use tools

Vocabulary

fireworks

Aim & Color

With a black crayon in hand, children search for all the ants to color. Then, with a red crayon they find ladybugs to color. Finally, with a yellow crayon they color the bees.

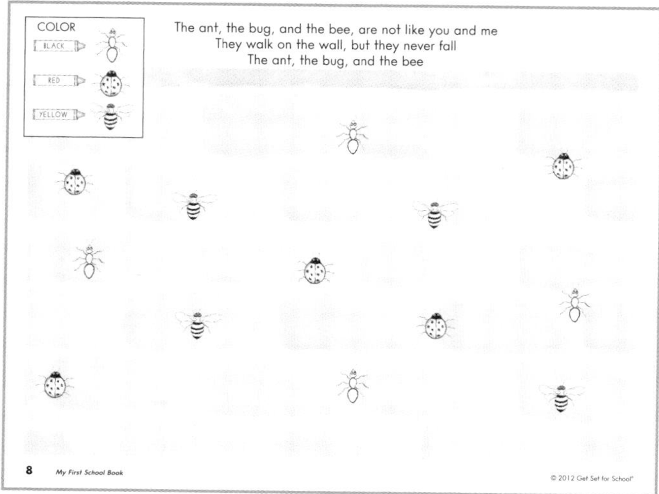

Activity

Have you ever seen ants? What color are they? Have you ever seen ladybugs? What color are they? Have you ever seen bees? What color are they?

Look and Learn

Let's find the top of the page. Let's find the insects in the corner. Where is the ant? Point. **Where is the ladybug?** Point. **Where is the bee?** Point.

Color

Let's color the insects in the top corner. Find a black crayon. Color the ant black. Find a red crayon. Color the ladybug red. Find a yellow crayon. Color the bee yellow. Lets' color all the ants. What color do we need? Let's color all the ladybugs now. What color do we need? Let's color all the bees. What color do we need?

✔ Check

Check children's crayon choices and grip.

Support/ELL

Teachers may color the crayons on the insect chart to show the color to use for each insect.

More To Learn

Look for things around the room that are black, red, and yellow.

Look What We're Learning

Foundation Skills

- Recognize and identify basic colors
- Listen to oral directions to attend to a simple task

Oral Language

- Respond to simple questions
- Learn words linked to content being taught

Writing

- Use helping hand to stabilize objects and papers

Sensory Motor

- Use same hand consistently to hold crayons
- Use fingers to hold crayons
- Use the right amount of pressure to hold and use tools

Vocabulary

ladybug
bee
black
red
yellow

Aim & Trace

With a black crayon in hand, children color each ant and then walk it up the wall. Ladybugs will walk down and bees will fly around. Children learn to follow the crayon strokes up, down, and around.

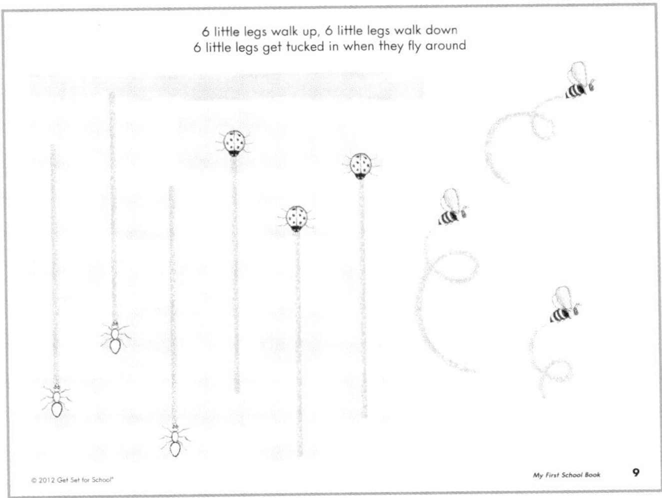

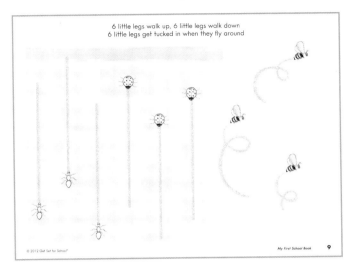

Activity

What are the ants doing? The ants are walking up the wall. What are the bugs doing? The bugs are walking down the wall. What are the bees doing? The bees are flying around.

Look and Learn

Where are the ants? Point. **Let's find ladybugs.** Point. **Let's find the bees.** Point.

Trace

Find a black crayon. Color the ant black. Use the crayon to walk the ant up the wall. Find a red crayon. Color the ladybug red. Make the ladybug walk down the wall. Find a yellow crayon. Color the bee yellow. Make the bee fly around. Follow the flying line.

✔ Check

Check start. The insects give a good starting place. Notice stop. It takes control to end the stroke.

Support/ELL

Help children finger trace the strokes before they crayon trace them.

More To Learn

Act out "The Ant, the Bug and the Bee" from the *Sing Along* CD, track 14. Hold up 3 fingers on each hand for 6 little legs.

Look What We're Learning

Foundation Skills

- Recognize and identify basic colors
- Listen to oral directions to attend to a simple task

Oral Language

- Respond to simple questions
- Learn words linked to content being taught

Writing

- Use helping hand to stabilize objects and papers

Sensory Motor

- Use same hand consistently to hold crayons
- Use fingers to hold crayons
- Use the right amount of pressure to hold and use tools

Vocabulary

up
down

Red

Help children choose a RED crayon or the RED/GREEN Flip Crayon®. Children do not have to finish this page before they color on the GREEN page. They may change crayons or flip the crayon to GREEN.

Activity

Where is the crayon? Point. **Let's color the crayon red. Do you know anything that is red?**

Look and Learn

Let's find the apple. Point. **Let's find the stop sign.** Point. **Let's find the barn.** Point. **Let's find the shapes. Where is the circle? The circle is under the apple.** Continue.

Color

Let's sing the "Crayon Song" (see page 29). **This is a page for red. Use red to color the apple, stop sign, or barn red. Color the shapes red too.**

Trace

Let's finger trace the circle. The circle is under the apple. Make a Magic C to start the circle.

✔ Check

Observe how children finger trace circles. Help them start at the top and make C for Circle.

Support/ELL

Use toys or objects to add interest. STOP signs are familiar. Some children may know them as ALTO signs. Find pictures of ALTO signs online to share.

More To Learn

Bring in red, green, and yellow apples. Say the names: perhaps Granny Smith or Red Delicious, sizes, and shapes.

Look What We're Learning

Foundation Skills

- Recognize and identify basic colors
- Recognize familiar two-dimensional shapes
- Listen to oral directions to attend to a simple task

Oral Language

- Respond to simple questions
- Learn words linked to content being taught

Writing

- Use helping hand to stabilize objects and papers

Sensory Motor

- Use same hand consistently to hold crayons
- Use fingers to hold crayons
- Use index finger to trace shapes

Vocabulary

red, apple, stop sign, barn, circle, octagon, square, pictures, over, under

Children choose a GREEN crayon or the RED/GREEN Flip Crayon®. Children develop fine motor skills when they flip to change colors and pages.

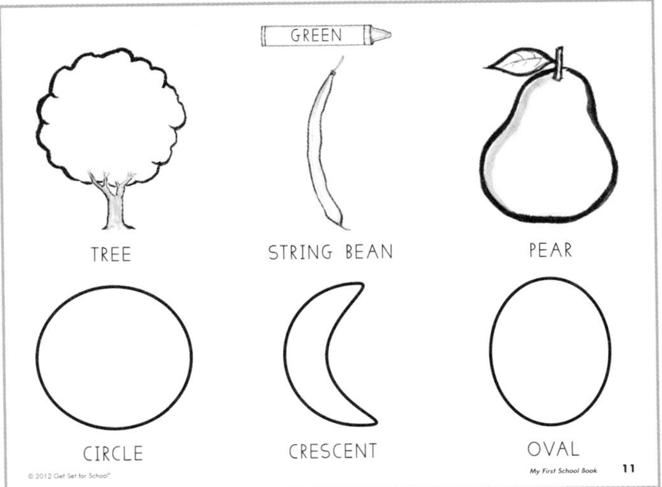

Activity

Where is the crayon? Point. **Let's color the crayon green. Do you know anything that is green?**

Look and Learn

Let's find the tree. Point. **Let's find the string bean.** Point. **Let's find the pear.** Point.

Let's find the shapes. Where is the oval?. The oval is under the pear. Continue.

Color

On this page, use green to color the tree, string bean, and pear. Color the shapes green too.

Trace

Let's trace the string bean. Start at the top. Now, let's trace the crescent. It is under the string bean. Start at the top.

✔ Check

Observe children as they select their crayons. Did they choose the color green?

Support/ELL

Model how to answer "Where is..." questions. Use question words in the answer. Where is the oval? The oval is ______. Practice this when asking where each shape is located.

More To Learn

Go on a "Green Hunt" with your students, and have them search for things around the classroom that are green.

Look What We're Learning

Foundation Skills

- Recognize and identify basic colors
- Recognize familiar two-dimensional shapes
- Listen to oral directions to attend to a simple task

Oral Language

- Respond to simple questions
- Learn words linked to content being taught

Writing

- Use helping hand to stabilize objects and papers

Sensory Motor

- Use same hand consistently to hold crayons
- Use fingers to hold crayons
- Use index finger to trace shapes

Vocabulary

green
tree
string bean
pear
circle
crescent
oval

Help children choose a YELLOW crayon or the YELLOW/PURPLE Flip Crayon®. Children do not have to finish this page before they color on the PURPLE page. They may change crayons or flip crayons for the PURPLE page.

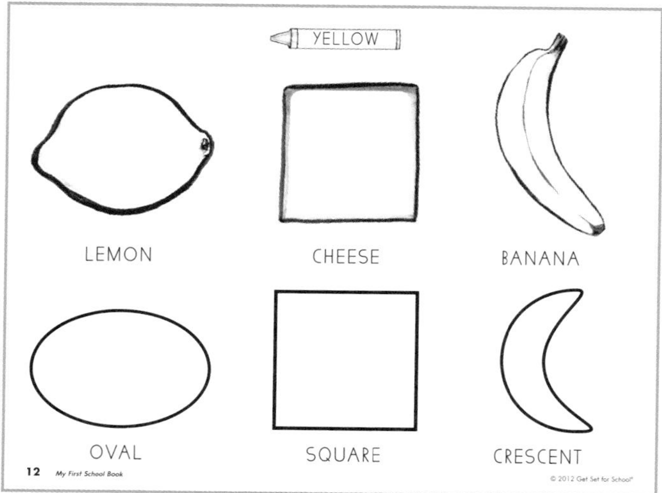

Activity

Where is the crayon? Point. **Let's color the crayon yellow. Do you know anything that is yellow?**

Look and Learn

Let's find the lemon. Point. **Let's find the cheese.** Point. **Let's find the banana.** Point.

Let's find the shapes. Where is the oval? The oval is under the lemon. Continue.

Color

This is a page for yellow. Use yellow to color the lemon, cheese, or banana. Color the shapes yellow too.

Trace

Let's finger trace the square. Stop at the corners to turn.

✔ Check

Observe children as they choose their crayons. Did they select the color yellow?

Support/ELL

Use real or plastic lemons and bananas to add interest. Let children feel the shape with their eyes closed. They can even taste the fruit if there is time.

More To Learn

Look at crescent and full moons in books and in the sky. Draw the moon they'll see at night: crescent, full, or half moon.

Look What We're Learning

Foundation Skills
- Recognize and identify basic colors
- Recognize familiar two-dimensional shapes
- Listen to oral directions to attend to a simple task

Oral Language
- Respond to simple questions
- Learn words linked to content being taught

Writing
- Use helping hand to stabilize objects and papers

Sensory Motor
- Use same hand consistently to hold crayons
- Use fingers to hold crayons
- Use index finger to trace shapes

Vocabulary

yellow
lemon
cheese
banana
oval
square
crescent

Children choose a PURPLE crayons or the YELLOW/PURPLE Flip Crayon®. They flip the crayon to change colors and develop coordination and crayon grip.

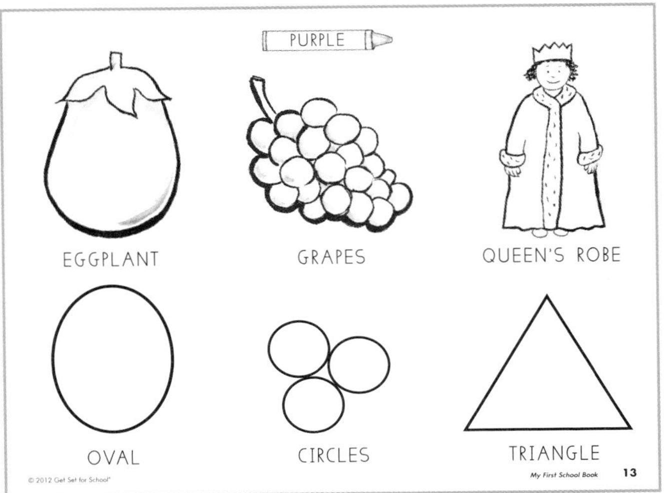

Activity

Where is the crayon? Point. **Let's color the crayon purple. Do you know anything that is purple?**

Look and Learn

Let's find the eggplant. Point. **Let's find the grapes.** Point. **Let's find the queen and her robe. Let's find the shapes. Where are the circles? The circles are under the grapes.** Continue.

Color

This is a page for purple. Use purple to color the eggplant, the grapes, or the queen's robe. Color the shapes purple too. Watch me make little circular strokes for the grapes or circles.

Trace

Let's finger trace the oval. Are there any corners?

✔ Check

Observe children as they hold their crayons. Do they hold them correctly?

Support/ELL

Make paper crowns. Play dress up as kings or queens. Use a purple cloth for a robe.

More To Learn

Ask about other colors for grapes. Mix red and blue paint to make purple. Eat purple grapes for a snack.

Look What We're Learning

Foundation Skills

- Recognize and identify basic colors
- Recognize familiar two-dimensional shapes
- Listen to oral directions to attend to a simple task

Oral Language

- Respond to simple questions
- Learn words linked to content being taught

Writing

- Use helping hand to stabilize objects and papers

Sensory Motor

- Use same hand consistently to hold crayons
- Use fingers to hold crayons
- Use index finger to trace shapes

Vocabulary

purple
eggplant
grapes
queen
oval
circles
triangle

Blue

Help children choose a BLUE crayon or the BLUE/ORANGE Flip Crayon®. Children do not have to finish this page before they color on the orange page.

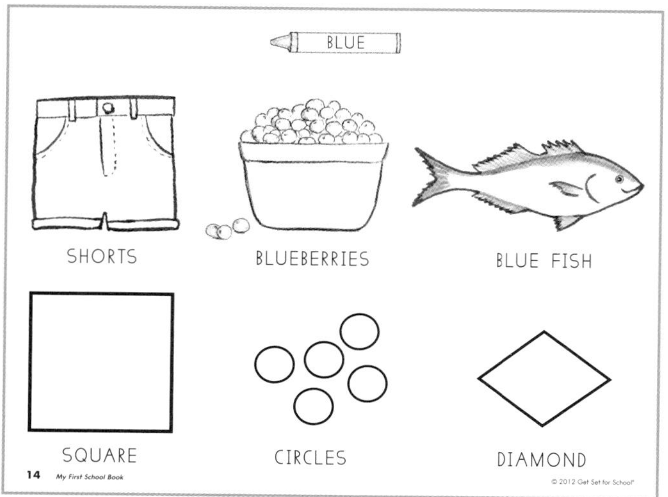

Activity

Where is the crayon? Point. **Let's color the crayon blue. Do you know anything that is blue?**

Look and Learn
Let's find the shorts. Point. **Let's find the blueberries.** Point. **Let's find the blue fish.**
Let's find the shapes. Where is the square? The square is under the shorts. Continue.

Color
Let's sing the "Crayon Song." (Lyrics and activities on page 29.) **Color the crayon blue. Use blue to color the shorts, blueberries, or blue fish. Color the shapes blue too.**

Trace
Let's finger trace the diamond. Stop and turn at the corners. Make four stops.

✔ Check

Observe children as they choose their crayons. Do they correctly select the blue crayon?

Support/ELL

Color with some children and help them begin with small circular strokes.

More To Learn

Ask about the pictures. What can we eat? We can eat blueberries. Ask this question on other pages to encourage children to think and sort.

Look What We're Learning

Foundation Skills
- Recognize and identify basic colors
- Recognize familiar two-dimensional shapes
- Listen to oral directions to attend to a simple task

Oral Language
- Respond to simple questions
- Learn words linked to content being taught

Writing
- Use helping hand to stabilize objects and papers

Sensory Motor
- Use same hand consistently to hold crayons
- Use fingers to hold crayons
- Use index finger to trace shapes

Vocabulary

shorts
blueberries
blue fish
square
circles
diamond

Children choose an ORANGE crayon or the BLUE/ORANGE Flip Crayon®. When children flip ORANGE to BLUE to color on the BLUE page, it doesn't matter how they flip the crayon. They may use two hands or one.

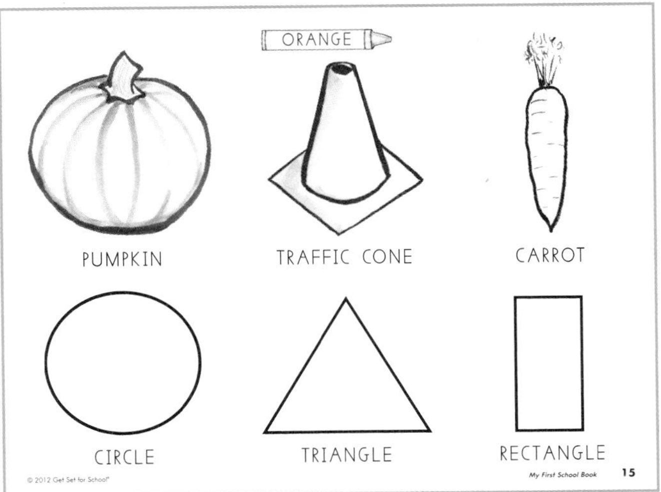

Activity

Where is the crayon? Point. **Let's color the crayon orange. Do you know anything that is orange?**

Look and Learn

Let's find the pumpkin. Point. **Let's find the carrot.** Point. **Let's find the traffic cone.** Point. **Let's find the shapes. Where is the rectangle? The rectangle is under the carrot.** Continue.

Color

Color the crayon orange. Use orange to color the pumpkin, traffic cone, or carrot. Color the shapes orange too.

Trace

Let's finger trace the triangle. Stop and turn at the corners. Make three stops.

✔ Check

Observe children as they choose their crayons. Do they correctly select the orange crayon?

Support/ELL

Remember to model answers to "Where is" questions.

Where is the circle? The circle is under ______.

More To Learn

Bring in a carrot with a top. Children may not recognize the carrot or know that carrots grow in the ground. Eat carrots for a snack. Mix yellow and red paint to make orange.

Look What We're Learning

Foundation Skills

- Recognize and identify basic colors
- Recognize familiar two-dimensional shapes
- Listen to oral directions to attend to a simple task

Oral Language

- Respond to simple questions
- Learn words linked to content being taught

Writing

- Use helping hand to stabilize objects and papers

Sensory Motor

- Use same hand consistently to hold crayons
- Use fingers to hold crayons
- Use index finger to trace shapes

Vocabulary

orange
pumpkin
carrot
traffic cone
carrot
circle
triangle
rectangle

Pink

Help children choose PINK and BROWN crayons or the PINK/BROWN Flip Crayon®. This Flip Crayon is ideal for coloring skin tones. Children may skip from page to page, coloring what interests them.

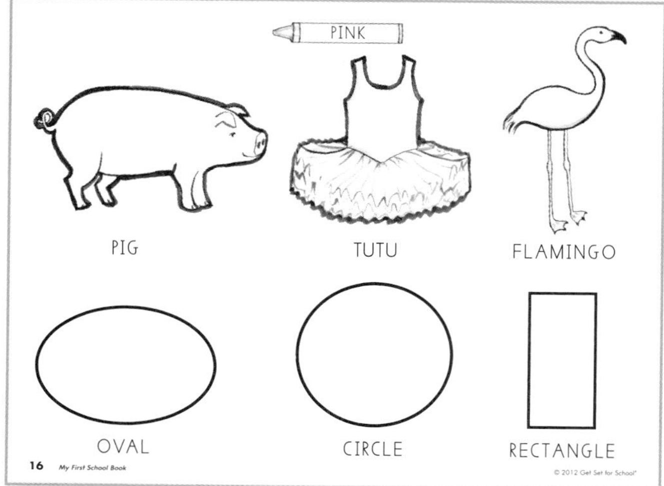

Activity

Where is the crayon? Point. **Let's color the crayon pink. Do you know anything that is pink?**

Look and Learn

Let's find the pig. Point. **Let's find the tutu.** Point. **Let's find the flamingo.** Point.

Let's find the shapes. Where is the oval? The oval is under the pig. Continue.

Color

Use pink to color the pig, tutu, and flamingo. Color the shapes pink too.

Trace

Let's finger trace the circle. The circle is under the tutu. Make a Magic C to start the circle.

✔ Check

Observe children choosing their crayons. Do they correctly select the pink crayon?

Support/ELL

Stand on one leg like flamingos do. Introduce FLAMINGO with changing voices. Children repeat your high, low, loud, or soft voice. FLUH (repeat) FLUH - MING (repeat) FLUH - MING - GOH (repeat).

More To Learn

Add one drop of red paint to white paint. Stir to make pink. That's a tint. Find flamingos in a bird book.

Look What We're Learning

Foundation Skills

- Recognize and identify basic colors
- Recognize familiar two-dimensional shapes
- Listen to oral directions to attend to a simple task

Oral Language

- Respond to simple questions
- Learn words linked to content being taught

Writing

- Use helping hand to stabilize objects and papers

Sensory Motor

- Use same hand consistently to hold crayons
- Use fingers to hold crayons
- Use index finger to trace shapes

Vocabulary

pink
pig
tutu
flamingo
oval
circle
rectangle

Children choose a BROWN crayon or the PINK/BROWN Flip Crayon®.

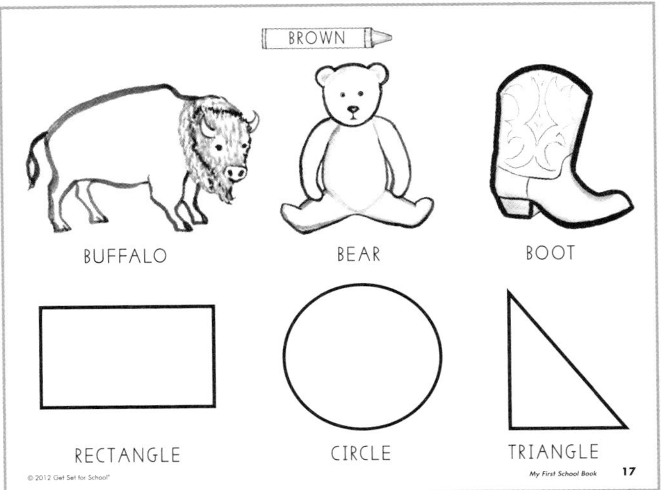

Activity

Where is the crayon? Point. **Let's color the crayon brown. Do you know anything that is brown?**

Look and Learn

Let's find the buffalo. Point. **Let's find the bear.** Point. **Let's find the boot.** Point.

Let's find the shapes. Where is the circle? The circle is under the bear. Continue.

Color

Use brown to color the buffalo, bear, and boot. Color the shapes brown too.

Trace

Let's trace shapes. Put finger on shape and trace.

✔ Check

Observe children choosing their crayons. Do they correctly select the brown crayon?

Support/ELL

If children liked using voices for flamingo, then repeat that voice activity for "BUF - FA - LO." Use a high voice the first time you build the word, then a low voice the next time.

More To Learn

Read books about brown bears and polar bears. **Look, letter B is the first letter in BUFFALO, BEAR, and BOOT.** Mix red and green to make brown.

Look What We're Learning

Foundation Skills
- Recognize and identify basic colors
- Recognize familiar two-dimensional shapes
- Listen to oral directions to attend to a simple task

Oral Language
- Respond to simple questions
- Learn words linked to content being taught

Writing
- Use helping hand to stabilize objects and papers

Sensory Motor
- Use same hand consistently to hold crayons
- Use fingers to hold crayons
- Use index finger to trace shapes

Vocabulary

brown
buffalo
bear
boot
rectangle
circle
triangle

Gray

Help children choose GRAY and BLACK crayons or the GRAY/BLACK Flip Crayon®.

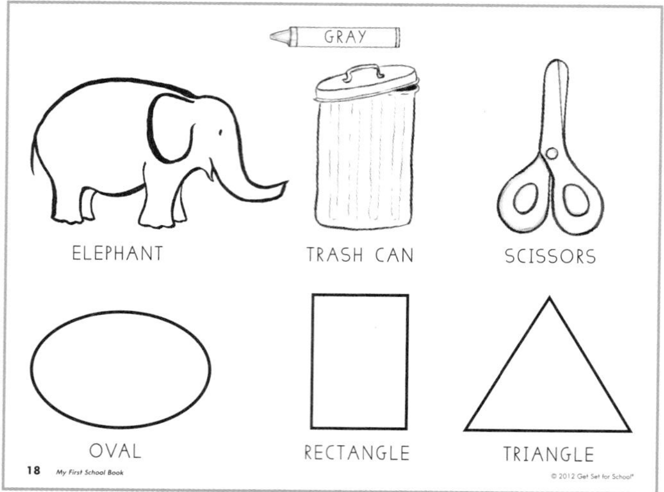

Activity

Where is the crayon? Point. **Let's color the crayon gray. Do you know anything that is gray?**

Look and Learn

Where is the elephant? Point. **Let's find the trash can.** Point. **Let's find shapes. Where is oval? The oval is under the elephant. The rectangle is under the trash can.** Continue.

Color

Color the elephant, trash can, and scissors gray. Color the shapes below gray.

Trace

Let's trace shapes. Put finger on shape and trace.

✔ Check

Observe children choosing their crayons. Do they correctly select the gray crayon?

Support/ELL

Show children pictures of things that are gray.

More To Learn

Point to gray items in the room. Make gray by mixing black and white.

Look What We're Learning

Foundation Skills

- Recognize and identify basic colors
- Recognize familiar two-dimensional shapes
- Listen to oral directions to attend to a simple task

Oral Language

- Respond to simple questions
- Learn words linked to content being taught

Writing

- Use helping hand to stabilize objects and papers

Sensory Motor

- Use same hand consistently to hold crayons
- Use fingers to hold crayons
- Use index finger to trace shapes

Vocabulary

gray
elephant
trash can
scissors
oval
rectangle
triangle

Black

The BLACK crayon is a good choice for tracing letters and numbers, but children may choose any color they like.

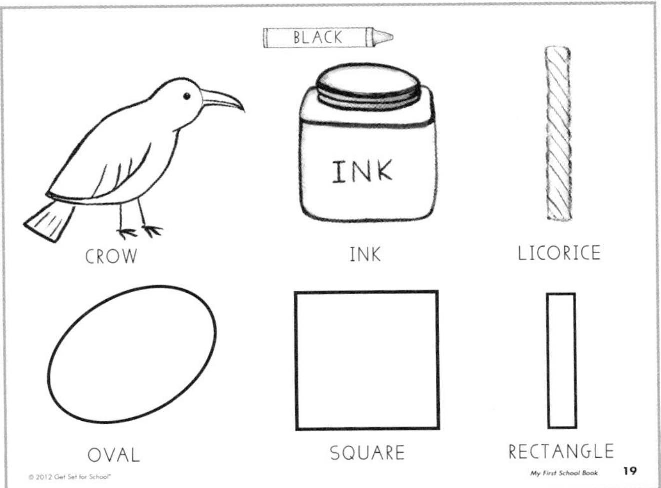

Activity

Where is the crayon? Point. **Let's color the crayon black. Do you know anything that is black?**

Look and Learn

Let's find the crow. Point. **Let's find the ink.** Point. **Repeat until you have found all items.**

Color

Color the crow, ink, and licorice black. Color the shapes below black. Let's sing the "Crayon Song." (Lyrics and activities on page 29.)

Trace

Let's trace shapes. Put finger on shape and trace.

✔ Check

Observe children choosing their crayons. Do they correctly select the black crayon?

Support/ELL

Show children pictures of things that are black.

More To Learn

Point to black items in the room. See who's wearing black shoes.

Look What We're Learning

Foundation Skills
- Recognize and identify basic colors
- Recognize familiar two-dimensional shapes
- Listen to oral directions to attend to a simple task

Oral Language
- Respond to simple questions
- Learn words linked to content being taught

Writing
- Use helping hand to stabilize objects and papers

Sensory Motor
- Use same hand consistently to hold crayons
- Use fingers to hold crayons
- Use index finger to trace shapes

Vocabulary

black
ink
crow
licorice
oval
square
rectangle

Pre-Writing

Writing skills depend on instruction. Without instruction, children improvise. They go to kindergarten "drawing" letters any which way. Their bad habits (starting at the bottom, making strokes in the wrong order, using awkward grip) go with them to kindergarten and hurt their academic performance. Children's play writing enthusiasm disappears when they can't meet expectations or write well.

A playful, developmentally based approach is the most effective way to develop readiness and beginning handwriting skills (Amundson 2001). We've done a task analysis of the skills children need—there are many! Children need social/school behaviors to imitate their teachers and learn with others. They need vocabulary to understand directions, alphabet knowledge, and familiarity with letters and numbers. They need fine motor (small muscle) skills, and awareness of size, shape, and position (Yakimishyn & Magill-Evans 2002).

And they need you—a teacher who can meet them where they are and get them ready for handwriting with music, movement, Wood Pieces, and hands-on letter play. This active approach is easy and fun for them and for you. Here's how to get them ready.

Objectives

- Participate in pre-writing activities
- Imitate teacher movements and words
- Learn letter parts (Wood Piece words: Big Line, Little Line, Big Curve, Little Curve)
- Learn position words (top, middle, bottom, up, down, under, over...)
- Imitate the teacher's letter building
- Build letters with Wood Pieces step by step
- Build letters right-side up
- Make letters with multisensory materials
- Orient letters to face the right way

Below is some of the significant research for Pre-Writing. For additional Pre-Writing research, see the reference section at the end of this teacher's guide.

Amundson, S.J. 2001. "Prewriting and Handwriting Skills." In *Occupational Therapy for Children*, 4th ed., edited by J. Case-Smith, 545-570. Sydney, Australia: Mosby.

Yakimishyn, J.E., & J. Magill-Evans. 2002. "Comparisons Among Tools, Surface Orientation, and Pencil Grasp for Children 23 Months of Age." *American Journal of Occupational Therapy* 56:564-572.

Wood Piece Play

Wood Piece Play has no entry requirements. Every child can play regardless of readiness level. Wood Piece Play takes children from the very beginning to teach everything they need for readiness and pre-writing. To children, it's just play–but this is play that leads directly to school readiness skills.

Music with Wood Pieces

Children take very naturally to music. They learn the words of the songs you play. Then when you introduce the "Wood Piece Pokey," or the "Big Line March," they're eager to participate. That sense of familiarity builds memory.

Polish, Sort, and Trade Wood Pieces

Call Wood Pieces by their names as children polish them. They pick up the pieces and pick up the words! They also pick up manners, "Please, may I have that Little Line?"

Wood Pieces in a Bag

Children get a feel for Wood Pieces when they polish them. Now they reach into a bag and say what they feel (tactile discrimination). Just for fun, you may put something else (a spoon, for example) in the bag.

Wood Pieces in a Box

This is a different tactile activity. Children feel for a certain piece. The piece to find is displayed on the Sound Around Box™. Children's fingers search for a matching Magnetic Piece.

Positions and Body Parts with Wood Pieces

Children quickly move a Big Line like you do. They also say your words: Big Line UNDER my arm, OVER my arm. It's easy to learn position words and body parts.

Curves and Circles

Children explore and create as they combine two big curves for a big **O**. It's even more fun for children to put the **O** up to their faces and say "OOOOOH," or "zeeero." A big curve by itself can be a smile or a rainbow.

Vertical, Horizontal, and Diagonal Positions

As children imitate these positions, they're getting ready for writing! So many letters are made with vertical, horizontal, and diagonal lines.

Wood Pieces with Music

Wood Piece Play starts with music because children learn so naturally and respond so positively to music. Music serves them emotionally and cognitively. When you sing to children, you know that they follow routines, co-operate, and engage more readily. Teach the Wood Pieces with music!

Materials/Setup

- *Sing Along* CD
  - "Golden Slippers," track 20
  - "Wood Piece Pokey," track 25
  - "Tap, Tap, Tap," track 19
- *Rock, Rap, Tap & Learn* CD
  - "Hey, Hey! Big Line," track 4
  - "Big Line March," track 6
- Wood Pieces

Grouping

Whole group; small group

Support/ELL

For "Wood Piece Pokey," use the CD just for familiarity. Then sing without CD at the right tempo for your children.

Video Lesson

View the video lesson, Tap, Tap, Tap Song: Body Awareness, at **getsetforschool.com/videos**

Activity

1. Introduce children to the names of the Wood Pieces.
   This is a Big Line. Hold it up in the air.
   Can you show me a Big Line? Children hold it up in the air.
2. Repeat for other shapes.
   This is a Little Line. Can you show me a Little Line?
   This is a Big Curve. Can you show me a Big Curve?
   This is a Little Curve. Can you show me a Little Curve?
3. Play songs from the CDs and have children participate as the music plays. Note: For "Golden Slippers," use two Big Lines. Children follow as you move the Big Lines in different ways.

✔ Check

Check handedness (which hand does the tapping?). Observe as children listen and follow directions.

More To Learn

Make up your own verses to extend a song. For Wood Piece Pokey, the ideas are endless.

Look What We're Learning

Foundation Skills

- Imitate teacher's body movements
- Listen to oral directions to attend to a simple task
- Listen to and repeat songs

Oral Language

- Learn words linked to content being taught

Sensory Motor

- Use large muscle groups to maintain posture/position and mobility
- Use both sides of the body in activities
- Tolerate motion in activities
- Handle play materials without an avoidance response
- Notice and attach meaning to visual information

Vocabulary

big
little
line
curve

Wood Pieces Set

Wood Pieces Set for Capital Letters

Set includes 26 pieces:

- 8 Big Lines
- 6 Little Lines
- 6 Big Curves
- 6 Little Curves

Buy from Get Set for School® or make your own.

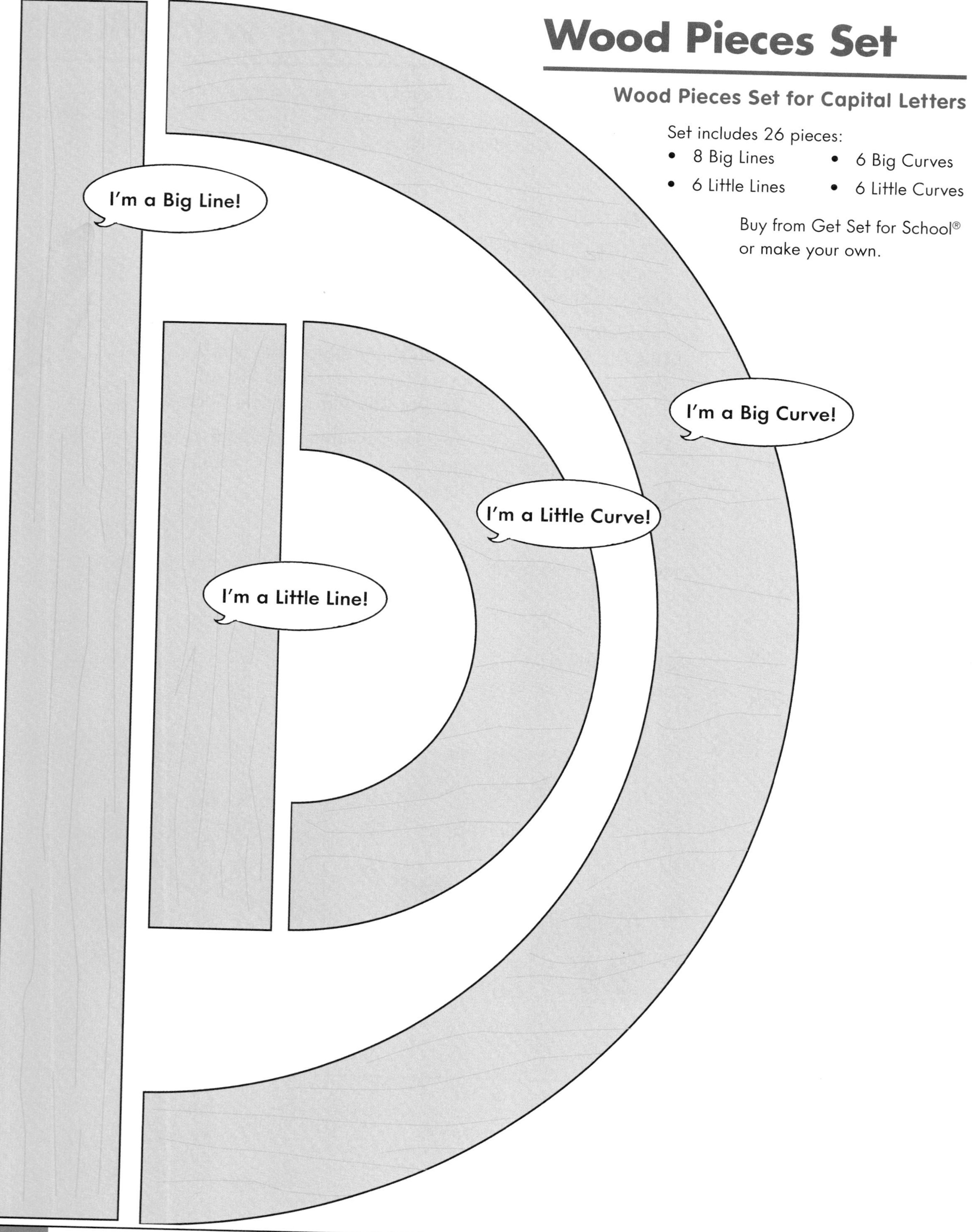

Polish, Sort & Trade Wood Pieces

Children love to feel like they belong. Spread the Wood Pieces on the floor and have children sit around them as a group. Show them how.

Materials/Setup
- Wood Pieces
- Old socks or paper towels

Grouping
Whole class

Support/ELL
Make up songs as children rub the pieces to reinforce the various concepts you are teaching. Try this one that goes to "Row, Row, Row Your Boat":

Rub, rub, rub Big Line
Rub your Big Line
Rub, rub, rub Big Line
It looks just like mine

Rub, rub, rub Big Curve
It is nice and round
Rub, rub, rub Big Curve
Now put it on the ground

Activity

1. Show children how to polish, stack, and sort the Wood Pieces. This is a friendly, relaxed, and worthwhile activity that they love.
2. Talk about the pieces. Gradually, they will pick up the important words (Big Line, Little Line, Big Curve, Little Curve) along with the pieces. You can say:

   You have a Big Curve. I have a Big Curve. We picked the same pieces.
   You have a Big Line. I have a Big Curve. Do you want to trade?
   Let's polish lines. Do you want to polish a Big Line or a Little Line?
   It's time to collect the Wood Pieces. Who has a Big Line?

✔ Check

Observe children to see which hand they use to rub the Wood Pieces. Generally, it will be the dominant hand. Do children name the Wood Pieces correctly?

More To Learn

Collect and put away pieces by type and size. Finding the right pieces among others is a figure-ground activity. Stacking requires turning and positioning.

Look What We're Learning

Oral Language
- Learn words linked to content being taught
- Communicate thoughts with words
- Speak in sentences made up of three or more words

Foundation Skills
- Imitate teacher's body movements
- Share with peers and adults
- Participate in school routines
- Listen to oral directions to attend to a simple task
- Observe and sort

Sensory Motor
- Use same hand consistently to hold crayons
- Look at hands and use visual cues to guide reaching for, grasping, and moving objects

Vocabulary

big
little
curve
line

Wood Pieces in a Bag

When fingers can identify a Wood Piece by feel alone, that's tactile discrimination. Children develop manipulative skills when they use their fingers to explore size and shape. However, they need to know the names of the Wood Pieces before you introduce this activity.

Materials/Setup

- Wood Pieces
- Bag

Grouping

Small group; whole class

Support/ELL

To make it easier for children to feel differences, use only two types of Wood Pieces in Big Curves and Little Lines, or Big Lines and Little Curves.

Activity

1. Put Wood Pieces and one surprise object in the bag.
2. Child reaches inside, feels one Wood Piece, guesses which piece it is, and takes it out to see. If the child feels the surprise (spoon, marker, ball, cup, etc.) first, child guesses that and removes the object from the bag to confirm. Let the child have another turn.

✔ Check

Observe if children remember the names of the Wood Pieces. If they don't, then think out loud with them: **He's wondering if it's a Big Curve or a Little Line.**

More To Learn

Sit in a circle and pass the bag. Children close their eyes and have to find what their classmates suggest.

Look What We're Learning

Oral Language

- Use words linked to content being taught
- Communicate thoughts with words
- Speak in complete sentences made up of three or more words
- Use words to describe an object

Sensory Motor

- Handle play materials without an avoidance response
- Perceive the size, shape, or identity of an object by sense of touch

Social-Emotional

- Take turns with peers
- Treat property with respect

Vocabulary

Big Line
Little Line
Big Curve
Little Curve
names of small objects

Wood Pieces in a Box

When fingers feel around to find and match a certain piece to another, that's tactile discrimination too. This activity doesn't require children to name the piece—only to find it.

Materials/Setup
- Sound Around Box™
- Magnetic Pieces for Capitals
- Wood Pieces

Grouping
Small group; whole class

Support/ELL
To make it easier for children to feel differences, use only two kinds of Wood Pieces in Big Curves and Little Lines, or Big Lines and Little Curves.

Activity

1. Put Magnetic Pieces for Capitals (or Wood Pieces) in the Sound Around Box™.
2. Put one Magnetic Piece on the side of the box.
3. Children take turns reaching into the box to feel for a matching piece.
4. Display found Magnetic Pieces beside the piece on the box. Stack found Wood Pieces in front of the box. Put any non matching piece back and try again.

✔ Check

Observe if children find this easier or harder than the Wood Pieces in a Bag activity. What makes the difference for children?

More To Learn

Use box for a "feel and guess" activity with shapes (circles, squares, triangles) or small items (toothbrush, comb, soap, toothpaste...).

Look What We're Learning

Oral Language
- Demonstrate active listening by attending to instruction
- Talk about experiences and observations
- Learn words linked to content being taught

Social-Emotional
- Take turns with peers
- Treat property with respect

Sensory Motor
- Handle play and art materials without an avoidance response
- Perceive the size, shape, or identity of an object by sense of touch
- Notice and attach meaning to visual information

Vocabulary

Big Line
Little Line
Big Curve
Little Curve
names of shapes/small objects

Positions & Body Parts with Wood Pieces

It's so much fun to follow you, "Big line UP in the air, UNDER your chair, OVER your head, UNDER your arm." All can play, and as they do, they learn POSITION words and body parts. Children need words like top, middle, bottom for a future lesson. They need other position words to follow directions. And as they follow you, they learn to imitate, focus, and respond quickly.

Materials/Setup
- Wood Pieces

Grouping
Whole class; small group

Support/ELL
Point to body parts with a Wood Piece. Slowly say the body part name. Have children repeat with you.

Activity

1. Say the name of each position or body part as you demonstrate. Have children join in.
2. Teach other position words such as: BEHIND my back, BETWEEN my fingers, BESIDE me, THROUGH my arm (put hand on hip first), ON my lap, ON my shoulder.
3. When teaching TOP, BOTTOM, MIDDLE, use a big line. Hold the big line with just one hand at the BOTTOM, then changes hands and positions, naming the position each time. Children imitate.

✔ Check

Name positions and see if children can move their Wood Piece to that position.

More To Learn

Play "Teacher Says" (just like Simon Says) and move Wood Pieces in different positions.

Big Line. . .UP in the air
UP and DOWN

Big Line. . .UNDER my chair
UNDER my arm
OVER my arm

Big Line. . .OUT to my side
AROUND in circle

Big Line in FRONT of me
BEHIND my back, BETWEEN my fingers
Hold it at the BOTTOM, It's VERTICAL

Climb UP and DOWN
Hold it at the TOP, MIDDLE, and BOTTOM

Big Line is HORIZONTAL
Move it SIDE to SIDE

Look What We're Learning

Foundation Skills
- Name body parts
- Recognize and use common prepositions in speech
- Imitate teacher's body movements
- Listen to oral directions to attend to a simple task

Comprehension
- Listen to perform a task

Oral Language
- Repeat teacher's words
- Learn words linked to content being taught

Sensory Motor
- Tolerate motion in activities
- Use both sides of the body in activities
- Move naturally and place body to perform tasks

Vocabulary

top	under
middle	on
bottom	between
above	head
below	eyes
over	hands

Curves & Circles

By imitating you, children prepare for capitals made with curves: **B C D G O P Q R S U**. Children learn that **O** can be letter O, number 0, or an O shape. When children rotate their arms to make circles, they prepare to write O and draw anything with a circular shape: snowmen, wheels, faces.

Materials/Setup

- Wood Pieces:
  2 Big Curves or 2 Little Curves per child

Grouping

Whole class; small group

Support/ELL

One symbol O has three different names: circle, zero, letter O. Help children understand that all three names belong. Focus on each concept individually.

Activity

1. Give each child two Big Curves or two Little Curves.
2. Say the name of each position as you demonstrate. Have children say it too.
3. Teach O as a letter, a number, and a shape.

✔ Check

Are the children able to distinguish circle, O, and zero?

More To Learn

With "Somewhere Over the Rainbow," children learn the rainbow shape and the concept OVER. Go on an O Hunt around the room.

APART
Hold the Big Curves apart.

TOGETHER
Bring them together.

O or ZERO
Say "O" or "Zeeeero."
Children hold two Big Curves up to their faces. Look at a friend's **O**.
Make circles in the air now.

RAINBOW
Hold UP a Big Curve.
Hold the Big Curve and then trace OVER the rainbow with the other hand.

SMILE
Hold Big Curve UP to make a happy face. Turn it DOWN to make a sad face.

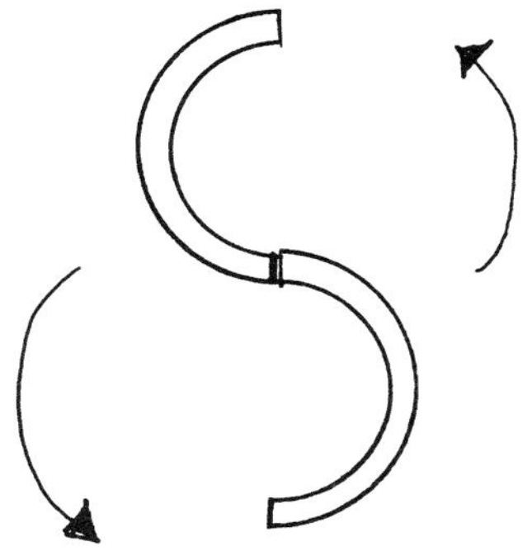

SQUIGGLE—WIGGLE
Hold curves with just one end touching. Move them alternately UP or DOWN.

Look What We're Learning

Foundation Skills
- Imitate teacher's body movements

Comprehension
- Listen to perform a task

Oral Language
- Repeat teacher's words
- Learn words linked to content being taught

Sensory Motor
- Tolerate motion in activities
- Use both sides of the body in activities
- Handle play materials without an avoidance response
- Notice and attach meaning to visual information

Vocabulary

apart	letter
together	O
rainbow	number
smile	zero
squiggle	shape
wiggle	circle

Vertical, Horizontal & Diagonal Positions

By imitating you, children learn the concepts of vertical, horizontal, and diagonal. They need to know how to place lines horizontally and vertically for letters **E F H I L T**. Diagonals prepare children for capitals **A K M N R V W X Y Z**.

Materials/Setup
- Wood Pieces
  - 2 Big Lines per child
  - 1 Little Line per child

Grouping
Whole class; small group

Support/ELL
Encourage children to speak with you. The words vertical, horizontal, and diagonal are fun to say with the motions. Teach tactile and kinesthetic concepts one at a time.

Activity
1. Give each child two Big Lines.
2. Use position words VERTICAL, HORIZONTAL, and DIAGONAL and have children say them as they imitate you.
3. Introduce the capitals **V T A X** as they make them with you.

✔ Check
Observe handedness as children play. Do most move their Wood Pieces with their dominant hand?

More To Learn
Show two children holding **V** how to make them touch for **W**.

Hold two Big Lines TOGETHER in one hand.

Open them! Hold them out. Say, Voilà! It's a **V**. Help children finger trace **V**.

Hold two Big Lines END to END diagonally. Move and say, DIAGONAL, DIAGONAL.

Make a Big Line stand up. It's VERTICAL. Make it walk on your arm.

Now it's tired. Make it lie down. It's HORIZONTAL.

One Big Line is standing UP. One Little Line ACROSS the TOP. It's capital **T**.

Hold one big line in each hand. They are VERTICAL.

Put them TOGETHER at the TOP. Looks like a tee-pee or the start of **A**.

Together at the MIDDLE— It's **X**! **X** marks the spot!

Look What We're Learning

Foundation Skills
- Recognize and use common prepositions in speech
- Imitate teacher's body movements

Comprehension
- Listen to perform a task

Oral Language
- Repeat teacher's words
- Learn words linked to content being taught
- Use new words linked to content being taught

Sensory Motor
- Tolerate motion in activities
- Use both sides of the body in activities
- Handle play materials without an avoidance response
- Notice and attach meaning to visual information

Vocabulary

verticle
horizontal
diagonal
letter names: A T V W X

Hands-On Letter Play

Hands-On Letter Play is the child friendly way to teach four-year-olds to write. They can learn to write before they write. They can learn how to make letters right-side up and facing correctly. Hands-On Letter Play provides all the fun of multisensory play with the bonus of enabling you to teach correct writing habits from the start.

Here's Hands-On Letter Play! Children learn letters with....

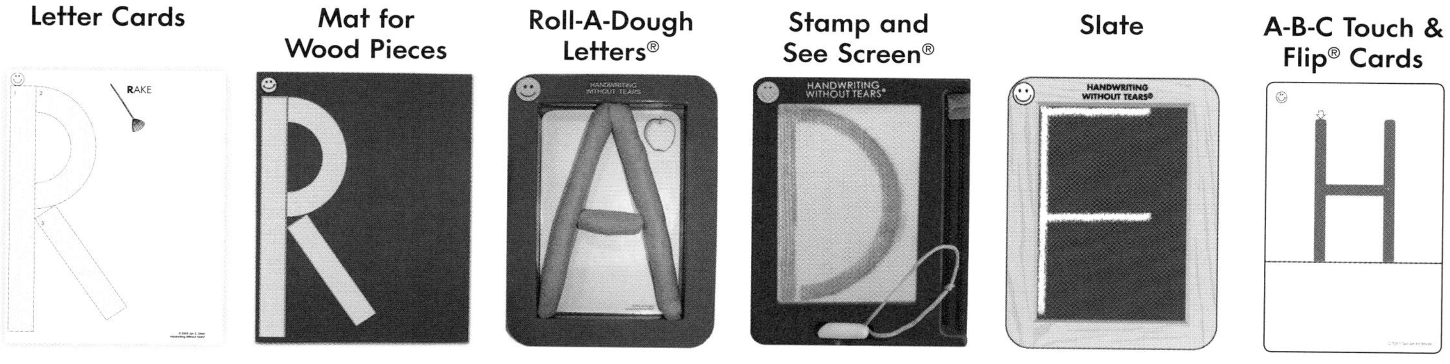

Smile and teach good habits! The smiley face in the top left corner helps children orient letters to make letters right-side up and facing correctly. The teacher uses the smiley face as a cue to show where to start and how to build letters correctly.

Capital Letter Cards for Wood Pieces

Each card shows a different letter made with Wood Pieces. Children use real Wood Pieces, to cover the letter, in the correct order, piece by piece. These cards are ideal for teaching the first letters in children's names. Each child has his/her own letter. The teacher helps each child choose the correct Wood Pieces and place them in order. The teacher and children always use the correct Wood Piece words. Letter R is made with a Big Line, then a Little Curve, then a Little Line.

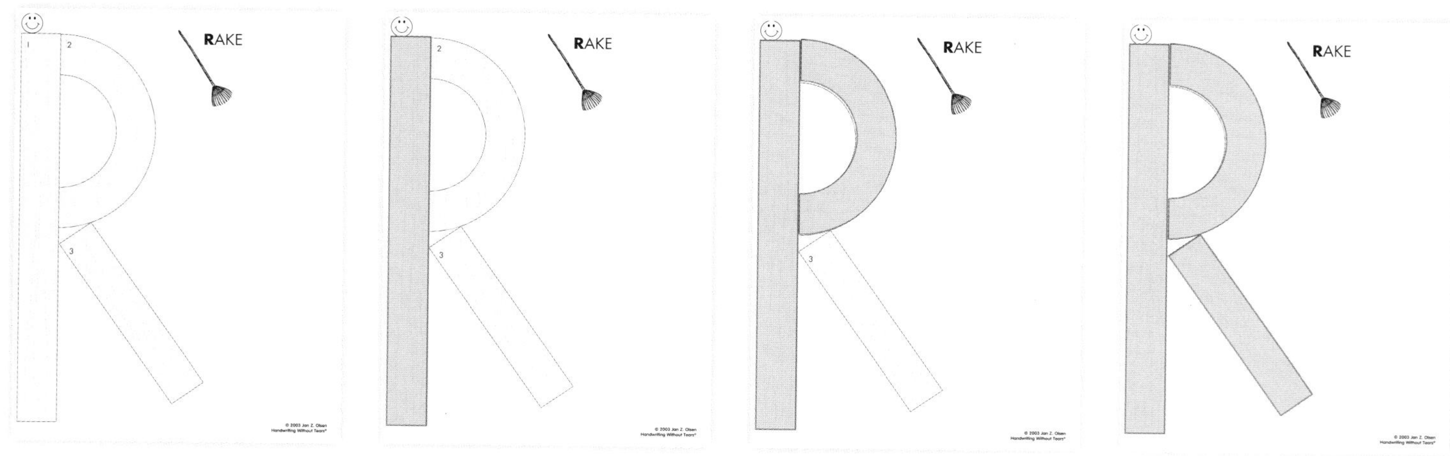

The set includes 26 double sided 8.5" x 11" cards. One side has a capital letter. The other side has related letter and picture matching activities.

Capitals on the Mat for Wood Pieces

The Mat is a place to build Wood Piece letters. It has a smiley face in the top left corner. That is the cue children need to place the Wood Pieces and make letters correctly. You build each letter correctly step by step and children imitate.

Sometimes you may keep the name of the letter a secret. Children like a surprise. This is an easy way for four-year-olds to learn letter names and good habits for making letters and is a favorite Hands-On Letter Play activity. You'll see it on most letter pages in *My First School Book*.

Teacher first:

Child imitates each step.

The blue, fabric covered mat has a yellow smiley face in the top left corner. It measures 8" x 11".

The Wood Pieces Set for Capital Letters includes 26 pieces:

8 Big Lines	6 Big Curves
6 Little Lines	6 Little Curves

Hands-On Letter Play

Roll-A-Dough Letters®

This is a way for children to develop fine motor skills as they learn letters. Children like to roll big dough snakes. Those snakes will be big lines or big curves for letters. Little snakes will be little lines or little curves. You help children roll dough and make letters step by step.

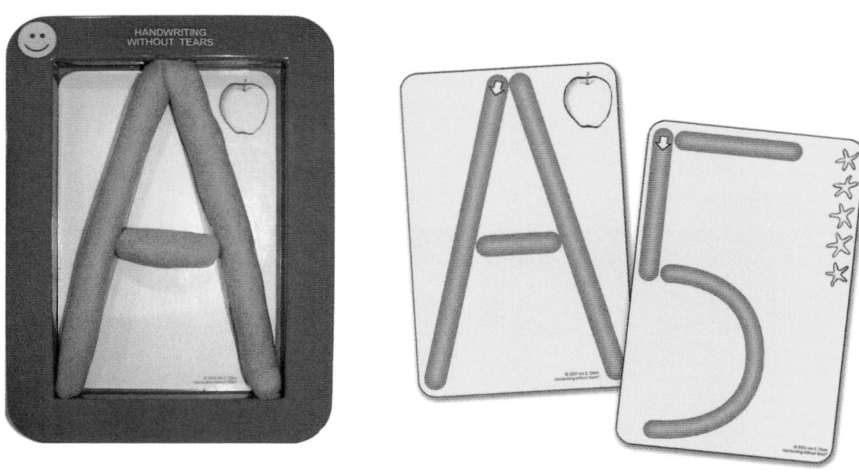

Set includes 13 double sided laminated Letter Cards (26 capitals) and 5 double sided Number Cards (1-10). The cards are 4" x 6". The tray is recessed to hold cards, or sensory material (sand, cream, etc.).

Stamp and See Screen®

Children enjoy stamping and learning letters with magnetic pieces: they use a magnetic Big Line, Little Line, Big Curve, Little Curve. They use the attached magnetic chalk to trace letters. It's easy to erase a letter and make another.

Roll-A-Dough Letters and Stamp and See Screen also work together. Put the Roll-A-Dough cards on the screen and trace them with the magnetic chalk. Then lift off the card to see the letter.

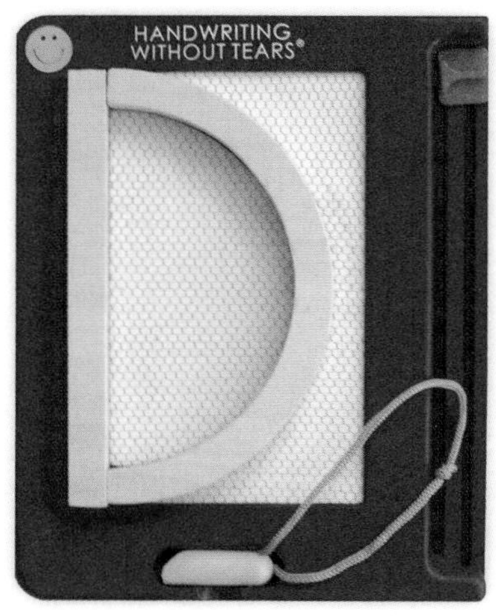

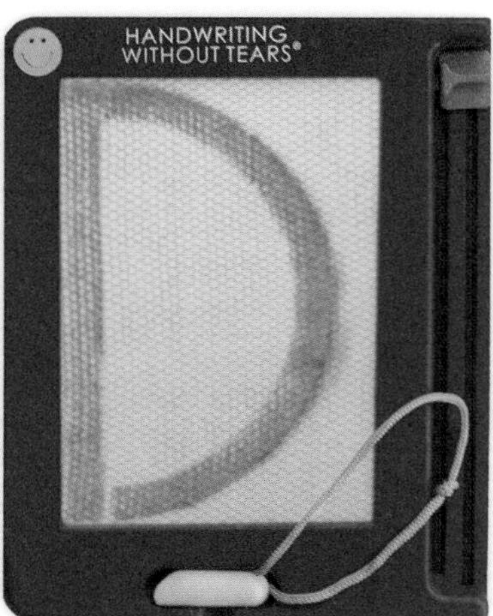

Set includes 4" x 6" screen, 4 magnetic stamps (Big Line, Little Line, Big Curve, Little Curve) and a string attached magnetic chalk.

Wet-Dry-Try on the Slate Chalkboard

Children light up when they see little sponge cubes in a cup of water. What's this? It's Wet-Dry-Try. This multisensory activity engages every child. It's visual, auditory, kinesthetic, and tactile. You write a chalk letter. Children then wet, dry, and try the letter with chalk. You can also use the Slate "dry" for review. Simply write and erase with a tissue and write again.

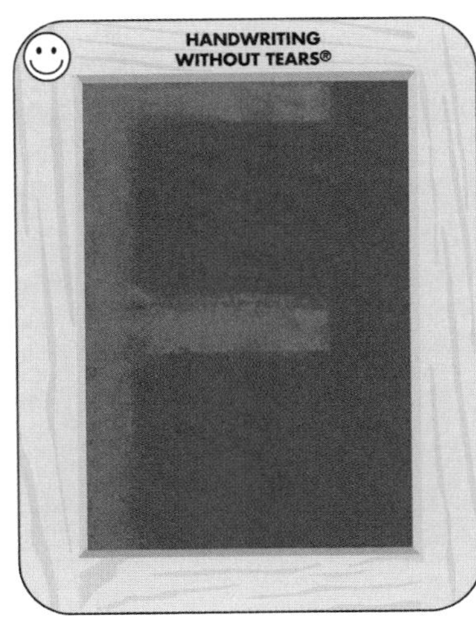

The 4" x 6" Slate Chalkboard features the smiley face in the top left corner. This is another favorite Hands-On Letter Play product. The Slate is real slate; the frame is real wood.

A-B-C Touch & Flip® Cards

Children learn better when they can feel letters. These tactile ABC Touch & Flip Cards feel good to touch. The arrow on the cards helps you teach children as they finger trace each letter with the correct strokes. Children are guided to finger trace exactly the way they'll write a letter. The tactile cards have an animal puzzle on the reverse side. You'll find that side described in the Alphabet Knowledge section.

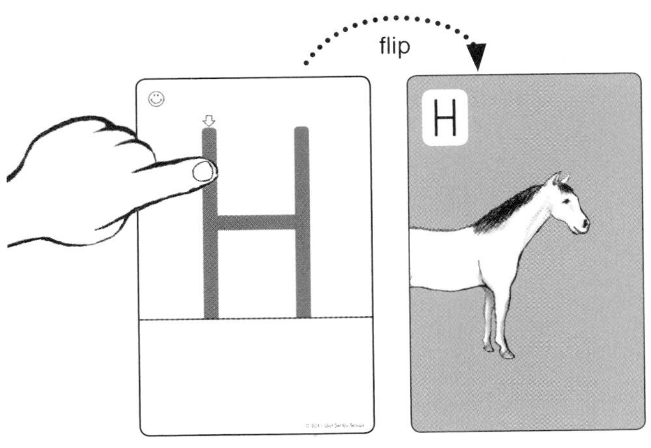

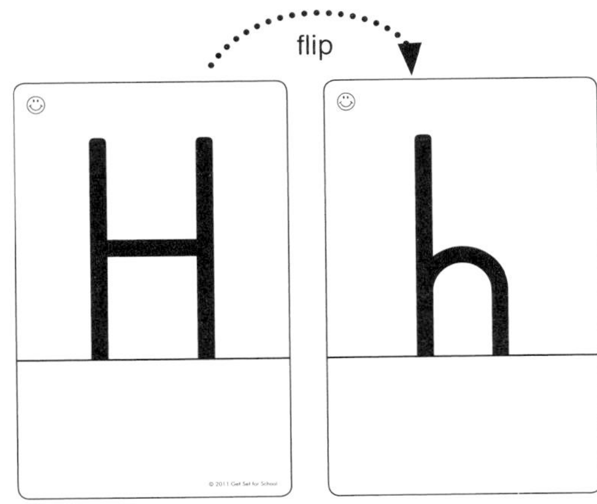

A-B-C Touch & Flip Cards includes two sets. Each set has double sided cards:

27 Picture Cards - Capital + Animal Puzzle (this set has the tactile capitals)

26 Letter Cards - Capital + Lowercase letter

Capitals with Letter Cards

Letter Cards show a capital made with Wood Pieces. Children simply put real Wood Pieces on the card. This is a fine first Letter Play activity, especially for children who are just learning to turn and place pieces. Children build the letters in order, piece by piece. It's also a beginning activity for observation and organization.

Materials/Setup

- Capital Letter Cards for Wood Pieces
- Wood Pieces

Grouping

1 - 5 children

Support/ELL

Placing each piece requires fine motor control and spatial awareness. Help to place a piece, take it away, and then let a child try.

Video Lesson

View the video lesson, Building Capitals with Capital Letter Cards, at **getsetforschool.com/videos**

Activity

1. Place a different Letter Card in front of each child. Have them point to the smiley face. The face shows the letter is right-side up.
2. Point to each child's Letter Card. Say, **This is capital ________. What pieces do you need for ________? That's right. Collect the pieces. Put them near your card. Then wait until everyone is ready.**
3. Place the pieces as a group, like this:
   Pick up the first piece for your letter. Wait for everybody.
   Put it in place.
   Pick up the second piece. Wait... everyone ready? Put it in place.
   Pick up the third piece. Wait... everyone ready? Put it in place.
   You made ________.

✔ Check

Observe if children choose the correct pieces. Do they count and name the pieces correctly?

More To Learn

Instead of building letters, give children the card for their names. Have them build the first letter in their name.

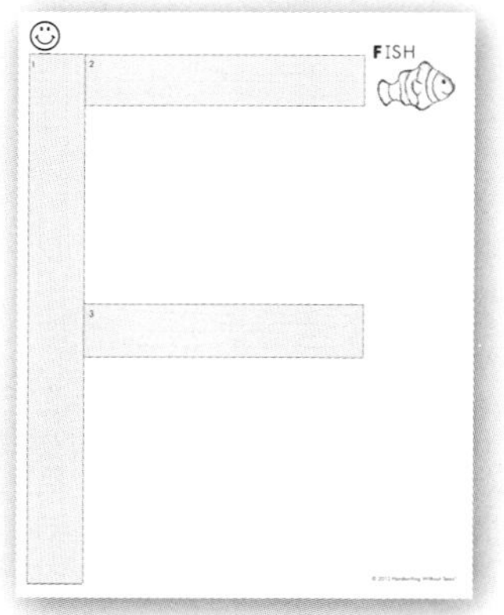

Look What We're Learning

Foundation Skills
- Sequencing

Alphabet Knowledge
- Point to and name capital letters
- Position capitals right-side up

Comprehension
- Listen to perform a task

Number & Operations
- Verbally count a set of objects

Sensory Motor
- Move an object in one hand to position it for use, placement, or release
- Look at hands and use visual cues to guide reaching for, grasping, and moving objects

Vocabulary

Capital F
Big Line
Little Line
smiley face
first
second
third

Capitals with the Mat

The Mat for Wood Pieces is blue with a yellow smiley face in the top left corner. The smiley face is in the top left corner. That's the starting corner for **B D E F H K L M N P R U V W X Y Z**. Many of them (**B D E F H K L M N P R**) start with a Big Line on the left of the Mat. When the Big Line is on the left of the Mat, the next part is always on the right side.

Materials/Setup

- Wood Pieces
- Mat for Wood Pieces (1 per child)

Grouping

Whole class; small group

Support/ELL

Start with simple two- or three-piece letters.

Video Lesson

View the video lesson, Building Capitals Letters on Mat, at **getsetforschool.com/videos**

Activity

1. Scatter Wood Pieces on the floor in front of children.
2. Give each child a Mat to place right-side up. The smiley face will be at the top.
3. Build a letter, piece by piece for children to imitate. Generally, letters are built in top-to-bottom, left-to-right order. To see the order for any letter, just find that letter page in this guide.
4. Describe each step as you build the letter:
   I put the Big Line here, under the ☺. Your turn.
   I put a Little Line at the top. Your turn.
   I put another Little Line at the middle. It's letter ______!

✔ Check

Your Mat should be upside down for you so that your letter model is right-side up for the children. Do children know the letter when it's finished?

More To Learn

Teach all the letters except **U** and **J** on the Mat. Letters **A C G I O Q S T** start at the top center of the Mat.

Demonstrate

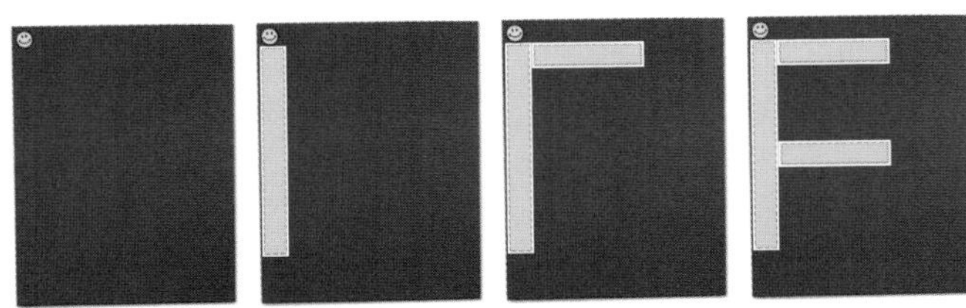

Look What We're Learning

Foundation Skills

- Sequencing
- Listen to oral directions to attend to a simple task

Sensory Motor

- Move an object in one hand to position it for use, placement, or release
- Notice and attach meaning to visual information
- Look at hands and use visual cues to guide reaching for, grasping, and moving objects

Alphabet Knowledge

- Point to and name capital letters
- Position capitals right-side up

Social-Emotional

- Interact easily with familiar adults

Vocabulary

right-side up
smiley face
Big Line
Little Line
top
middle

Roll-A-Dough Letters®

Children love to roll dough snakes and make capitals and numbers. They can build them on the cards or in the tray. This activity helps them build strength in their fingers as they learn letters and numbers.

Materials/Setup

- Roll-A-Dough Tray
- Tray Cards
- Dough

Grouping

Small group

Support/ELL

Help children with hand skills. Roll a ball first, and then use flat hands to roll snakes back and forth.

Video Lesson

View the video lesson, Building with Roll-A-Dough, at **getsetforschool.com/videos**

Activity

1. Give each child a letter card and have dough for all to use.
2. Show children how to roll big and little dough snakes. Show them step by step how to place the dough on the card.
3. Show children how to make a letter in empty trays. Place the letter card to copy above the empty tray.

✔ Check

Be sure all children place their cards and trays right-side up. The cards have images to orient them and arrows to show where to begin.

More To Learn

Use the tray to trace letters in sand, shaving cream, pudding, or finger paint. Simply place the card above the tray, or even in the tray!

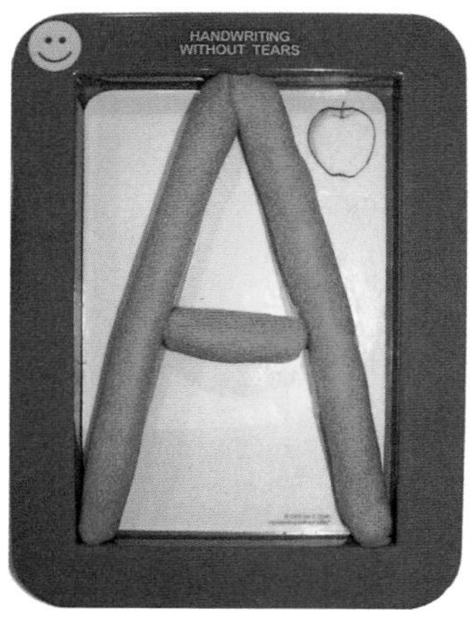

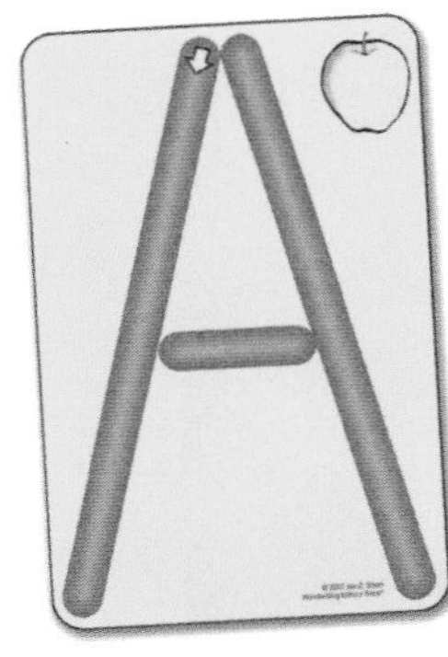

Look What We're Learning

Foundation Skills

- Sequencing
- Listen to oral directions to attend to a simple task

Alphabet Knowledge

- Point to and name capital letters
- Position capitals right-side up

Sensory Motor

- Move an object in one hand to position it for use, placement, or release
- Use both sides of the body in activities
- Look at hands and use visual cues to guide reaching for, grasping, and moving objects
- Reach across midline to get an object from other side

Vocabulary

snake

roll

Stamp and See Screen®

Here's another sensory activity. Children stamp a capital with magnetic stamps: Big Lines, Little Lines, Big Curves, Little Curves. After that, they can trace the stamped capital with magnetic chalk (included and attached). Tracing the letter is a first taste of writing the letter with strokes.

Materials/Setup
- Stamp and See Screen®
- Roll-A-Dough Tray Cards

Grouping
Small group

Support/ELL
Use just the first two steps of the activity. Model the next two steps for exposure.

Video Lesson
View the video lesson, Forming Letters with Stamp and See, at **getsetforschool.com/videos**

Activity
1. Show children how to stamp the first piece on the screen. Erase and let children try.
2. Show children how to stamp the complete letter, step by step. Erase and let children try.
3. Show children how to use the magnetic chalk to trace the strokes. Erase the letter.
4. Children stamp with magnetic pieces or write with magnetic chalk to make letter from memory.

✔ Check
Watch children as they trace. If you have Roll-A-Dough, put one of those cards on the screen. Children trace the Roll-A-Dough card with the magnetic chalk. When the card is taken off the screen, the letter is on the screen.

More To Learn
Play Boss of the Board. One person builds a letter as the other guesses it. Switch roles.

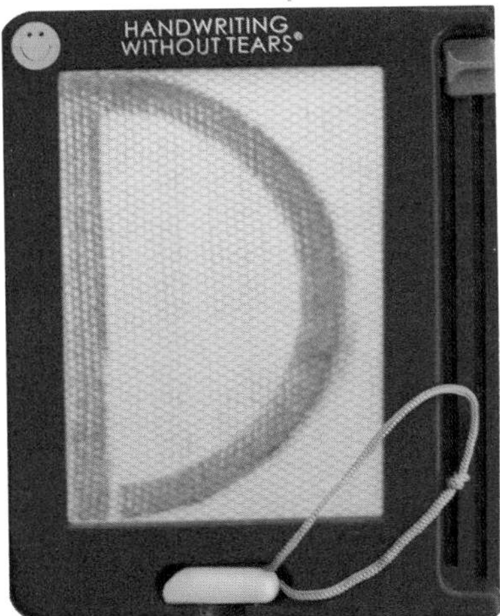

Look What We're Learning

Foundation Skills
- Sequencing
- Listen to oral directions to attend to a simple task

Writing
- Enjoy writing and engage in writing activities
- Hold a crayon with proper grip to write
- Use helping hand to stabilize objects and papers

Alphabet Knowledge
- Point to and name capital letters
- Position capitals right-side up

Sensory Motor
- Use same hand consistently to perform skilled tasks
- Use fingers to hold crayons, etc.
- Notice and attach meaning to visual information

Vocabulary
Big Line
Little Line
Big Curve
Little Curve
top
middle
bottom
smiley face
stamp
erase

A-B-C Touch & Flip® Cards

Writing is the trace of movement. Think about it! Children hold a crayon and move it on paper. Those actions create letters. We want children to move the crayon correctly. We teach them to move their fingers correctly. As they move and touch, they learn the correct way to write letters.

Materials/Setup

- A-B-C Touch & Flip® Cards (Picture cards - tactile side)

Grouping

Small groups of 3-4

Support/ELL

Let children who need support watch others first. Extra exposure prepares them. Start with easier letters (those with horizontal and vertical strokes).

Activity

1. Choose a capital that's familiar from Letter Play or from a child's name. Sit at a table with children standing beside you.
2. Finger trace H as you say the Wood Piece words: **Big Line down, Big Line down, Little Line across. That's.... H. Your turn!**
3. Children take turns finger tracing the letter. Say the words with them as they trace. Waiting children watch others trace.
4. Continue with two or three more letters, perhaps the first letter in each child's name.

✔ Check

Observe if children finger trace accurately. Do they name the letters as they trace?

More To Learn

After they finger trace on A-B-C Touch & Flip cards, have children finger trace the letters from memory on the Mat for Wood Pieces.

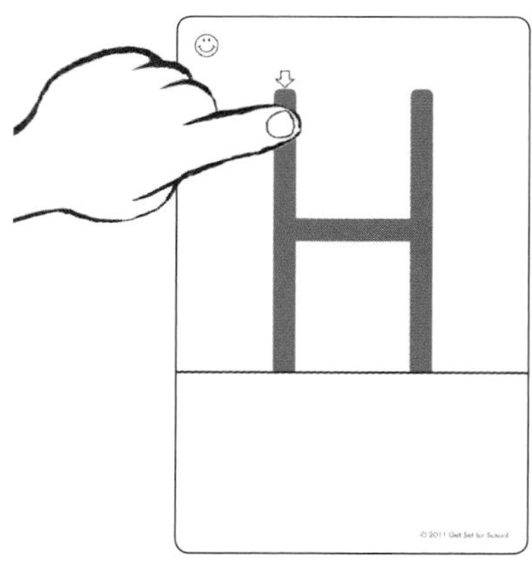

Look What We're Learning

Foundation Skills
- Sequencing

Oral Language
- Repeat teacher's words
- Use new words linked to content being taught

Alphabet Knowledge
- Point to and name capital letters
- Position capitals right-side up

Sensory Motor
- Use index finger to trace numbers on cards
- Use same hand consistently to perform skilled tasks
- Perceive the identity of an object by sense of touch

Social-Emotional
- Interact easily with familiar adults

Vocabulary

letter names
top
smiley face
arrow

Wet-Dry-Try on the Slate

This is a favorite activity because it teaches so many skills. You write a chalk letter and teach each step. Children wet the letter, dry it, and then try it with chalk. The little bits of sponge and chalk reinforce correct grip.

Materials/Setup
- Slate (1 per child)
- Little Chalk Bits
- Little Sponge Cubes
- Little cups of water
- Paper towels

Grouping
1 - 5 children

Support/ELL
You say the words for each step slowly. Children join in when they can.

Video Lesson
View the video lesson, Letter K on the Slate Chalkboard, at **getsetforschool.com/videos**

Activity

Teacher's Part – Write F with chalk
Start in the starting corner.
Big Line down. Jump to the ☺.
Little Line across the top.
Little Line across the middle.

Child's Part – Wet-Dry-Try
Wet **F** with sponge. Say the words with the teacher. Wet **F** with finger, the same way.
Dry **F** with crumbled towel. Say the words.
Try **F** with chalk. Say the words.

✔ Check
Observe if children follow directions. Do they complete the steps to make a letter?

More To Learn
Review already learned letters with chalk. You demonstrate on one slate. Children imitate on their slates. Erase with a tissue.

Teacher's Part

Start in the starting corner
Big Line down, Jump to ☺
Little Line across the top
Little Line across the middle

Child's Part

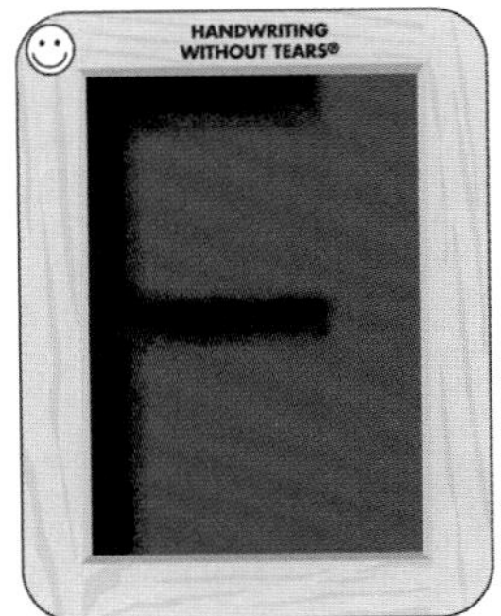

WET: Wet **F** with sponge,
Wet **F** with wet finger,
Say the words

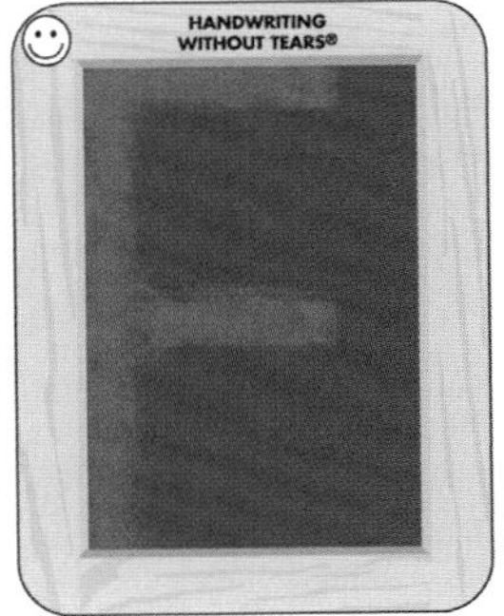

DRY: Dry **F** with towel,
Dry **F** with gentle blow,
Say the words

TRY: Try **F** with chalk,
Say the words

Look What We're Learning

Foundation Skills
- Sequencing
- Listen to oral directions to attend to a simple task

Oral Language
- Repeat teacher's words
- Learn words linked to content being taught
- Use new words linked to content being taught

Writing
- Use helping hand to stabilize objects and papers

Sensory Motor
- Use same hand consistently to perform skilled tasks
- Use index finger to trace numbers

Social-Emotional
- Interact easily with familiar adults

Vocabulary

letter F	across
Big Line	wet
Little Line	dry
jump	try
top	sponge
smiley face	squeeze

Teaching Letters with Technology

Infusing simple technology into our daily classroom experiences can make learning letters engaging and fun. This process also exposes young children to the world of technology at an early age.

Materials/Setup

- Computer
- Digital Teaching Tools (available online at hwtears.com)

Grouping

Whole class

Support/ELL

Making large movements can help children remember letter names. For children who do not know the letters in their names, use the Digital Teaching Tools to introduce letters. Children can Air Write the letters in their names using a visual model.

Activity

1. Prepare Digital Teaching Tools for the letter to demonstrate.
2. Children point their pointer fingers at the screen.
3. As children trace the letter, say the parts of letter. **We are going to trace F in their air. Say the parts of F with me, Big Line, Little Line, Little Line. We made an F.**

✔ Check

Observe children tracing letters in the air following the model on the screen. Observe if children are saying the correct parts of the letter.

More To Learn

Using the Digital Teaching Tool, you may play lowercase letters for children for naming and recognition.

Look What We're Learning

Sensory Motor

- Use same hand consistently to perform a task
- Notice and attach meaning to visual information

Alphabet Knowledge

- Point to and name letters

Oral Language

- Demonstrate active listening by attending to instruction

Vocabulary

capital letter names
lowercase letter names

Door Tracing

Doors can do more than open in and out. They can help you teach lessons. Just put a smiley face in the top left corner, and the door is ready to help! Where do you start your letters? At the top. The smiley face brings a child's eye to the top and to the starting corner.

Materials/Setup

- Bright yellow smiley face mounted on top left corner of door
- Small Laser Pointer

A Click Away
getsetforschool.com/click

Grouping

Whole class

Support/ELL

Make children wait until you have traced the letter three times before they guess.

Activity

1. Write a laser letter on the door for all to see. What letter will it be? Write a familiar starting corner letter, perhaps **B D E F H K L P R V X** or **Z** (hide beam when jumping back to starting corner).
2. Children hold a crayon and pretend to write on the door, by following the laser beam.
3. Children guess the letter.

✔ Check

Do they follow your beam with their crayons?

More To Learn

Play Guess My Letter! Children guess the letter as you trace it on the door.

Look What We're Learning

Foundation Skills
- Imitate teacher's body movements

Alphabet Knowledge
- Point to and name capital letters

Oral Language
- Use new words linked to content being taught
- Communicate thoughts with words

Sensory Motor
- Use same hand consistently to hold crayons
- Use fingers to hold crayons, etc.
- Tolerate motion in activities
- Notice and attach meaning to visual information

Social-Emotional
- Cooperate with other children

Vocabulary

door
smiley face
laser

Writing

Children who know how to write–who have good handwriting–have an educational advantage, especially in the early grades (Lust & Donica 2011).

Good handwriting starts now, but not with pencil and paper. Good handwriting starts with crayons and with capital letters. Capitals are the first letters children learn to write, and you'll teach them in developmental order (NAEYC & IRA 1998). *My First School Book* starts with easy letters like **L F E H T** before it progresses to more difficult letters like **R K A X Z**. But what about names like AVA? Make exceptions to teach letters out of order for a child's name. Just look at the alphabet across the Table of Contents to find the letters you need.

What matters is how children write and their first habits for writing. This is the year for children to learn writing habits: how to hold a crayon and write letters. Writing habits are easy to remember. We read and write the same way: from top to bottom and left to right.

Play writing is also important. Let children have access to paper, crayons, envelopes, stickers, and other materials. They need an opportunity to play with what they know and to pretend what they don't (Neuman & Roskos 2005).

Objectives

- Establish handedness for writing
- Hold the crayon correctly
- Use the helping hand to hold a paper or book
- Sit with good posture (furniture must fit child)
- Start letters at the top
- Trace letters correctly, step by step
- Write on page from left to right
- Write all capitals
- Write NAME in all capitals
- Write Name in title case
- Write some lowercase letters
- Enjoy writing

Below is some of the significant research for Writing. For additional Writing research, see the reference section at the end of this teacher's guide.

Lust, C.A., and D. K. Donica. 2011. "Effectiveness of a Handwriting Readiness Program in Head Start: A Two-Group Controlled Trial." *Research Scholars Initiative* 65(5):560-568.

Neuman, S.B., and K. Roskos. 2005. "Whatever Happened To Developmentally Appropriate Practice in Early Literacy?" *Young Children* 60:22-26. Accessed September 2011. http://journal.naeyc.org/btj/200507/02Neuman.pdf

National Assocation for the Education of Young Children & International Reading Assocation. 1998. "Learning to Read and Write: Developmentally Appropriate Practices for Young Children." *Young Children* 53(4):30-46. Accessed August 2011. http://www.naeyc.org/files/naeyc/file/positions/PSREAD98.pdf

Writing in *My First School Book*

You are helping children hold crayons correctly, and they're coloring in *My First School Book*. They know the Wood Piece words and how to build a few letters. Your children are now ready to start writing in *My First School Book*. Look at how *My First School Book* supports young writers and your teaching.

My First School Book is part of the Readiness & Writing curriculum.

Readiness comes first with Pre-Writing activities to prepare children for writing pages. The illustrations at the top remind children of how they built the letter. They've already made the letter (with Wood Pieces, dough, magnets, or chalk). Now they can focus on writing strokes, starting and stopping, and making the strokes in the correct order.

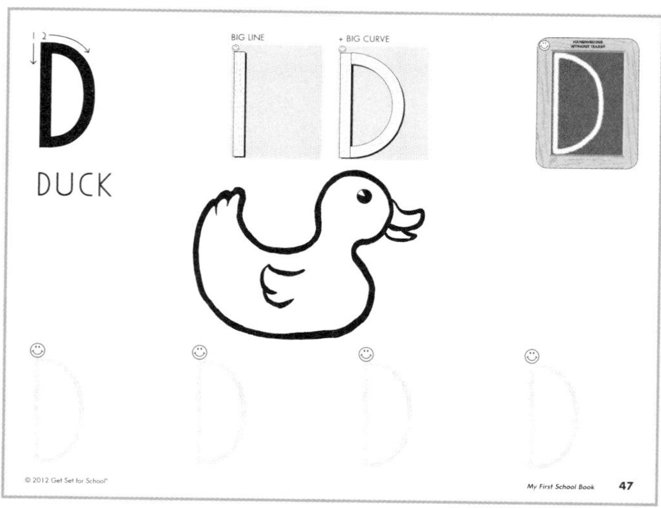

My First School Book uses consistent words for instruction.

What are the words? They're Wood Piece words. Children already know these words. When you say that we write **D** with a Big Line and a Big Curve, all children know what you mean.

My First School Book keeps children coloring and drawing.

Coloring and drawing are part of written expression for young children. The simple pictures make children want to color, but also give them enough space and freedom to make the page their own.

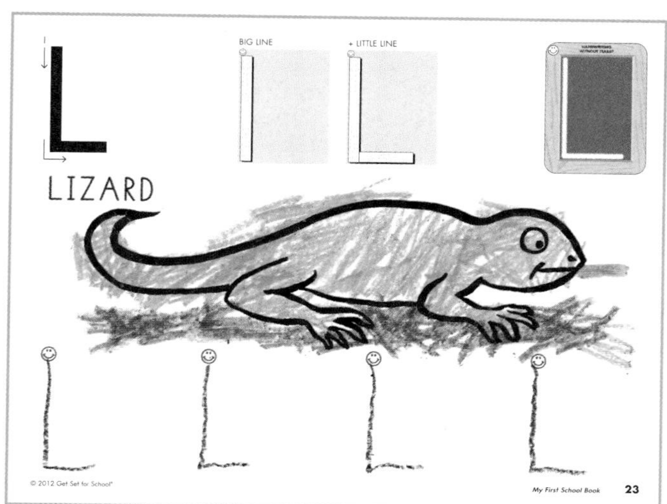

My First School Book has unique crayon strokes.

Get Set for School® has developed the unique gray crayon stroke because we have found that the typical dot to dot exercises found in other workbooks are ineffective. With the gray crayon stroke, there's a surprise. When children write, the underlying gray strokes disappear. The page then shows just children's letters or numbers. Children are so proud of their work.

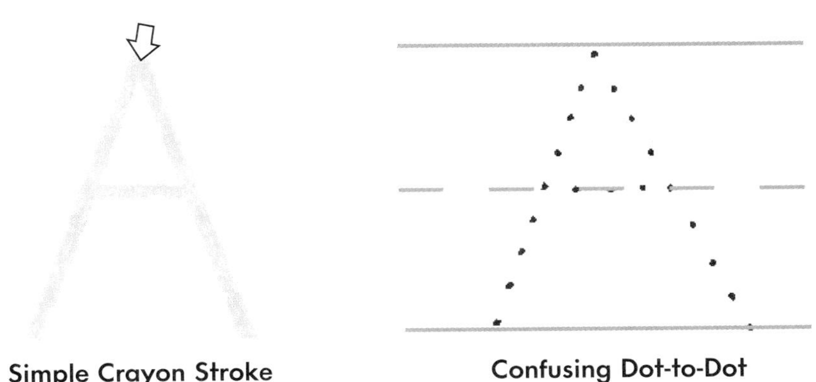

Simple Crayon Stroke **Confusing Dot-to-Dot**

My First School Book prepares children for lowercase letters.

When you are teaching capitals, you are teaching more. The good habits for capitals are the same habits children need for writing all the same and similar lowercase letters. That's 13 letters.

Cc Oo Ss Vv Ww Xx Zz Jj Kk Pp Tt Uu Yy

Before kindergarten, children learn to write even more lowercase letters when they learn to write their names in title case. Both *My First School Book* and Alphabet Knowledge activities teach lowercase recognition for all lowercase letters.

My First School Book is developmentally based.

Letters are taught in developmental order: easy vertical and horizontal letters first, then letters with curves, and finally those with diagonals. Review the research and teaching order on the next pages

Developmental Stages in Writing

Some strokes are developmentally easier to write than others.* Children gradually develop their ability to copy forms in a very predictable order.

* Gesell, A.,H.M. Halverson, H. Thomson, F.L. Ilg, B.M. Castner, L.B. Ames, and C.S. Amatruda. (1940). *The First Year of Life: A Guide to the Study of the Pre-school Child.* New York: Harper and Brothers.

DEVELOPMENTAL ANALYSIS – Capitals vs. Lowercase letters

This is the capital/lowercase analysis that informs our developmental teaching order.

Capital letters are easy

- All start at the top.
- All are the same height.
- All occupy the same vertical space.
- All are easy to recognize and identify (compare **A B D G P Q** with **a b d g p q**).
- Capitals are big, bold, and familiar.

Lowercase letters are more difficult

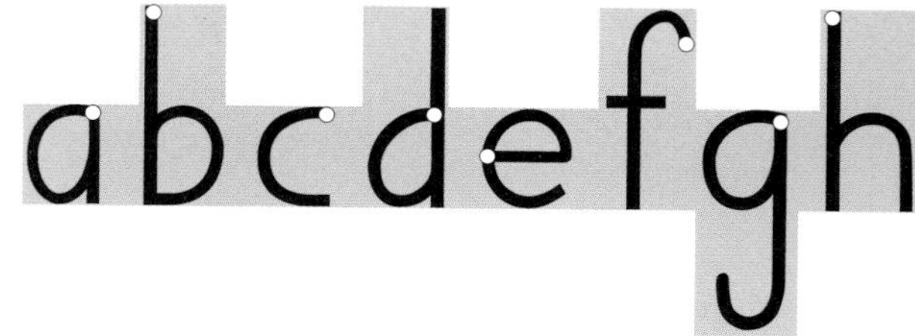

- Lowercase letters start in four different places (**a b e f**).
- Lowercase letters are not the same size. Fourteen letters are half the size of capitals. Twelve are the same size as capitals.
- Lowercase letters occupy three different vertical positions: small, tall, descending.
- Lowercase letters are more difficult to recognize because of subtle differences (**a b d g p q**).

Let's do the math

You can see at a glance that capitals are easier for children. Students have fewer chances to make mistakes when they write capital letters. They aim the pencil at the top and get it right. With lowercase, there are many more variables.

When you teach handwriting, start with capitals. You will save yourself time, make life easier for children, and get better handwriting results.

CAPITAL AND LOWERCASE LETTER ANALYSIS

	Capitals	Lowercase
Start	1	4
Size	1	2
Position	1	3
Appearance	• Familiar • Distinctive A B D G P Q	• Many similiar • Easy to confuse a b d g p q

Developmental Teaching – Capitals First

Capitals are developmentally easier than lowercase letters, so most young children naturally begin writing capitals as their first recognizable letters. Stay with capitals and teach them well. A strong foundation with capitals is the key to both alphabet knowledge (rapid letter recognition and naming) and handwriting skill.

This is what we teach with capitals:

- Letter recognition and naming
- Top-to-bottom, left-to-right habits
- Top start for letters
- Correct letter formation
- Correct letter orientation

When children learn capitals first and learn them well, they have many advantages:

- They avoid capital/lowercase confusion.
- They learn lowercase letters more easily because **c o s v w x y z** are the same as their capitals; **j k t p** and **u** also are similar to their capitals. If we teach capitals correctly, children will be skilled with all capitals and nearly half of the lowercase alphabet.

DEVELOPMENTAL ORDER – *MY FIRST SCHOOL BOOK*

Diagonals

R K A M N V W X Y Z

Numbers - They are already in a good order

1 2 3 4 5 6 7 8 9

Top to Bottom

English is a top-to-bottom, left-to-right language. The top-to-bottom habit is the secret to handwriting success. Children who start letters at the top will develop speed and neatness. Those who start from the bottom will struggle to write.

Often, we judge a young child's writing only by how the letters look. However, habits are more important than the look of the letters. Wobbly, skinny, or fat letters are not worrisome, but letters that start at the bottom are. Try this experiment:

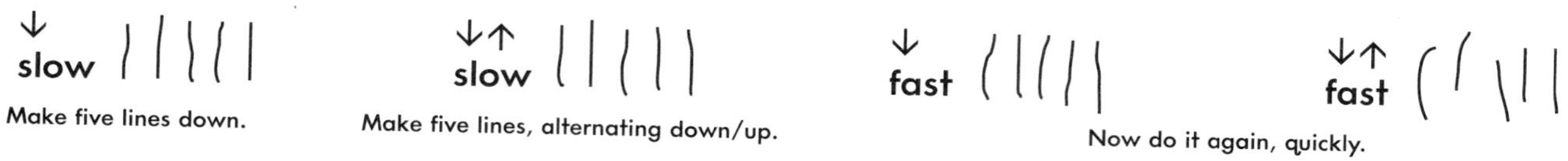

Notice that when you make lines down slowly, it doesn't really matter where you start. But when you add speed, it does matter where you start. Children who start at the top can be fast and neat! Tell parents about this. Send children home singing this song to remind parents to help children start at the top.

Chords
F = C F A
C7 = C E G B♭
B♭ = F B♭ D

Where Do You Start Your Letters?

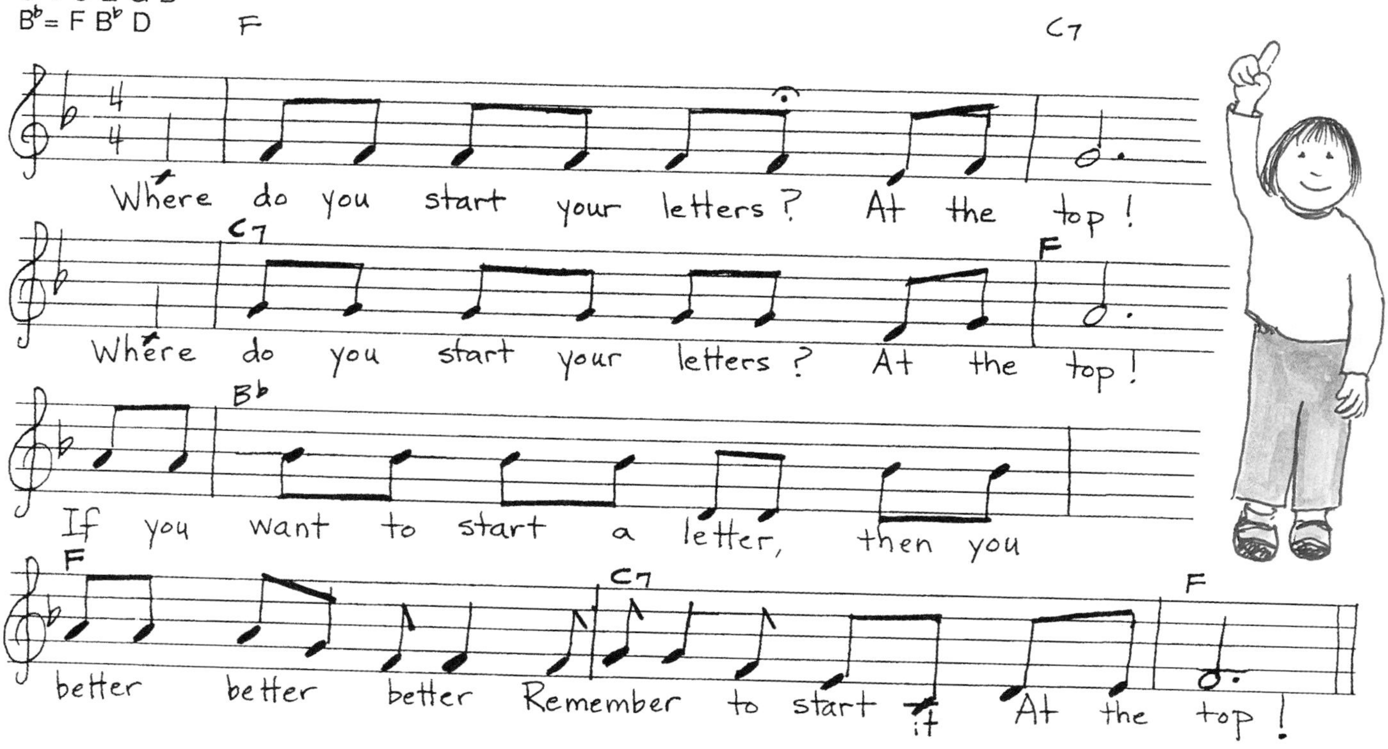

F ... C7
Where do you start your letters? At the top!

C7 ... F
Where do you start your letters? At the top!

B♭
If you want to start a letter, then you

F ... C7 ... F
better better better Remember to start it At the top!

Where Do You Start Your Letters?

Children never forget where to start their letters with this fun song.

Materials/Setup
- *Sing Along* CD, "Where Do You Start Your Letters?" track 1

Grouping
Whole class

Support/ELL
Teach Top with Wood Piece Play. See Pre-Writing section, pages 90-91.

Activity

1. Play the CD in the background as children play so that they will become familiar with the lyrics. They'll know the tune from "If You're Happy and You Know It."
2. Sing the song with children, making a questioning gesture with hands for "Where?" and pointing high for "At the Top!"
3. End by writing a letter on the board.

✔ Check
Observe children as they build a letter with Wood Pieces. Can they identify the top/correct starting point?

More To Learn
Make a lyric change with "Where Do You Start Your Numbers?" Try the rock version: *Rock, Rap, Tap & Learn* CD, track 2.

Look What We're Learning

Foundation Skills
- Recognize and use common prepositions in speech
- Listen to and repeat songs

Geometry
- Identify position or location using top

Sensory Motor
- Notice and attach meaning to visual information

Oral Language
- Repeat teacher's words
- Demonstrate active listening by attending to instruction
- Respond to simple questions

Vocabulary

top

Chicks & Ducks

These pages give experience with vertical and horizontal lines. Verticals are made with down strokes. Horizontals are made like this ⇨ for right-handed children and like this ⇦ for left-handed children.

Activity

How many chicks do you see? How many ducks do you see?
How many legs do chicks have? How many wings do ducks have?
How many legs do you have? How many wings do you have? None!

Look and Learn

The fence has posts. The posts go down into the dirt. The fence has rails. The rails go across.

Trace, Color, and Draw

Trace posts down. Start on the arrows. Trace the bird and duck legs down. Trace rails across. Right-handed children trace ⇨ but left-handed children may trace ⇦. Color the grass with little down strokes and the rest freely.

✔ Check

Observe children as they trace. Can they distinguish and form vertical and horizontal lines?

Support/ELL

Help with crayon grip. If too many children need help, use small bits of crayon. Small bits can be picked up only with a good fingertip grip.

More To Learn

Compare birds and ducks. Look at beaks and bills, feet and webbed feet.

Look What We're Learning

Oral Language
- Demonstrate active listening by attending to instruction
- Learn words linked to content being taught
- Respond to simple questions

Writing
- Hold a crayon with proper grip to write
- Use helping hand to stabilize papers

Number & Operations
- Verbally count a set of objects
- Recognize that the last number said is the total

Sensory Motor
- Use the same hand consistently to hold crayons
- Use fingers to hold crayons

Vocabulary

chick
duck
wings
rails
posts

Bird Legs

Children learn to count two, and they also learn about birds as they chirp and fly around.

Materials/Setup
- *Sing Along* CD, "Bird Legs," track 12

Grouping
Whole class

Support/ELL
What sounds do birds make in other languages? Roosters may say "kikiriki" instead of "cock-a-doodle-doo. " Little chicks may say "pio pio" instead of "peep peep."

Activity

1. Play CD in background days before this activity to familiarize children with the tune and lyrics.
2. Children stand to sing along with you and the CD. You show motions: wings (arms) flap for the beginning of each verse.
3. When each verse ends with the refrain, "When we count the legs on birds, we always count 1 2", children enthusiastically make two down strokes in the air for 1, 2.

✔ Check

Observe children as they pick up the words from the CD. Do they begin to join in on the repeated refrain?

More To Learn

Expose children to tally marks. How many legs on a bird? I I = 2. Table? I I I I = 4. Let children make tally marks at the boards.

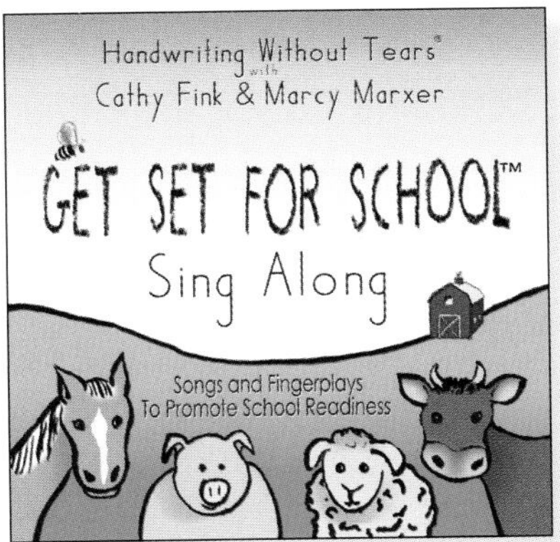

Look What We're Learning

Foundation Skills
- Listen to and repeat songs

Number & Operations
- Verbally count a set of object
- Recognize that the last number said is the total

Oral Language
- Demonstrate active listening by attending to instruction

Sensory Motor
- Use large muscle groups to maintain posture/position and mobility
- Use both sides of the body in activities
- Know where the body is in relation to space
- Tolerate motion in activities
- Play with body awareness, balance, and regard for people and equipment
- Move naturally and place body to perform tasks

Shape – Cross

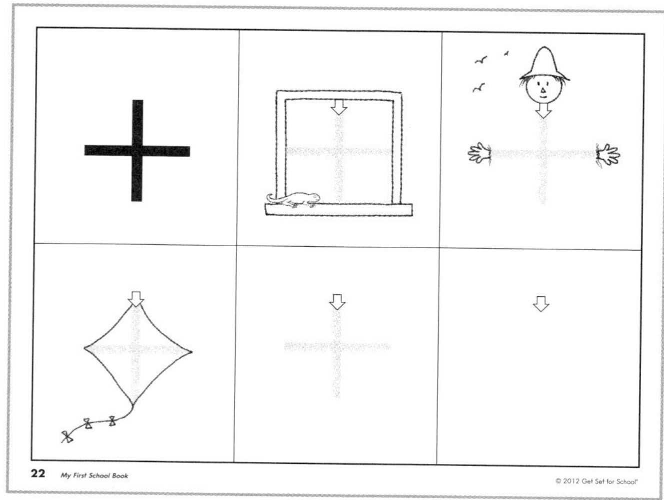

Three-year-olds can make a circle before they can make a cross. For four-year-olds, we use the cross to prepare them to write letters with vertical and horizontal strokes. Teach the vertical from top to bottom and the cross from left to right.

Activity

This is a shape page. This shape is a cross.

Look and Learn

Look at the pictures and name them together: **cross, window, scarecrow, kite, cross.** Then say together: **This is a cross. The window has a cross; the scarecrow has a cross,** etc. This strategy helps children learn words and left-to-right reading. The window has something else—a lizard.

Trace, Color, and Draw Crosses

Demonstrate how to draw a cross: **Little line down, little line across.** Trace the first cross together. Children put their crayons on the arrow, little line down, little line across. Children trace, color, and draw as they like.

✔ Check

Check for who needs help with crayon grip. Notice handedness and use of helping hand.

Support/ELL

Children who are not ready for crayon tracing can finger trace over each cross.

More To Learn

Show children pictures of scarecrows and crows. **Scarecrow is a big word, a compound word. It is made with two little words: scare, crow. Put them together.**

Look What We're Learning

Foundation Skills
- Recognize familiar two-dimensional shapes
- Draw simple shapes
- Use correct top-to-bottom, left-to-right directionality for symbols

Oral Language
- Learn words linked to content being taught

Writing
- Hold a crayon with proper grip to write
- Use helping hand to stabilize objects and papers

Sensory Motor
- Use same hand consistently to hold crayons
- Use fingers to hold crayons

Vocabulary

cross
window
scarecrow
kite

Activity

This is the L page. L is a letter. Do you know: L words? L names? L sounds? Have you ever seen a lizard?

Look and Learn

Let's find Ls on this page. Look. There's a lizard. Lizard starts with L. Is a lizard an animal or a person? Where do lizards live? What do lizards have?

Color and Draw

Let's color the lizard. Show pictures. **Lizards can be any color. They can have spots or stripes. Draw rocks or grass for the lizard too.** Demonstrate. **The lizard needs a tongue!**

Trace and Write L

Finger trace the L at the top of the page. (Say directions.)
Let's write L. Put the crayon on the ☺. Big line down. Little line across.

✔ Check

Check for those who need help with crayon grip. Notice handedness and use of the helping hand.

Support/ELL

Help children make a sharp corner on **L**. Make the big line go straight down to a full stop, and then make the little line.

More To Learn

Look for lizards in reptile books. Find other animals in the reptile family.

Look What We're Learning

Foundation Skills
- Use correct top-to-bottom, left-to-right directionality for letters
- Sequencing

Oral Language
- Respond to simple questions
- Learn words linked to content being taught

Writing
- Hold a crayon with proper grip to write
- Use helping hand to stabilize objects and papers
- Trace capital letters

Sensory Motor
- Use same hand consistently to hold crayons
- Use fingers to hold crayons

Vocabulary

lizard
spots
stripes

Shape – Square

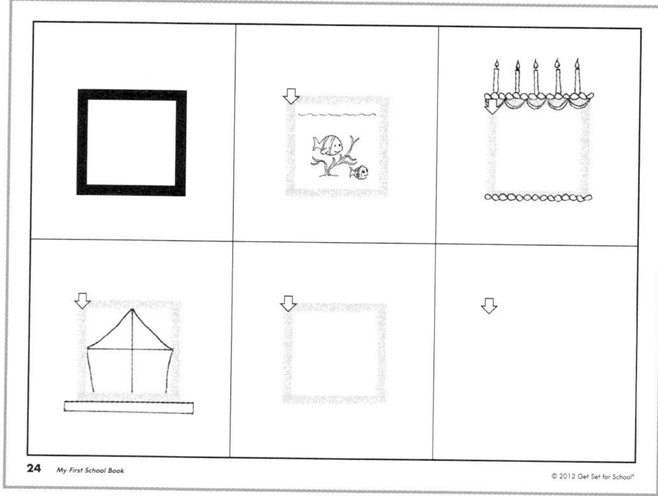

Developmentally, the square comes after the cross. This shape contains vertical and horizontal strokes.

Activity

This is a shape page. This shape is a square.

Look and Learn

Look at the pictures and name them together: **square, fish tank, birthday cake, window, square.** Say, together: **This is a square. The fish tank has a square. The present has a square. . . .** This helps children learn words and left to right reading.

Trace, Color and Draw Squares

Demonstrate how to draw a square. **Start at the top: little line down, little line across the bottom, little line up, little line across the top.** Trace the first square together. Children put their crayons on the arrow. Say the words for them. Children trace and copy the squares. They color and draw.

✔ Check

Observe children as they start to trace or draw squares. Do they start at the top?

Support/ELL

Build squares with four big lines. Build a square in one corner of the room. That will help with one of the right angles.

More To Learn

Use beans to teach four corners on a square. Three beans won't cover all corners. Five will have one extra. Four is perfect.

Look What We're Learning

Foundation Skills
- Recognize familiar two-dimensional shapes
- Draw simple shapes
- Use correct top-to-bottom, left-to-right directionality for symbols

Oral Language
- Learn words linked to content being taught

Writing
- Hold a crayon with proper grip to write
- Use helping hand to stabilize objects and papers

Sensory Motor
- Use same hand consistently to hold crayons
- Use fingers to hold crayons

Vocabulary

square
stripes

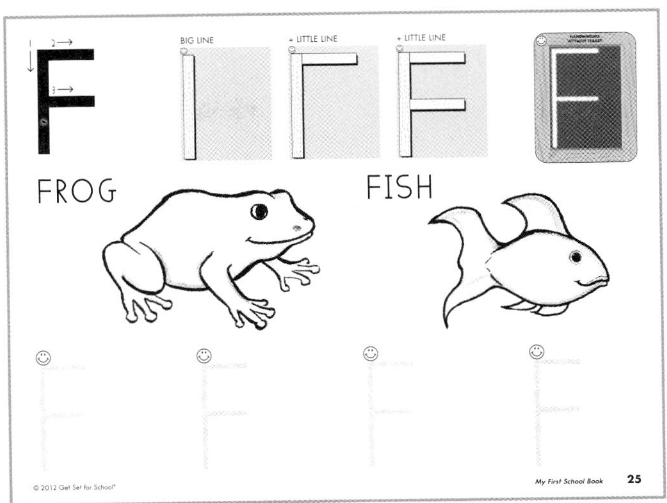

Activity

This is the F page. Do you know: F words? F names? F sounds? F month?

Look and Learn

Let's find Fs on this page. Look. There's a frog and a fish. Frog and fish start with F. How do frogs move? They jump. How do fish move? They swim. What do they use to move?

Color and Draw

Let's color the frog and fish. Show different ways to color. **You can also draw water or grass.**

Trace and Write F

Finger trace the F at the top of the page. (Say directions.)

Let's write F. Put the crayon on the ☺. Big line down. Jump to the ☺. Little line across the top. Little line across the middle.

✔ Check

Observe if children can stop with increasing control. The crayon letters and numbers are at the bottom of pages to help them anticipate when to stop.

Support/ELL

If children are not ready to trace letters, save that part of the page for another time. Practice **F** on the Slate instead of tracing **F**.

More To Learn

Find two words: FROG and FISH. Compare a frog's body to a fish's body. Act out hopping and swimming.

Look What We're Learning

Foundation Skills

- Use correct top-to-bottom, left-to-right directionality for letters
- Sequencing

Oral Language

- Respond to simple questions
- Learn words linked to content being taught

Writing

- Hold a crayon with proper grip to write
- Use helping hand to stabilize objects and papers
- Trace capital letters

Sensory Motor

- Use same hand consistently to hold crayons
- Use fingers to hold crayons

Vocabulary

frog
fish

Pre-Stroke for E

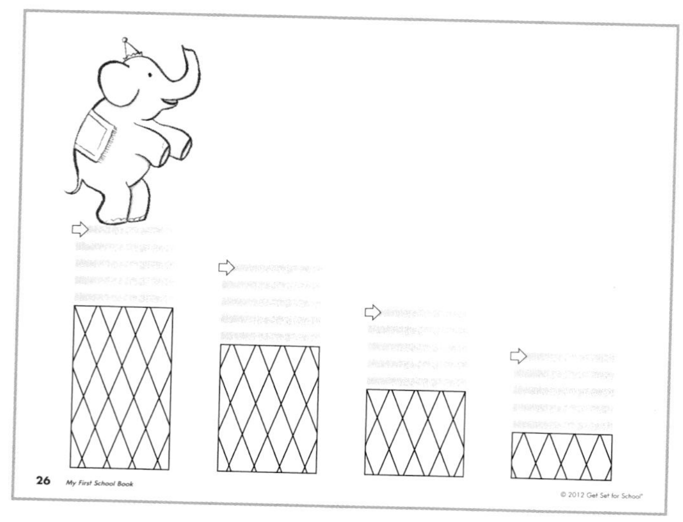

Prepare children for **E** with this pre-stroke page, which has horizontal lines to trace. Developmentally, the horizontal line is one of the easiest strokes for a child. Focus on left-to-right tracing and stopping.

Activity

This is a line page. The lines are horizontal. The floor is horizontal.

Look and Learn

Look at the elephant. This is a circus elephant. How can we tell?

Trace and Color Pre-Strokes for E

Demonstrate how to write lines. Children put their crayons on the arrow as you say: **Big line across. Slow down, get ready to stop. Look, we made a line.** They color the page as they like. It is a circus, so encourage bright colors.

✔ Check

Observe children as they trace and color. Do they know about bright and dull colors? Earth colors, the colors of dirt, are considered dull. Flowers usually have bright colors.

Support/ELL

Use an oven rack to help children learn to make horizontal lines. Just pull the crayon along the rungs. The rack also helps children to stop.

More To Learn

Show picture books about elephants. Some tame elephants work to lift and carry heavy loads. Children may know cartoon or storybook elephants.

Look What We're Learning

Foundation Skills

- Listen to oral directions to attend to a simple task

Oral Language

- Respond to simple questions
- Learn words linked to content being taught
- Communicate thoughts with words

Writing

- Hold a crayon with proper grip to write
- Use helping hand to stabilize objects and papers

Sensory Motor

- Use same hand consistently to hold crayons
- Use fingers to hold crayons
- Notice and attach meaning to visual information

Vocabulary

horizontal

circus

Activity

This is the E page. Do you know: E words? E names? E sounds? Have you seen an elephant?

Look and Learn

Let's find the Es. Look. There's an elephant. Elephant starts with E. Compare body parts of a person and an elephant: nose/trunk, ears/ears, two legs/four legs, no tail/one tail. **How do elephants pick up things? What do you have that elephants don't have? Hands and fingers!**

Color and Draw

Color the elephant any color you like. You can also draw trees and grass.

Trace and Write E

Finger trace the E at the top of the page. (Say directions.)

Let's write E. Put the crayon on the ☺. Big line down. Jump to the ☺. Little line across the top, middle, and bottom.

✔ Check

Observe if children use just three little lines for **E**. Do they sometimes use extra lines?

Support/ELL

Crayon trace the Wood Pieces at the top of the page. Do each one step by step, saying the Wood Piece words.

More To Learn

Find the word ELEPHANT on the page. Act like an elephant: bend over, put hands together as a trunk, and swing side to side. Compare heavy and light.

Look What We're Learning

Foundation Skills

- Name parts of the body
- Use correct top-to-bottom, left-to-right directionality for letters
- Sequencing
- Listen to oral directions to attend to a simple task

Writing

- Hold a crayon with proper grip to write
- Use helping hand to stabilize objects and papers
- Trace capital letters

Sensory Motor

- Use same hand consistently to hold crayons
- Use fingers to hold crayons

Vocabulary

elephant
trunk

Shape – Rectangle

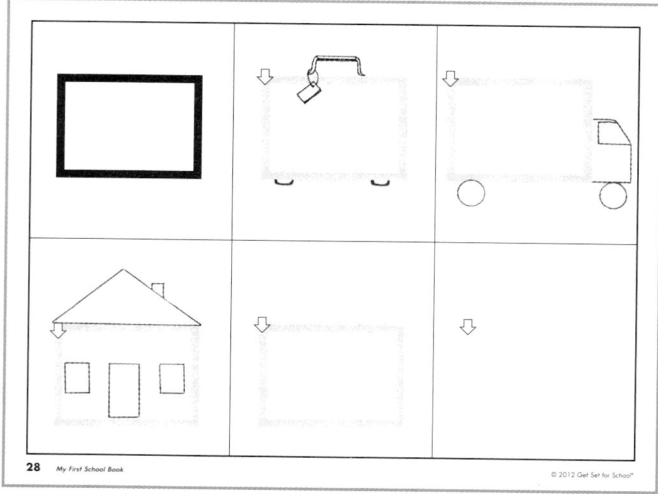

28 My First School Book
© 2012 Get Set for School®

Rectangles are like squares but different. Square sides are equal. Rectangle sides are not equal. Two are long, two are short. Rectangles are more common. Children will find them easily in the classroom.

Activity

This is a shape page. This shape is a rectangle.

Look and Learn

Look at the pictures and name them together: **rectangle, suitcase, truck, house, rectangle.** Then say together: **This is a rectangle. The suitcase has a rectangle. The truck has a rectangle. The house has a rectangle. This is a rectangle.**

Trace, Color and Draw Rectangles

Demonstrate how to draw a rectangle. **Start at the top. Little line down, big line across the bottom, little line up, big line across the top.** Trace the first rectangle together. Children put their crayons on the arrow. Say the words for them. Children trace and copy the rectangles. They color and draw.

✔ Check

Observe children as they trace. Do they start to trace on the ⇨? The ⇨ is there to encourage them to start at the top.

Support/ELL

If children need help to find the starting arrows, simply use a yellow highlighter to mark them. Practice saying rectangle with different voices: slow, high, low, loud, etc.

More To Learn

Use rectangle shape sticky notes. Give each child a rectangle note to stick on a rectangle in the room. You'll find so many because most books are rectangles.

Look What We're Learning

Foundation Skills

- Recognize familiar two-dimensional shapes
- Draw simple shapes
- Use correct top-to-bottom, left-to-right directionality for symbols

Oral Language

- Learn words linked to content being taught

Writing

- Hold a crayon with proper grip to write
- Use helping hand to stabilize objects and papers

Sensory Motor

- Use same hand consistently to hold crayons
- Use fingers to hold crayons

Vocabulary

rectangle
suitcase
truck

Activity

This is the H page. H is a letter. Do you know H words? H names? H sounds? Have you seen a house? Have you seen a chimney? What does a chimney do?

Look and Learn

Let's find the Hs. Look. There's a house. House starts with H. Talk about the outside parts of a house: walls, roof, doors, windows. Talk about what's inside.

Color and Draw

Color the house any color. Encourage children to add grass, bushes, window panes, etc.

Trace and Write H

Finger trace the H at the top of the page. (Say directions.)

Let's write H. Put the crayon on the ☺. Big line down. Big line down. Little line across. Right-handed children pull the little line like this ⇨. Left-handed children pull the little line like this ⇦.

✔ Check

Observe handedness. Are children using the dominant hand consistently?

Support/ELL

If children are not ready to trace letters, save that part of the page for another time. Practice **H** on the Slate instead.

More To Learn

Find the word HOUSE on the page. Tell the story of the *Three Little Pigs.* They built three different houses: straw, stick, and brick.

Look What We're Learning

Foundation Skills

- Recognize and use common prepositions in speech
- Use correct top-to-bottom, left-to-right directionality for letters
- Sequencing
- Listen to oral directions to attend to a simple task

Writing

- Hold a crayon with proper grip to write
- Use helping hand to stabilize objects and papers
- Trace capital letters

Sensory Motor

- Use same hand consistently to hold crayons
- Use fingers to hold crayons

Vocabulary

outside
inside
roof
chimney
window panes

BIG LINE + LITTLE LINE

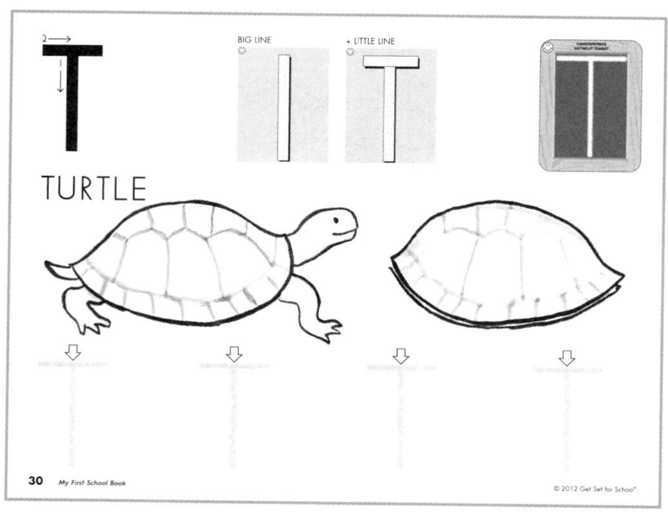

This is the capital **T** page. Capital **T** is crossed at the TOP. Lowercase **t** is crossed lower.

Activity

This is the T page. Do you know T words? T names? T sounds? T days? Have you seen a turtle?

Look and Learn

Let's find the Ts. Turtle starts with T. Talk about opposites (in/out, hard/soft), and how turtles go in and out from their shells.

Color and Draw

Sing the "Crayon Song" (page 29). Children color the turtles and add grass, water, or rocks.

Trace and Write T

Finger trace the T at the top of the page. (Say directions.)

Let's write T. Put the crayon on the arrow ⇩. Big line down. Little line across the top. Right-handed children pull little line like this ⇨ Left handed children pull the little line like this ⇦.

✔ Check

Do children trace the top of the T correctly with one stroke? A common error is doing one side, then the other.

Support/ELL

T is the first letter that starts in the top center of the Mat or Slate.

More To Learn

Make turtles as a craft project. Make **T** for "Time Out" with your hands, just like a referee.

Look What We're Learning

Foundation Skills

- Use correct top-to-bottom, left-to-right directionality for letters
- Sequencing

Oral Language

- Respond to simple questions
- Learn words linked to content being taught

Writing

- Hold a crayon with proper grip to write
- Use helping hand to stabilize objects and papers
- Trace capital letters

Sensory Motor

- Use same hand consistently to hold crayons
- Use fingers to hold crayons

Vocabulary

turtle
shell
opposite

Letter I

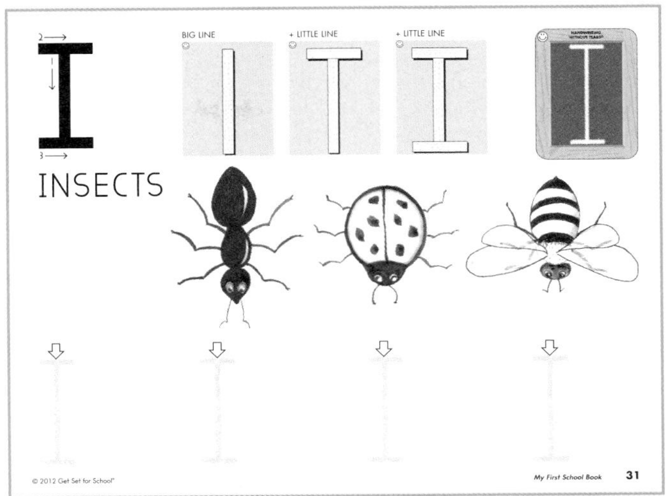

Remind children about "The Ant, the Bug and the Bee." Show them pages 8-9 from *My First School Book*.

Activity

This is the I page. Do you know I words? I names? I sounds? Have you seen insects?

Look and Learn

Let's find the Is. Look. There are insects. Insects start with I. Discuss where insects live and their body parts: six legs, two antenna, and wings to fly.

Color and Draw

Color the ladybug red and the bee yellow. Make tiny scribbles for more insects.

Trace and Write I

Finger trace the I at the top of the page. (Say directions.)

Let's write I. Put the crayon on the arrow ⇩. Big line down. Little line across the top, and little line across the bottom. Right-handed ⇨ left-handed ⇦.

✔ Check

Observe as children trace. Remind children to start at the top. Model for them.

Support/ELL

Letter **I** is also a center starter. Help children find the top center of the Mat or the Slate.

More To Learn

Fly around like insects. Sing "The Ant, The Bug and The Bee," track 14, and show pages 8-9 from *My First School Book*.

Look What We're Learning

Foundation Skills
- Use correct top-to-bottom, left-to-right directionality for letters
- Sequencing

Oral Language
- Respond to simple questions
- Learn words linked to content being taught

Writing
- Hold a crayon with proper grip to write
- Use helping hand to stabilize objects and papers
- Trace capital letters

Sensory Motor
- Use same hand consistently to hold crayons
- Use fingers to hold crayons

Vocabulary

insect
antenna
firefly

The Rain Song

This is a coloring page to use with the "Rain Song," *Sing Along* CD, track 24.

Activity

What kind of page is this? Is it a shape page? Is it a letter page? It's a coloring page.

Look and Learn

This coloring page is about rain. Explain that the pictures at the top are repeated below. Read the words for the children as they name the pictures. **The words name what is in each picture: rain, puddle, raincoat, boots, boat, rainhat. There are three rain words.**

Color and Draw

Children color the page as they like. Demonstrate how to make little down strokes for the rain. They may add more elements to the picture, perhaps grass or flowers.

✔ Check

Observe if children can tell pictures from words. Do they know that the words tell what is in the picture? The words are like labels.

Support/ELL

Use this page for word practice. Point to something at the top. Children find the same thing in the picture below. Say the name together.

More To Learn

Raincoat is a compound word. Have half the class say rain and the other half say coat. Then all say raincoat together.

Look What We're Learning

Foundation Skills
- Listen to and repeat songs

Alphabet Knowledge
- Tell the difference between letters, pictures, and other symbols

Concepts About Print
- Understand that print can be read and has meaning

Oral Language
- Learn words linked to content being taught

Writing
- Use helping hand to stabilize objects and papers

Sensory Motor
- Use same hand consistently to hold crayons
- Use fingers to hold crayons

Vocabulary

puddle
boots
boat

Activity

This is the U page. Do you know U words? U names? U sounds? Have you used an umbrella?

Look and Learn

Let's find the Us. Look. There's an umbrella. Umbrella starts with U. Up starts with U. Talk about opposites: open/shut, up/down, wet/dry.

Color and Draw

Color the umbrella. What about using different colors for each section of the umbrella?

Trace and Write U

Finger trace the U at the top of the page. (Say directions.)

Let's write U. Put the crayon on the ☺. Big line down. Turn and go across the bottom. Big line up.

✔ Check

Check for those who need help with crayon grip. Notice handedness and use of the helping hand.

Support/ELL

Letter **U** is not made with Wood Pieces. To prepare for **U**, use Wet-Dry-Try on the Slate. Letter **U** starts in the starting corner.

More To Learn

Make an umbrella, raincoat, and boots for Mat Man®. Use toy cars and make U turns.

Look What We're Learning

Foundation Skills
- Use correct top-to-bottom, left-to-right directionality for letters

Sequencing
- Listen to oral directions to attend to a simple task

Oral Language
- Respond to simple questions

Writing
- Hold a crayon with proper grip to write
- Use helping hand to stabilize objects and papers
- Trace capital letters

Sensory Motor
- Use same hand consistently to hold crayons
- Use fingers to hold crayons

Vocabulary

umbrella

Make a Magic C Bunny

It's easy to engage children and get them to listen with the help of a puppet. Invite a puppet to co-teach with you. You can use the Magic C Bunny puppet, or simply make one with a paper napkin.

The Magic C Bunny helps you teach these very important handwriting habits:
Magic C starts every circle, **O**, and oval.
Magic C starts every number zero 0.
Magic C starts every capital **C O Q G S**.
Magic c starts every lowercase letter **a d g o q**.

Make Your Own Magic C Bunny

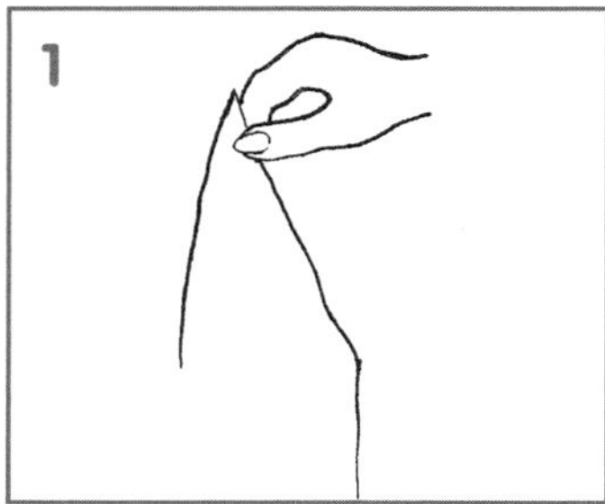

Open paper napkin.
Hold by one corner.

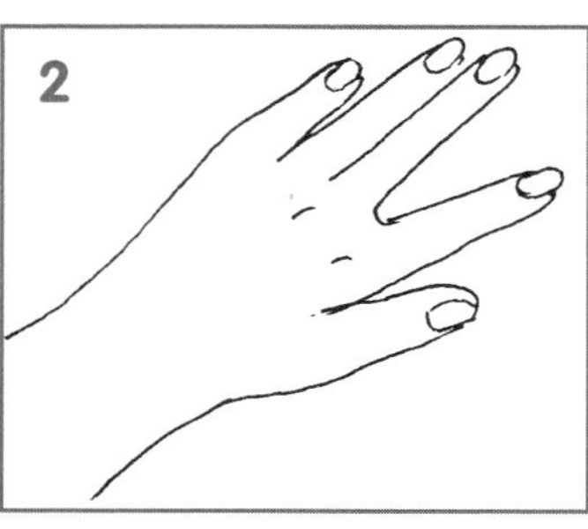

Spread index and middle fingers apart.

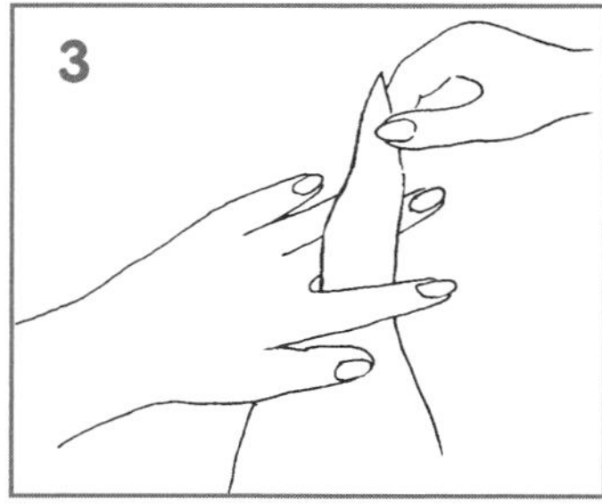

Pull corner between your index and middle fingers. (First ear)

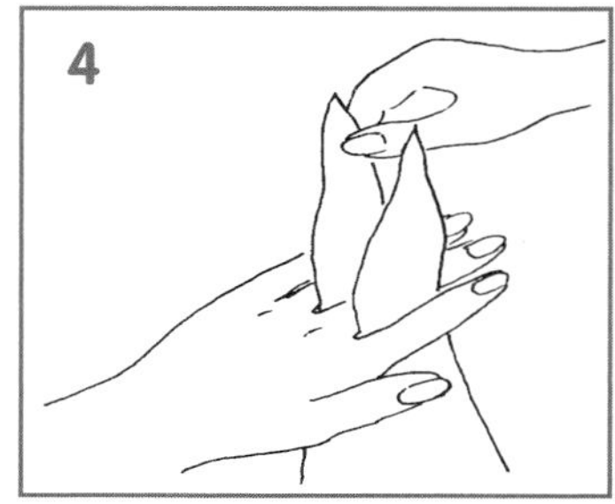

Take the next corner.
Pull corner between your middle and ring fingers. (Second ear)

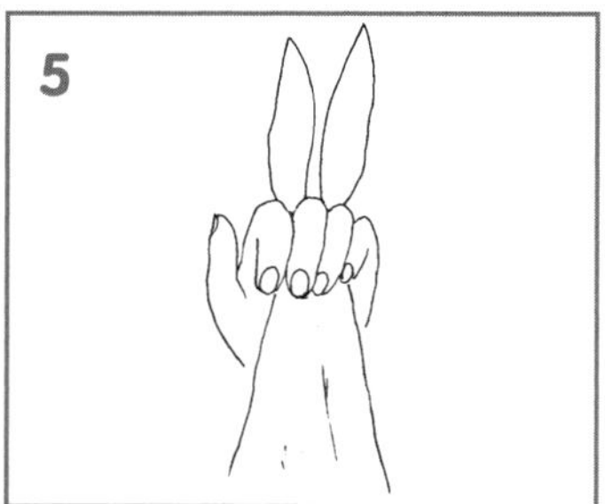

Fold fingers into palm.

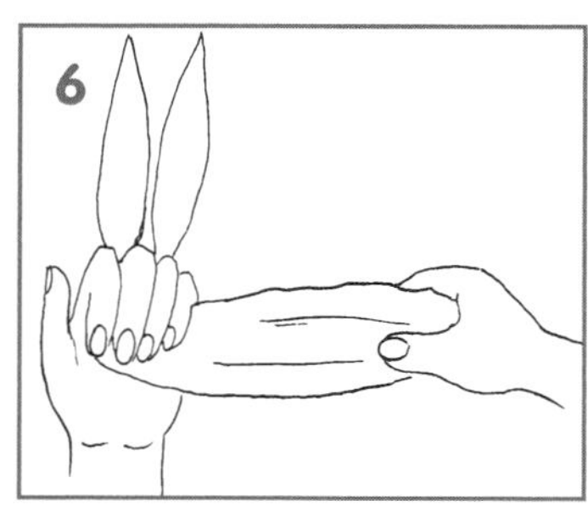

Pull napkin out to side.

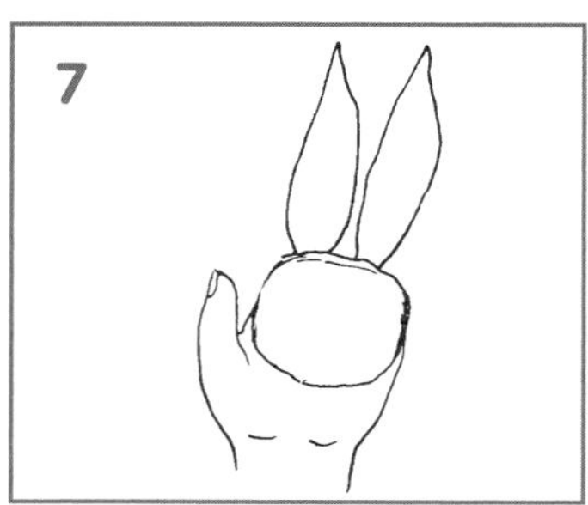

Wrap napkin over fingers and tuck into hand.

Add the face with a pen.
It's Magic C Bunny!
Slip the bunny off and give him to a child. Tape or staple the napkin to hold it.

Materials/Setup

- Magic C Bunny puppet
- Crayons

Grouping

Whole class

Support/ELL

Put children who may need help right in front of or close to you. Move slowly. Trace a **C** on an easel to provide a visual model.

Activity

1. Hold Magic C Bunny in your left hand. Listen to him. He'll tell you and the children what to do.
2. Magic C Bunny says, pick up a crayon and hold it correctly. Let me see!
3. Magic C Bunny says, follow the teacher.

   Start at the top, make a magic C. Stop.

   Start at the top, make a magic C... keep going to make a circle. Stop.

   Start at the top, make a magic C. Stop.

   Start at the top, make a magic C. Keep going, to make a zero. Stop.

   Start at the top, make a magic C. Stop.

   Start at the top, make a magic C. Keep going to make a letter O. Stop.

✔ Check

Observe children as they make **C**. Do they start at the top? Do they stop after they make a half circle?

More To Learn

Also start at the top, make a magic C. Stop. Start at the top, make a magic C turn into **G** or **Q** or **S** (little magic c).

Look What We're Learning

Foundation Skills

- Imitate teacher's body movements
- Listen to oral direction to attend to a simple task

Writing

- Hold a crayon with proper grip to write

Geometry

- Identify position or location using top

Sensory Motor

- Use same hand consistently to hold crayons
- Use fingers to hold crayons
- Use index finger to trace letters in the air
- Use large muscle groups to maintain posture/position and mobility
- Tolerate motion in activities
- Notice and attach meaning to visual information

Pre-Stroke for C

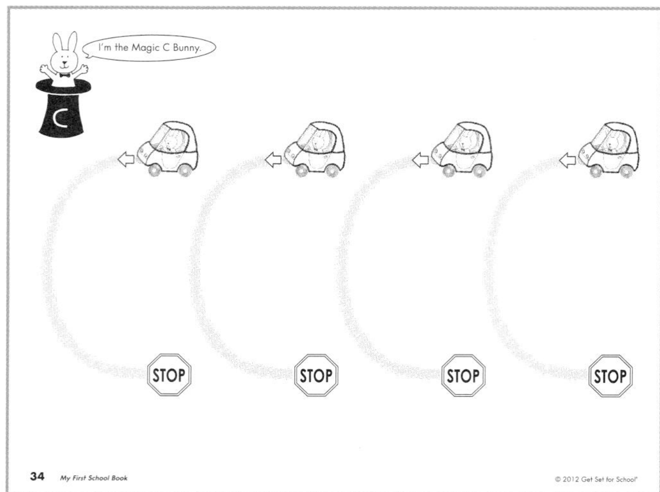

Use Magic C to prepare for **C**, **O**, **Q**, **G** and circles. They all start at the top with Magic C.

Activity

Magic C Bunny is on this page. There is also a bunny in every car.

Look and Learn

Children count the cars as they touch each one and say, "1, 2, 3, 4... 4 cars in all."

Color and Trace Pre-Stroke for C

Children choose a different color for each car. They color the STOP signs red. Then they drive the first car on the Magic C road to the STOP sign. Repeat with the 2nd, 3rd, and 4th car.

✔ Check

Observe children as they touch each car. Do they understand first, second, third, and fourth? Point out that the car by the Magic C Bunny is first.

Support/ELL

Before this page, use a Wood Piece Little Curve as a guide for **C**s. Right-handed children trace the inside curve. Left-handed children trace the outside curve.

More To Learn

Use the Magic C Bunny puppet to introduce **C** or make your own. Sing the "Magic C" song, track 6, on the *Sing Along* CD.

Look What We're Learning

Foundation Skills
- Recognize and identify basic colors
- Listen to oral directions to attend to a simple task

Sensory Motor
- Use same hand consistently to hold crayons
- Use fingers to hold crayons
- Perceive the size, shape, or identity of an object by sense of touch
- Notice and attach meaning to visual information

Writing
- Hold a crayon with proper grip to write
- Use helping hand to stabilize objects and papers

Number & Operations
- Verbally count a set of objects
- Recognize that the last number said is the total

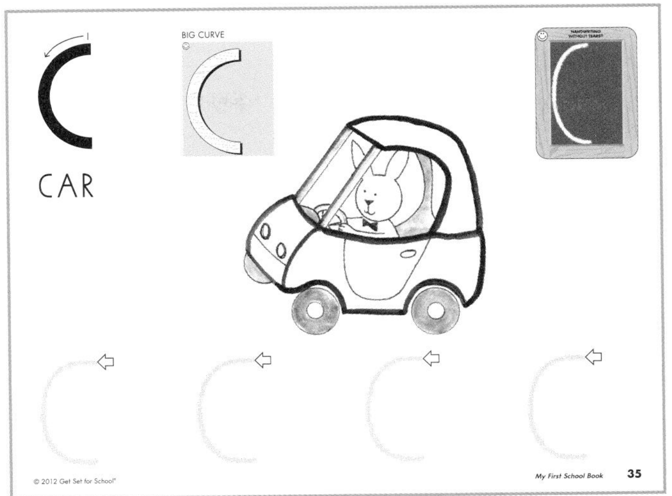

Activity

This is the C page. Do you know C words? C names? C sounds? Have you ever seen a car like this one?

Look and Learn

Let's find Cs on this page. Look. There's a car. Car starts with C. What do cars do? What color cars have you seen? Show pictures.

Color and Draw

Let's color the car. Show different ways to color. **Any designs? Does your car need a road?** Demonstrate.

Trace and Write C

Finger trace the C at the top of the page. (Say directions.)

Let's write C for car. Put the crayon on the arrow ⇦. Big curve. Stop at the bottom.

✔ Check

Observe children as they trace **C**. Do the children start correctly at the top on the arrow?

Support/ELL

Curve left hand to make **C**. Use right index finger to trace **C**.

More To Learn

If you're teaching letter sounds, teach two sounds for **c**. It's easy to remember the /k/sound in car. Think of **c** for circle to remember the /s/ sound. Circle starts with a /s/ sound.

Look What We're Learning

Foundation Skills

- Use correct top-to-bottom, left-to-right directionality for letters

Oral Language

- Respond to simple questions
- Learn words linked to content being taught
- Talk about experiences and observations

Writing

- Hold a crayon with proper grip to write
- Use helping hand to stabilize objects and papers
- Trace capital letters

Sensory Motor

- Use same hand consistently to hold crayons
- Use fingers to hold crayons

Vocabulary

road

Pre-Stroke for O

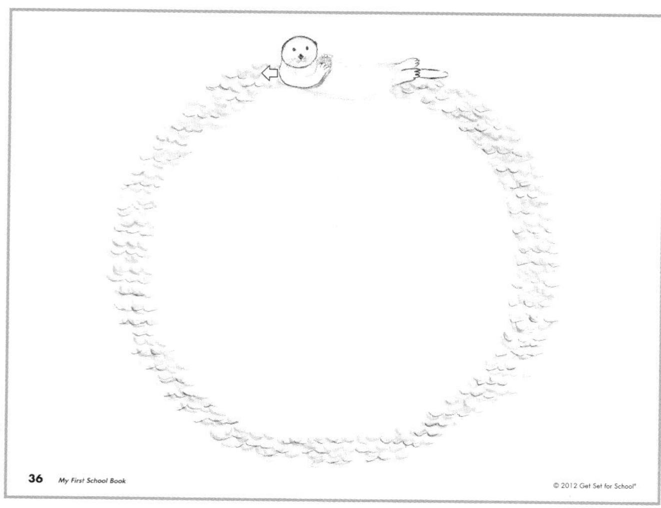

36 My First School Book
© 2012 Get Set for School®

Take the otter for a swim to get ready for **O**, **Q** and circles too.

Activity

There is an otter on this page. It is a sea otter. It swims on its back. It eats and sleeps on its back too.

Look and Learn

The otter is holding something. It's a sea urchin. It's lunch!

Color and Trace Pre-Stroke for O

Help children choose two crayons: brown for the otter and blue for the water. They take the otter for a swim by tracing around. Try different shades of blue for more swims.

✔ Check

Observe children as they trace around the waves. Do they know front and back? Have them lie down on their backs to float and kick.

Support/ELL

Help children rotate their arms from the shoulder to make big circles on easels. Wrists rotate for smaller circles. Circles aren't hard to make if they use their bodies.

More To Learn

A mother otter carries her baby on her chest. A baby sea otter is called a pup, but it's not a dog.

Look What We're Learning

Foundation Skills
- Recognize and identify basic colors
- Listen to oral directions to attend to a simple task

Writing
- Enjoy writing and engage in writing activities
- Hold a crayon with proper grip to write
- Use helping hand to stabilize objects and papers

Sensory Motor
- Use same hand consistently to hold crayons
- Use fingers to hold crayons
- Notice and attach meaning to visual information

Social-Emotional
- Interact easily with familiar adults
- Ask for help when needed

Vocabulary

otter

sea urchin

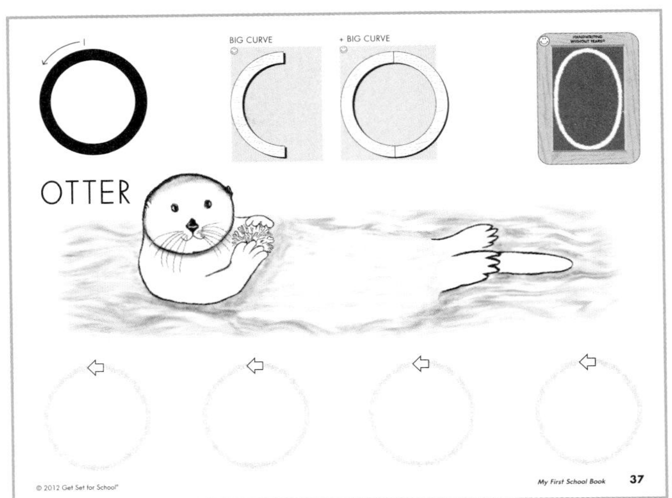

Activity

This is the O page. Do you know O words? O names? O months? O sounds? Have you seen an otter?

Look and Learn
There's an otter. Otter starts with O. Look at the otter's head. It has an O, or a circle shape.

Color and Draw
Otters have brownish gray hair that looks dark when it's wet. Let's find a picture and color the otter.

Trace and Write O
Finger trace the O at the top of the page. (Say directions.)
Let's write O. Put the crayon on the ⇦. Magic C. Keep going. See the C turn into an O. Stop at the top.

✔ Check

Observe children. Do they know which way the otter will go when it kicks? The arrow points that way too.

Support/ELL

Your mouth makes an O shape when you say **O**. Use big curves to make **O**s and say **O** to each other.

More To Learn

Find the word OTTER. Say the letters: **O - T - T - E - R**. **R** is the only letter we haven't learned.

Look What We're Learning

Foundation Skills
- Use correct top-to-bottom, left-to-right directionality for letters
- Recognize familiar two-dimensional shapes
- Sequencing
- Listen to oral directions to attend to a simple task

Oral Language
- Respond to simple questions

Writing
- Hold a crayon with proper grip to write
- Use helping hand to stabilize objects and papers
- Trace capital letters

Sensory Motor
- Use same hand consistently to hold crayons
- Use fingers to hold crayons

Shape – Circle

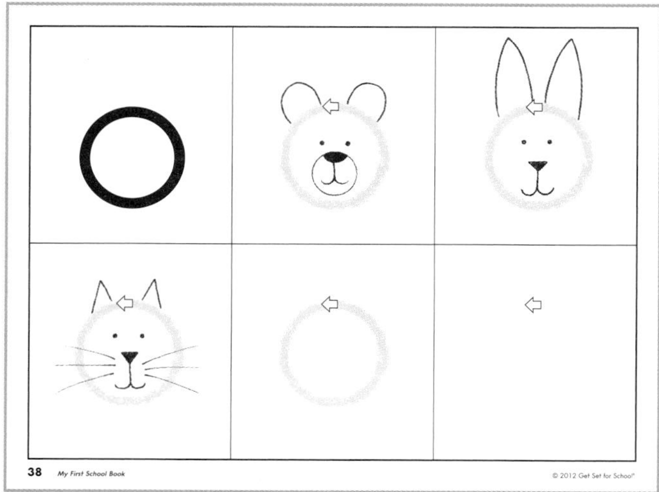

Developmentally, the circle comes after the horizontal. Demonstrate circles often for children. Always start with a **C** for circle stroke.

Activity

This is a shape page. This shape is a circle.

Look and Learn

Look at the pictures. Name them together: **circle, bear, bunny, cat.** Then say together: **This is a circle. The bear has a circle. The bunny has a circle. The cat has a circle. This is a circle.** Ask about ears. **Which animal has rounded ears? ...long ears? ...pointed ears?**

Trace, Color, and Draw

Demonstrate how to draw a circle. **Start at the top. Magic C. Keep going. Stop at the top.** Trace the first circle together. Children put their crayons on the arrow. Say the words for them. Children trace and copy the circles. They color and draw.

✔ Check

Help children start circles at the top, with a **C** stroke. Look out for left-handed children. They need that habit too, but it doesn't come naturally.

Support/ELL

Use the *Sing Along* CD, track 6 or 17, to teach simple drawings with circles.

More To Learn

Children make bear faces. Show them how to make a smaller circle inside the big circle. The nose goes at the top of the circle.

Look What We're Learning

Foundation Skills

- Recognize familiar two-dimensional shapes
- Draw simple shapes
- Use correct top-to-bottom, left-to-right directionality for symbols

Oral Language

- Learn words linked to content being taught

Writing

- Hold a crayon with proper grip to write
- Use helping hand to stabilize objects and papers

Sensory Motor

- Use same hand consistently to hold crayons
- Use fingers to hold crayons

Vocabulary

circle

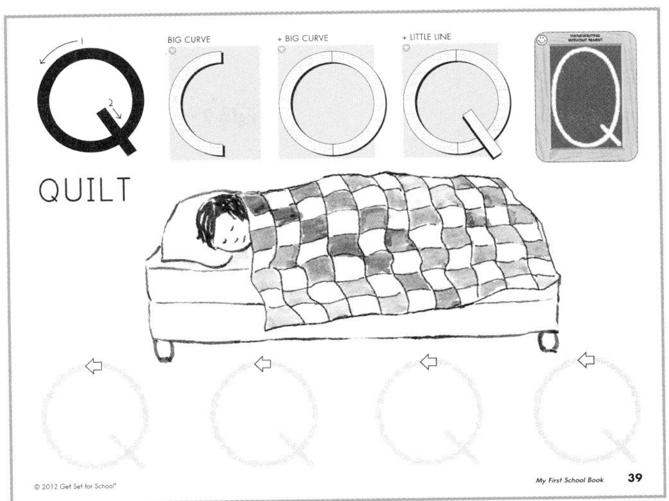

Activity

This is the Q page. Do you know: Q words? Q names? Q sounds? Have you seen a quilt?

Look and Learn

Let's find the Qs. Look. There's a quilt. Quilt starts with Q. Talk about how quilts keep us warm, are made of pieces, have many patterns and colors.

Color and Draw

Color the quilt. Use many colors to aim and scribble on the squares.

Trace and Write Q

Finger trace the Q at the top of the page. (Say directions.)

Let's write Q. Put the crayon on the ⇦. Magic C. Keep going. Stop at the top. Add a little line.

✔ Check

Help left-handed children start **O** and **Q** at the top, with a **C** stroke. This important habit doesn't come naturally to left-handed children.

Support/ELL

Introduce the /q/ sound as children act like ducks. Say, **QUACK, QUACK, QUACK**. Then mother duck says "QUIET."

More To Learn

Sit on the quilt for question time. Give question marks on paper. Help children give you the question mark and say, **I have a question**. Help children ask questions.

Look What We're Learning

Foundation Skills

- Use correct top-to-bottom, left-to-right directionality for letters
- Sequencing

Oral Language

- Respond to simple questions
- Learn words linked to content being taught

Writing

- Hold a crayon with proper grip to write
- Use helping hand to stabilize objects and papers
- Trace capital letters

Sensory Motor

- Use same hand consistently to hold crayons
- Use fingers to hold crayons

Vocabulary

quilt
pattern

Pre-Stroke for G

This pre-stroke page prepares children for **G**. They cut the grass to get ready.

Activity

There is a lady on the page. What is she pushing? The grass is growing into a letter.

Look and learn

She's ready to cut the grass. The grass is growing a letter G. She starts at the top to cut the grass.

Color and Trace Pre-Strokes for G

Children start at the top and color the lady first. They pretend to mow as they color the grass. **Put a green crayon on the lawnmower. Trace the Magic C. Trace the little line up. Stop and lift the crayon. Trace the little line like this ⇨.**

✔ Check

Check your teaching for the little line. Make it in one stroke like this ⇨. The exception is ⇦ for left-handed children.

Support/ELL

Help children lift the crayon before they make the little line. **G** is made in two steps.

More To Learn

Mow the lawn. Cut the grass. They both mean the same. What do you say? Talk about mow/cut and lawn/grass.

Look What We're Learning

Foundation Skills

- Recognize and identify basic colors
- Listen to oral directions to attend to a simple task

Writing

- Enjoy writing and engage in writing activities
- Hold a crayon with proper grip to write
- Use helping hand to stabilize objects and papers

Oral Language

- Respond to simple questions
- Learn words linked to content being taught

Sensory Motor

- Use same hand consistently to hold crayons
- Use fingers to hold crayons
- Notice and attach meaning to visual information

Vocabulary

lawnmower

Activity

This is the G page. Do you know G words? G names? G sounds? Have you seen a grasshopper?

Look and Learn

Let's find Gs. Look. There's a grasshopper in the grass. Find the words GRASS and GRASSHOPPER. They start with G. Grasshoppers have six legs. Two legs are big for hopping, cutting grass.

Color and Draw

Most grasshoppers are green, like grass. Consider adding a bug or a worm in the grass.

Trace and Write G

Finger trace the G at the top of the page. (Say directions.)

Let's write G. Put the crayon on the ⇦. Magic C. Little line up. Now pick up your crayon. Make a Little line across like this ⇨.

✔ Check

Check your teaching for the little line. Make it in one stroke like this ⇨. Exception ⇦ for left-handed children.

Support/ELL

Demonstrate tracing **G** with Line It Up Letter Card **G**.

G uses two strokes.

More To Learn

Grasshoppers are insects, like the ant, the bug, and the bee.

G makes a /g/ sound in Gail, goat, gas, goals.

G makes a /j/ sound in George, gym, gentle, giraffe.

Look What We're Learning

Foundation Skills
- Use correct top-to-bottom, left-to-right directionality for letters
- Sequencing

Alphabet Knowledge
- Tell the difference between letters, pictures, and other symbols

Writing
- Hold a crayon with proper grip to write
- Use helping hand to stabilize objects and papers
- Trace capital letters

Sensory Motor
- Use same hand consistently to hold crayons
- Use fingers to hold crayons

Vocabulary

grasshopper

Pre-Stroke for S

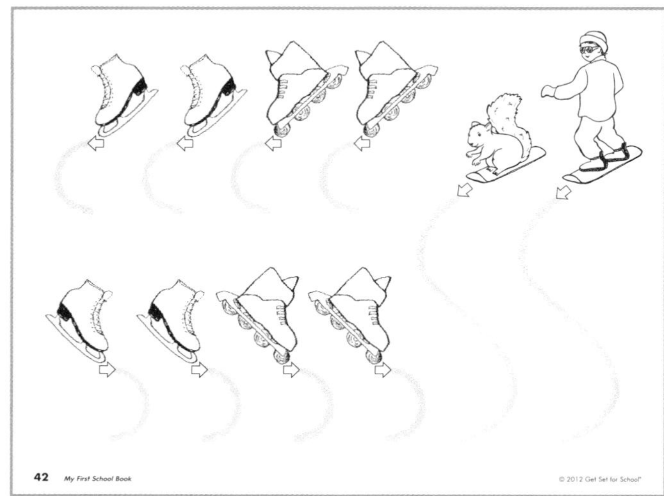

Letter **S** changes direction during a stroke. This page has little curves and curves in the shape of an **S** for tracing.

Activity

This is a skating and snowboarding page. The skates at the top make Magic c curves. The skates at the bottom curve the other way.

Look and Learn

The squirrel and the skateboarder put curves together. They make a Magic c curve and then turn to make another curve the other way. It's S.

Color and Trace Pre-Strokes for S

Children color the skates at the top first. They make little Magic c curves. Then they color the skates at the bottom that curve the other way. Now, they're ready to color the squirrel and skateboarder and take them down the hill.

✔ Check

Observe if children start at the top for every curve and for **S**.

Support/ELL

Demonstrate tracing **S** with Line It Up™ Letter Card **S**. Then let children trace too. Watching others trace first is helpful.

More To Learn

Do compound words: Boys say, "ice." Girls say, "skate." Then all say "ice-skate". Now girls go first. Girls say, "skate," boys say, "board." Then all say, "skateboard."

Look What We're Learning

Foundation Skills

- Listen to oral directions to attend to a simple task

Writing

- Enjoy writing and engage in writing activities
- Hold a crayon with proper grip to write
- Use helping hand to stabilize objects and papers

Oral Language

- Demonstrate active listening by attending to instruction
- Learn words linked to content being taught

Sensory Motor

- Use same hand consistently to hold crayons
- Use fingers to hold crayons
- Notice and attach meaning to visual information

Vocabulary

skateboard
snowboard
squirrel

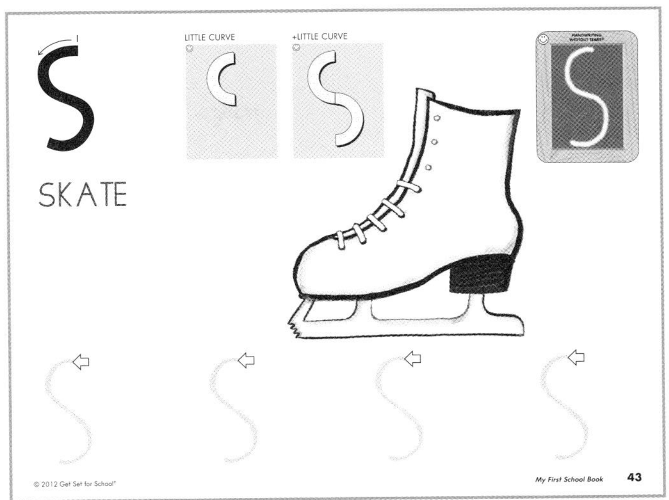

Activity

This is the S page. Do you know S words? S names? S sounds? S days? S months? Have you seen a skate?

Look and Learn

Let's find the Ss. Look. There's a skate. Skate starts with S. Talk about places you can skate. Ask who has skates and if they have seen anyone skate.

Color and Draw

Children color the skate. If you have any silver crayons, bring them out for the shiny skate blade.

Trace and Write S

Finger trace the S at the top of the page. (Say directions.)

Let's write S. Put the crayon on the ⇦. Make a little Magic c curve. Slide down to make a little curve turn the other way.

✔ Check

Observe handedness and use of the helping hand. Check for those who need help with crayon grip.

Support/ELL

Use hands-on letter play for **S**: Wood Pieces and Mat, and Wet-Dry-Try slate activity. Have children finger trace. Save crayon tracing until they are ready.

More To Learn

Children can make a dough snake into an **S**. Use two cones to set up an **S** path for children to pretend skate. Paper under shoes makes them skate.

Look What We're Learning

Oral Language
- Demonstrate active listening by attending to instruction
- Learn words linked to content being taught
- Respond to simple questions
- Talk about experiences and observations
- Use words to describe an object's traits

Writing
- Hold a crayon with proper grip to write
- Use helping hand to stabilize objects and papers
- Trace capital letters

Sensory Motor
- Use same hand consistently to hold crayons
- Use fingers to hold crayons

Vocabulary

skate
silver

Pre-Stroke for J

Letters **J** and **U** are not made with Wood Pieces. The Wet-Dry-Try activity is the best preparation for **J**.

Activity

Here are four skaters skating for you. What did they do? What will they do?

Look and Learn

The J skaters make a big line down, a turn, and then a stop. The skaters beside are ready to go.

Trace and Color Pre-Strokes for J

Children should trace J first, starting at the top. Say, **Big line down. Turn. Stop.** Children trace little lines. They put their crayons on the arrow. Say, **Little line across. Stop.** Finally, color the skaters and perhaps draw a new skater.

✔ Check

Observe how children start **J**. Is the big line straight? Pull down straight, then turn. This is a good habit for neat **J**s.

Support/ELL

Keep the little line at the top little. That makes it neat.

More To Learn

How can you tell a capital **J** from a lowercase j? The capital has a little line at the top. Lowercase j has a dot.

Look What We're Learning

Oral Language

- Demonstrate active listening by attending to instruction
- Respond to simple questions
- Communicate thoughts with words

Writing

- Enjoy writing and engage in writing activities
- Hold a crayon with proper grip to write
- Use helping hand to stabilize objects and papers

Sensory Motor

- Use same hand consistently to hold crayons
- Use fingers to hold crayons
- Notice and attach meaning to visual information

Activity

This is the J page Do you know J words? J names? J sounds? J months? Do you have a jacket?

Look and Learn

Let's find the Js. Look. There's a jacket. Jacket starts with J. Talk about January, June and July weather, hanging up jackets, parts of a jacket, and the number of sleeves.

Color and Draw

Color the jacket.

Trace and Write J

Let's finger trace J at the top of the page. (Say directions.)

Let's write J. Put the crayon on the ⇩. Big line down. Turn. Little line across the top.

✔ Check

Check your teaching for the little line. Make it in one stroke like this ⇨. This exception is ⇦ for left-handed children.

Support/ELL

Keep center starters **T I C O Q G S** in review with the slate. You write a letter on one side. The child watches, turns the slate over, and writes the same letter.

More To Learn

J is for jumping. Let's jump. **J** is for jogging. Let's jog. Practice putting on and taking off jackets. Practice zipping or buttoning. Teach up/down, on/off, and open/closed concepts.

Look What We're Learning

Foundation Skills
- Use correct top-to-bottom, left-to-right directionality for letters
- Sequencing

Oral Language
- Talk about experiences and observations
- Use words to describe an object's traits

Writing
- Hold a crayon with proper grip to write
- Use helping hand to stabilize objects and papers
- Trace capital letters

Sensory Motor
- Use same hand consistently to hold crayons
- Use fingers to hold crayons

Vocabulary

jacket
sleeve
January
June
July

Pre-Stroke for D, P, B, R

The letters, **D, P, B,** and **R** begin with a big line. The next part is a big curve (**D**) or a little curve (**P, B, R**). The curves go the way the ducks are facing, to the right. This page gives practice in tracing big and little curves.

Activity

Here are ducks. How many are big ducks? How many are little ducks?

Look and learn

Which way are the ducks facing? Point that way. That's right! They swim in big curves and little curves.

Color and Trace Pre-Strokes for D P B R

These ducks look like rubber ducks. Children may want them to be yellow with orange bills, but any color combination is fine. Children trace the curves the way the ducks swim. They start at the arrow.

✔ Check

Look at this page and earlier pages. Observe how children's coloring skills are developing. Do children show more control and creativity?

Support/ELL

Provide hand-over-hand assistance to get the child moving in the direction of the stroke.

More To Learn

Make children aware of which way pictures face. This book plans the way they face to help them make strokes go in the correct direction.

Look What We're Learning

Oral Language
- Demonstrate active listening by attending to instruction
- Communicate thoughts with words

Algebra
- Sort objects by size

Writing
- Hold a crayon with proper grip to write
- Use helping hand to stabilize objects and papers

Number & Operations
- Verbally count a set of objects
- Recognize that the last number said is the total

Sensory Motor
- Use same hand consistently to hold crayons
- Use fingers to hold crayons

Vocabulary

bills

duck

Activity

This is the D page. Do you know D words? D months? D names? D sounds? Have you ever seen a duck?

Look and Learn

Let's find Ds on this page. Look. There's a duck. Duck starts with D. Is a duck an animal or a person? Where do ducks live? What do ducks have? What color are ducks? Show pictures.

Color and Draw

Let's color the duck. Do you want it to be the same or different from the other ducks?

Trace and Write D

Let's finger trace D at the top of the page. (Say directions.)

Let's write D. Put the crayon on the ☺. Big line down. Jump back to ☺. Big curve to the bottom.

✔ Check

Check for those who need help with crayon grip. Notice handedness and use of helping hand.

Support/ELL

Help children with their physical approach to writing by ensuring that chair and table heights suit children's heights.

More To Learn

Make duck sounds. Fly or walk like ducks. Float a rubber ducky. Play with sinking and floating objects.

Look What We're Learning

Foundation Skills
- Use correct top-to-bottom, left-to-right directionality for letters
- Sequencing
- Listen to oral directions to attend to a simple task

Oral Language
- Respond to simple questions
- Talk about experiences and observations

Writing
- Hold a crayon with proper grip to write
- Use helping hand to stabilize objects and papers
- Trace capital letters

Sensory Motor
- Use same hand consistently to hold crayons
- Use fingers to hold crayons

Letter P

BIG LINE + LITTLE CURVE

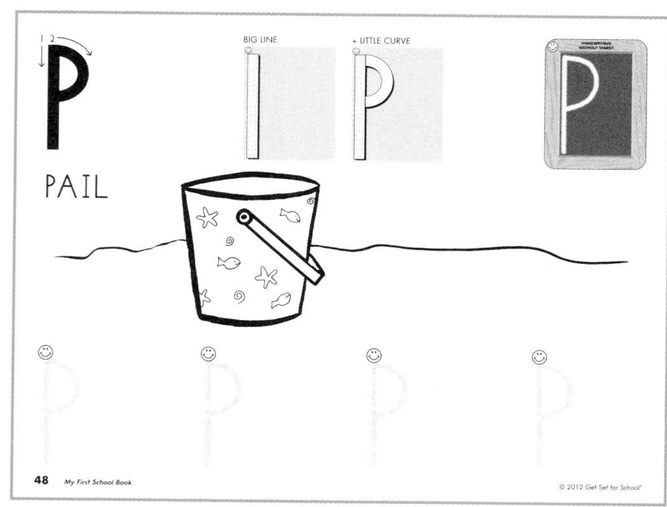

Activity

This is the P page. Do you know P words? P names? P sounds? Have you seen a pail?

Look and Learn

Let's find the Ps. Look. There's a pail. Pail starts with P. Talk about how pails are used, what goes in them, and the Jack and Jill nursery rhyme.

Color and Draw

Children color the pail, the sand, and water. Have children put details in the water: fish, bubbles, and so forth.

Trace and Write P

Let's finger trace P at the top of the page. (Say directions.)

Let's write P. Put the crayon on the ☺. Big line down. Jump to the ☺. Little curve to the middle.

✔ Check

Observe if children use the Wood Piece words: Big Line + Little Curve.

Support/ELL

Review position words. Use a Wood Piece Big Line to review top, middle, and bottom.

More To Learn

Teach in/out by placing things in pails. **P** is for peppermint. Smell peppermint. Make a bucket brigade and pass like firefighters did long ago.

Look What We're Learning

Foundation Skills

- Use correct top-to-bottom, left-to-right directionality for letters
- Sequencing
- Listen to oral directions to attend to a simple task

Oral Language

- Respond to simple questions

Writing

- Hold a crayon with proper grip to write
- Use helping hand to stabilize objects and papers
- Trace capital letters

Sensory Motor

- Use same hand consistently to hold crayons
- Use fingers to hold crayons

Vocabulary

pail

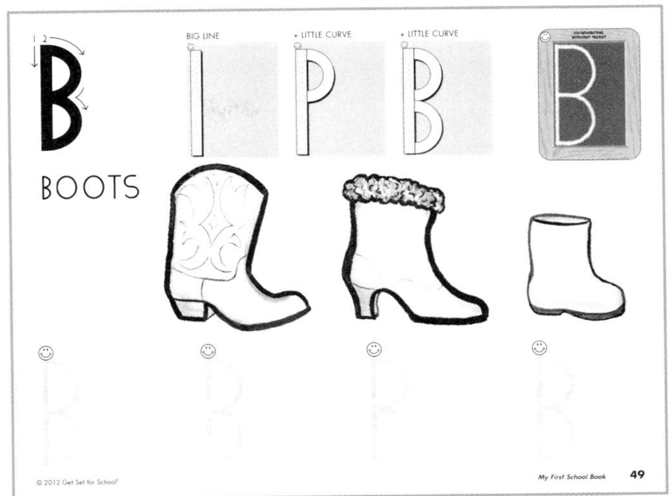

Activity

This is the B page. Do you know B words? B names? B sounds? Do you have boots?

Look and Learn

Let's find the Bs. Look. There are three boots. Boot starts with B. Talk about different purpose boots: baby booties, big and little boots.

Color and Draw

Color the boots any color. Consider adding mud, puddle, grass. Demonstrate.

Trace and Write B

Finger trace the B at the top of the page. (Say directions.)

Let's write B. Put the crayon on the ☺. Big line down. Jump to the ☺. Little curve to the middle.

✔ Check

Observe if children know how **p** and **b** are different. **P** has one little curve, and **B** has two little curves.

Support/ELL

When children write **B** for names, don't fret over skinny or fat **B**s. The order is what matters: big line, jump, little curve to middle, little curve to bottom.

More To Learn

B is for ball. Sort balls by color, type, and size. Talk about cowboy boots and pretend to ride horses.

Look What We're Learning

Foundation Skills

- Use correct top-to-bottom, left-to-right directionality for letters
- Sequencing
- Listen to oral directions to attend to a simple task

Oral Language

- Respond to simple questions

Writing

- Hold a crayon with proper grip to write
- Use helping hand to stabilize objects and papers
- Trace capital letters

Sensory Motor

- Use same hand consistently to hold crayons
- Use fingers to hold crayons

Vocabulary

boots
booties

Pre-Stroke for R

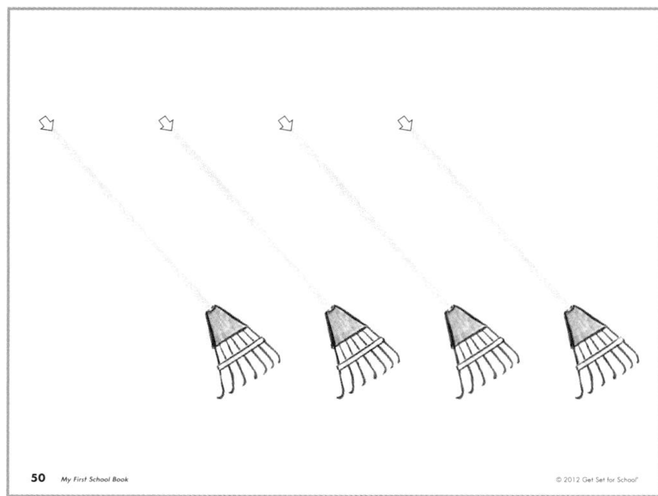

Prepare children for the diagonal in **R** with this pre-stroke page. Diagonal lines are the most difficult.

Activity

There are rakes on this page. Count the rakes and talk about raking leaves.

Look and Learn

Children can make their hands take on characteristics of tools. Use open fingers for a rake, closed fingers for a scoop or shovel, fisted fingers for a hammer.

Trace and Color Pre-Strokes for R

Children put their crayons on the arrow. Say, **Slide down the rake handle.** Stop. They may draw and color fall leaves.

✔ Check

Observe crayon grip. Use "Crayon Song" and pick-up activities. See page 29.

Support/ELL

Rakes are tools. Animals use body parts as tools. Bird beaks work like tools. Look at woodpecker beaks and pelican bills.

More To Learn

Use Wood Piece Big Lines to help children with diagonals. See the Wood Piece Play section of this guide, page 84.

Look What We're Learning

Foundation Skills
- Imitate teacher's body movements

Comprehension
- Listen to perform a task

Writing
- Hold a crayon with proper grip to write
- Use helping hand to stabilize objects and papers

Numbers & Operations
- Verbally count a set of objects
- Recognize that the last number said is the total

Sensory Motor
- Use same hand consistently to hold crayons
- Use fingers to hold crayons
- Move fingers for finger plays

Vocabulary

rake
shovel
hammer

Activity

This is the R page. Do you know R words? R names? R sounds? Have you seen a rake? Have you ever used a rake? What do rakes do?

Look and Learn

Let's find the Rs. Look. There's a rake. Rake starts with R. Talk about one handle.

Color and Draw

Color rake any color. Consider adding leaves and grass. Demonstrate.

Trace and Write R

Finger trace the R at the top of the page. (Say directions.)

Let's write R. Put the crayon on the ☺. Big line down. Jump to the ☺. Little curve to the middle. Little line to the corner.

✔ Check

Observe if children make **D P B R** with the big line first, and the next part on the right side. Do they use good habits when play writing? Don't criticize or correct. Continue to teach good habits.

Support/ELL

Demonstrate tracing **R** with Line It Up Letter Card **R**. Then let children trace too. It is helpful for them to watch others trace first.

More To Learn

Rake leaves. Use a rake to make patterns in a sandbox. R is for run. Go outside and run. Find everything that is red in the room. Who's wearing red?

Look What We're Learning

Foundation Skills

- Use correct top-to-bottom, left-to-right directionality for letters
- Sequencing
- Listen to oral directions to attend to a simple task

Oral Language

- Respond to simple questions

Writing

- Hold a crayon with proper grip to write
- Use helping hand to stabilize objects and papers
- Trace capital letters

Sensory Motor

- Use same hand consistently to hold crayons
- Use fingers to hold crayons

Vocabulary

rake

Pre-Stroke for K

Prepare children for **K** with this pre-stroke page. This page has little diagonal lines for children to trace. Because the stroke begins at the kite and ends at a child's hand, it provides practice with the ability to start and stop.

Activity

There are children and kites on this page. What makes the kite go up?

Look and Learn

The kite strings make lines on the page. They are diagonal lines. Use one arm as a straight line. Make arms be diagonal, vertical, or horizontal.

Trace and Color Pre-Strokes for K

Children put their crayons on the arrow. **Slide down the kite string to the hands. Make noises like the wind as you're making the strokes. Color the page. Use different color crayons.**

✔ Check

Observe children's helping hands and how they open and place their books. Be sure their writing tables and chairs are at a good height. Plan seating according to children's sizes.

Support/ELL

Use Big Lines from the Wood Pieces. Teach vertical, horizontal, and diagonal by moving Big Lines and saying the words. See Wood Piece Play.

More To Learn

Is the wind blowing? Which way? Consider making a wind sock to see.

Look What We're Learning

Foundation Skills

- Use correct top-to-bottom, left-to-right directionality for symbols
- Imitate teacher's body movements

Oral Language

- Demonstrate active listening by attending to instruction
- Respond to simple questions
- Learn words linked to content being taught

Writing

- Hold a crayon with proper grip to write
- Use helping hand to stabilize objects and papers

Sensory Motor

- Use same hand consistently to hold crayons
- Use fingers to hold crayons

Vocabulary

horizontal
vertical
diagonal

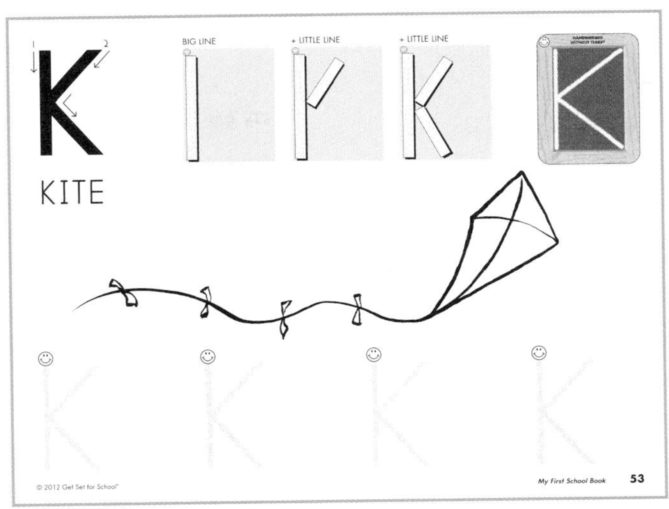

Activity

This is the K page. Do you know K words? K names? K sounds? Have you flown a kite?

Look and Learn

Let's find the Ks. Look. There's a kite. Kite starts with K. Talk about wind and different types of kites.

Color and Draw

Color the kites any color.

Trace and Write K

Finger trace the K at the top of the page. (Say directions.)

Let's write K. Put the crayon on the ☺. Big line down. Jump to the other corner. Little line slides to the middle, little line slides to the bottom.

✔ Check

Observe children as they write **K** in their names. Use the Line It Up™ Letter Card **K** to practice using a kick stroke for **K**'s diagonal lines.

Support/ELL

Review **D P B R** with the slate. You write a letter on one side. The child watches, turns the slate over, and imitates you.

More To Learn

Make kites. Wind string. Pretend to give the **K** a karate kick when making the letter.

Look What We're Learning

Foundation Skills

- Use correct top-to-bottom, left-to-right directionality for letters
- Sequencing
- Listen to oral directions to attend to a simple task

Oral Language

- Respond to simple questions

Writing

- Hold a crayon with proper grip to write
- Use helping hand to stabilize objects and papers
- Trace capital letters

Sensory Motor

- Use same hand consistently to hold crayons
- Use fingers to hold crayons

Vocabulary

kite

Pre-Stroke for A

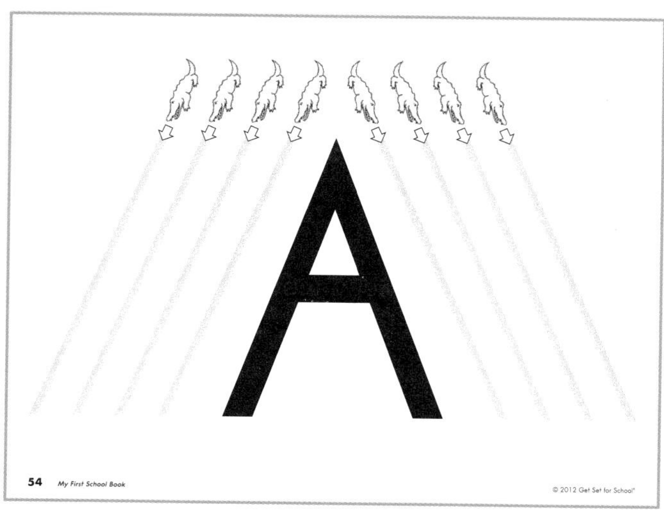

The first letter of the alphabet is one of the most difficult. Often, children mistakenly start at the bottom. That's why the pre-stroke page is so important.

Activity

Letter **A** is in the center of the page. Alligators are at the top to catch children's eyes and help them learn to make **A** with down strokes.

Look and Learn

Letter A uses two big lines. They are diagonal lines. Letter A uses one little line. The little line is horizontal.

Trace and Color Pre-Strokes for A

Demonstrate starting at the top where the alligators are. Put the crayon on the arrow and say, **Big line slides down. Stop.** Use a different color for every alligator and stroke to practice picking up crayons with correct grip.

✔ Check

Observe if children know the pieces they need for **A**. Do they know how many of each piece they need?

Support/ELL

For a child's name that begins with **A**, give individual help.

More To Learn

Have children make chomping noises as they trace, as if the alligator is eating the lines. Look at ABC books to find **A** animals.

Look What We're Learning

Foundation Skills

- Recognize and use common prepositions in speech
- Listen to oral directions to attend to a simple task

Comprehension

- Listen to perform a task

Oral Language

- Learn words linked to content being taught

Writing

- Hold a crayon with proper grip to write
- Use helping hand to stabilize objects and papers

Sensory Motor

- Use same hand consistently to hold crayons
- Use fingers to hold crayons
- Notice and attach meaning to visual information

Vocabulary

alligator

Activity

This is the A page. Do you know A words? A names? A sounds? A months? Have you seen an alligator?

Look and Learn

Let's find the As. Look. There's an alligator. Alligator starts with A. Talk about where alligators live, one tail, lots of teeth, four legs.

Color and Draw

Color the alligator green. What about adding water, a sun, rocks? Demonstrate.

Trace and Write A

Finger trace the A at the top of the page. (Say directions.)

Let's write A. Put the crayon on the ✐. Big line slides down. Jump back to the top. Big line slides down. Little line across.

✔ Check

Check the little line on **A**. Make it in one stroke like this ⇨. The exception is ⇦ for left-handed children.

Support/ELL

Use hands-on letter play in addition to pre-stroke practice for **A**.

More To Learn

Crawl like alligators. Make hand shadow alligator mouths.

A is for apple. Sort apples by color.

Look What We're Learning

Foundation Skills

- Use correct top-to-bottom, left-to-right directionality for letters
- Sequencing
- Listen to oral directions to attend to a simple task

Oral Language

- Respond to simple questions
- Communicate thoughts with words

Writing

- Hold a crayon with proper grip to write
- Use helping hand to stabilize objects and papers
- Trace capital letters

Sensory Motor

- Use same hand consistently to hold crayons
- Use fingers to hold crayons

Shape - Triangle

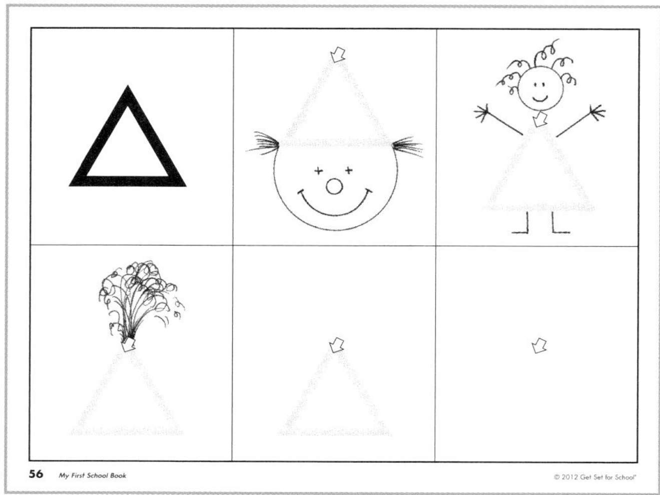

Developmentally, the triangle and diamond come after the circle and square. Motor experiences with slides, ramps, cones, and funnels make diagonal lines and these shapes easier for children.

Activity

This is a shape page. This shape is a triangle.

Look and Learn

Look at the pictures. Name them together: **triangle, clown, girl, volcano**. Say together: **This is a triangle. The clown has a triangle. The girl has a triangle.**

Trace, Color, and Draw Triangles

Demonstrate how to draw a triangle. Say, **Little line slides down, little line across the bottom, little line slides up to the top.** Trace the first triangle together. Children put their crayons on the arrow. Say the words for them. Children trace and copy the triangles. They color and draw.

✔ Check

Do children know how many sides? Do they know how many corners or angles?

Support/ELL

Play "My Teacher Draws" song, track 17, *Sing Along* CD.

More To Learn

Have children point to triangles in different shape books.
Build a triangle with Wood Pieces.

Look What We're Learning

Foundation Skills

- Recognize familiar two-dimensional shapes
- Draw simple shapes
- Use correct top-to-bottom, left-to-right directionality for symbols

Oral Language

- Learn words linked to content being taught

Writing

- Hold a crayon with proper grip to write
- Use helping hand to stabilize objects and papers

Sensory Motor

- Use same hand consistently to hold crayons
- Use fingers to hold crayons

Vocabulary

triangle
clown
volcano

Shape - Diamond

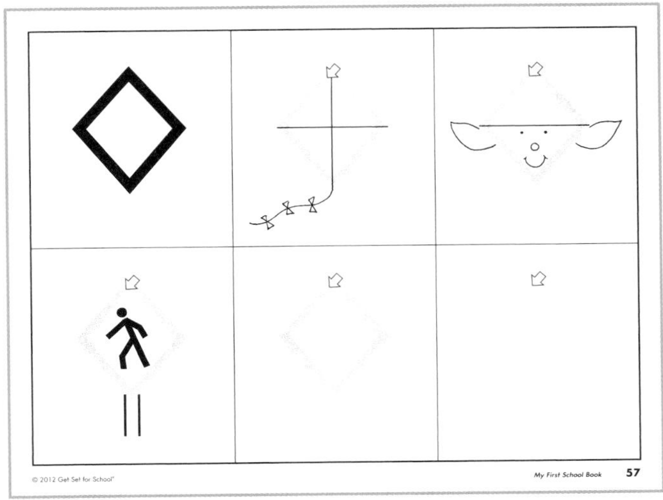

Activity

This is a shape page. This shape is a diamond.

Look and Learn

Look at the pictures. Name them together: **diamond, kite, elf, sign, diamond.** Say together: **This is a diamond. The kite has a diamond. The elf has a diamond. The sign has a diamond.** Pointing to each builds the top-to-bottom, left-to-right habit for reading and writing.

Trace, Color, and Draw Diamonds

Demonstrate how to draw a diamond. **Little line slides down to the side, little line slides down to the bottom, little line slides up to the side, little line slides up to the top.** Trace the first diamond together. Children put their crayons on the arrow. Say the words for them. Children trace and copy the diamonds. They color and draw.

✔ Check

Observe if children know the number of sides. Do they know the number of corners or angles?

Support/ELL

Make a diamond with hands. Flat hands touch at the top. Move thumbs down to touch.

More To Learn

Use a bottomless open box to make a diamond with obtuse and acute angles. That's 3rd grade vocabulary fun for dessert.

Look What We're Learning

Foundation Skills
- Recognize familiar two-dimensional shapes
- Draw simple shapes
- Use correct top-to-bottom, left-to-right directionality for symbols

Oral Language
- Learn words linked to content being taught

Writing
- Hold a crayon with proper grip to write
- Use helping hand to stabilize objects and papers

Sensory Motor
- Use same hand consistently to hold crayons
- Use fingers to hold crayons

Vocabulary

diamond
elf
sign

Pre-Stroke for M

Prepare children for **M** with this pre-stroke page. Two mice are looking for cheese.

Activity

Two mice look for cheese. The first mouse walks straight down to the cheese. The next mouse has to slide down, slide up, and then go straight down to the cheese.

Look and Learn

Mice have fronts and backs. Their noses are at the front. They're smelling the cheese. What's at the back?

Trace and Color Pre-Strokes for M

Help children find the first mouse. **Take the first mouse to the cheese. Big line down. Take the second mouse to the cheese. Big line slides down, big line slides up, big line down. Look, it looks like M.** Pretend to be mice with sniffing sounds searching for cheese. Trace more than once with different colors. Color the mice different colors.

✔ Check

Observe if children start in the correct places. The left-to-right habit should guide them.

Support/ELL

Help children stop to change direction. The second mouse stops to change direction. That will make nice sharp turns for **M**.

More To Learn

Discuss tails: long and short, smooth and hairy. It would be special to show children a violin bow. The bow uses hair from a horse's tail.

Look What We're Learning

Foundation Skills

- Use correct top-to-bottom, left-to-right directionality for symbols
- Recognize and use common prepositions in speech

Oral Language

- Demonstrate active listening by attending to instruction
- Respond to simple questions

Writing

- Hold a crayon with proper grip to write
- Use helping hand to stabilize objects and papers

Sensory Motor

- Use same hand consistently to hold crayons
- Use fingers to hold crayons

Vocabulary

mouse/mice

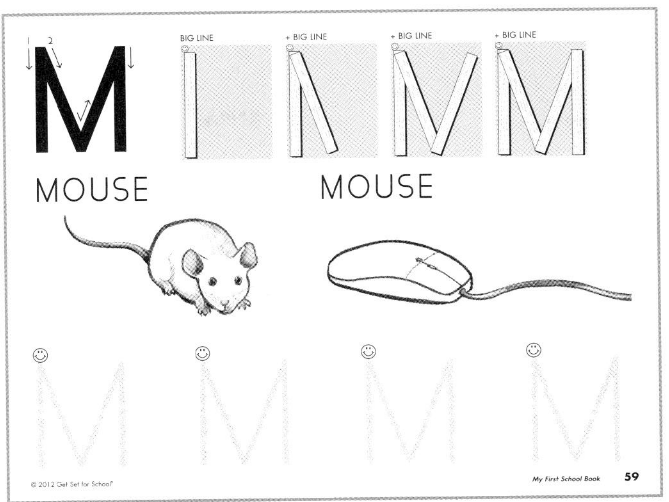

Activity

This is the M page. Do you know M words? M names? M sounds? M months? An M day? Have you seen a mouse?

Look and Learn

Let's find the Ms. Look. There's a mouse. Look, there's a different mouse—a computer mouse. Mouse starts with M. Talk about mice: their size, where they live, what they eat.

Color and Draw

Color both mice. What about adding cheese?

Trace and Write M

Finger trace the M at the top of the page. (Say directions.)

Let's trace M. Put the crayon on the ☺. Big line down. Jump to the ☺. Big line slides down... and up... and down.

✔ Check

Observe children whose names begin with **M**. It's very important that they start **M** at the top.

Support/ELL

Demonstrate how to trace **M** with Line It Up™ Letter Card **M**. After the first big line, jump to the ☺. Do not lift the crayon after that.

More To Learn

Use the "Three Blind Mice" nursery rhyme. **M** is for middle. Play with Mat Man® and put a belly button in the middle of his body.

Look What We're Learning

Foundation Skills

- Use correct top-to-bottom, left-to-right directionality for letters
- Sequencing
- Listen to oral directions to attend to a simple task

Oral Language

- Respond to simple questions
- Talk about experiences and observations

Writing

- Hold a crayon with proper grip to write
- Use helping hand to stabilize objects and papers
- Trace capital letters

Sensory Motor

- Use same hand consistently to hold crayons
- Use fingers to hold crayons

Pre-Stroke for N

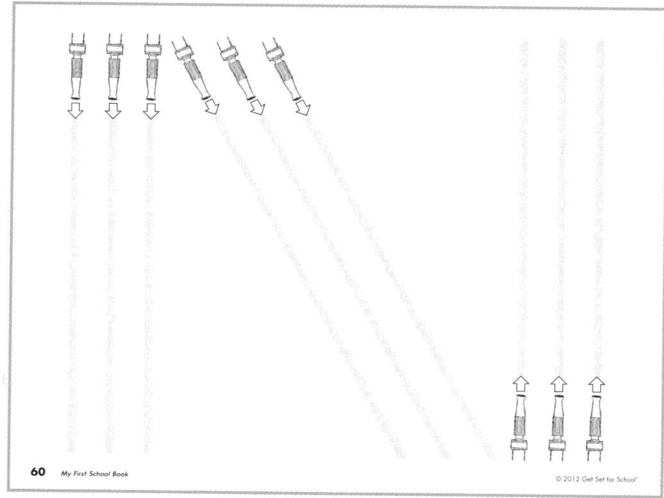

Prepare children for **N**. The last stroke of **N** makes a big line from the bottom. This is the only time children start a vertical big line from the bottom. All other vertical lines start at the top for **B D E F H I K L M P R T**.

Activity

This page has nozzles squirting water vertically and diagonally.

Look and Learn

Nozzles screw on to hoses. They can make sprays or squirts. These nozzles are squirting straight.

Trace and Color Pre-Strokes for N

Demonstrate lines in the air. **Big line down.** For diagonals, face children and point up to your right so children will point to the left. **Big line slides down. Big line goes straight up.** Children put blue crayons on the arrow to trace the water. **Big line down** (3 times). **Big line slides down** (3 times). **Big line up** (3 times). **Color the nozzles too.**

✔ Check

Observe if children start in the correct starting position. Which hand do they use for air writing?

Support/ELL

It's easier for children to follow your air demonstration if you hold a brightly colored ball in your hand.

More To Learn

Children know "At the top!" for starting letters. They need to watch you to start diagonals correctly. Most diagonal lines start at their top left.

Look What We're Learning

Foundation Skills

- Imitate teacher's body movements
- Listen to oral directions to attend to a simple task

Oral Language

- Learn words linked to content being taught

Writing

- Enjoy writing and engage in writing activities
- Hold a crayon with proper grip to write
- Use helping hand to stabilize objects and papers

Sensory Motor

- Use same hand consistently to hold crayons
- Use fingers to hold crayons
- Use index finger to trace objects in the air
- Notice and attach meaning to visual information

Vocabulary

nozzle

hose

straight

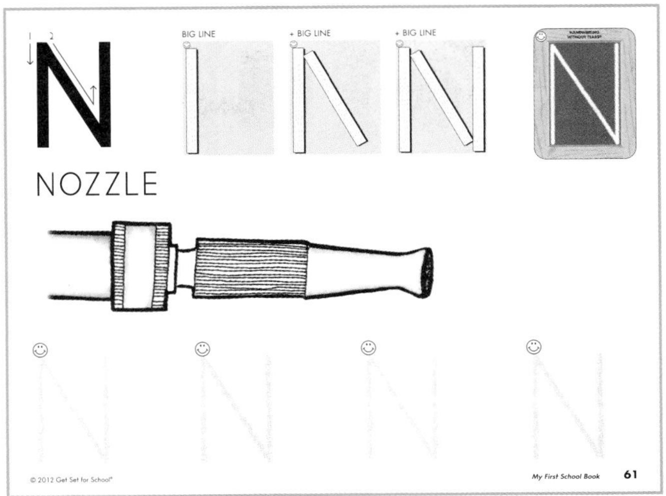

Activity

This is the N page. Do you know N words? N names? N sounds? Have you seen water squirted out of a nozzle?

Look and Learn

Let's find the Ns. Look. There's a nozzle. Nozzle starts with N. What do nozzles do? What comes out of a nozzle? Discuss on/off concepts and what you can water.

Color and Draw

Color the nozzle. Draw water squirting out of the nozzle.

Trace and Write N

Finger trace the N at the top of the page. (Say directions.)

Let's write N. Put the crayon on the ☺. Big line down. Jump to the ☺. Big line slides down. Big line goes up.

✔ Check

Observe children with **N** names. Do they start **N** at the top? It's tempting to begin at the bottom.

Support/ELL

Demonstrate tracing **N** with Line It Up™ Letter Card **N**. Then let children trace too. It is helpful for children to watch others trace first.

More To Learn

N is for no. Shake head for no. Nod head for yes. Play with hose and nozzle. Squirt water. **N** is for noise. Make car, truck, and airplane noises.

Look What We're Learning

Foundation Skills

- Use correct top-to-bottom, left-to-right directionality for letters
- Sequencing
- Listen to oral directions to attend to a simple task

Oral Language

- Respond to simple questions
- Talk about experiences and observations

Writing

- Hold a crayon with proper grip to write
- Use helping hand to stabilize objects and papers
- Trace capital letters

Sensory Motor

- Use same hand consistently to hold crayons

Vocabulary

squirt

Shapes Review

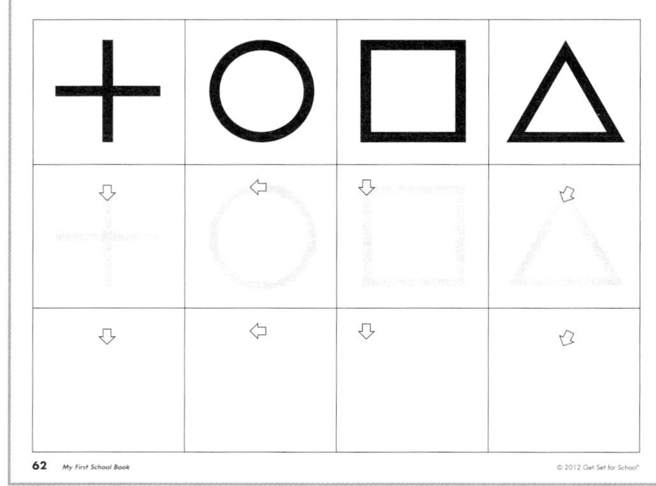

Here are two shape pages. Use each page by itself, and then enjoy them together. Match, name, describe, and compare the shapes from page to page.

Activity

Ask children to point to shapes in random order. **Where is the triangle... the cross... the circle... the square?** Then "read" the shapes together from left to right: **cross, circle, square, triangle.**

Look and Learn

Let children guess. **Which shape has three sides... four sides... no corners... two lines?**

Color, Trace, and Draw Shapes

Children color the shapes at the top. Demonstrate how to draw each shape:
Cross: **Little line down, little line across.**
Circle: **Start at the top. Magic C. Keep going. Stop at the top.**
Square: **Little line down, little line across the bottom, little line up, little line across the top.**
Triangle: **Little line slides down, across the bottom, slide up to the top.**

✔ Check

Observe habits for starting at the top. Highlight the arrows with yellow if children need extra help.

Support/ELL

Give children materials to play with shapes: Wood Pieces, shape puzzles, and Mix & Make Shapes™.

More To Learn

Teachers usually talk about corners, so teach children to use the word "angle" too.

Look What We're Learning

Foundation Skills
- Recognize familiar two-dimensional shapes
- Draw simple shapes
- Use correct top-to-bottom, left-to-right directionality for letters

Oral Language
- Demonstrate active listening by attending to instruction
- Respond to simple questions

Writing
- Hold a crayon with proper grip to write
- Use helping hand to stabilize objects and papers

Sensory Motor
- Use same hand consistently to hold crayons
- Use fingers to hold crayons

Vocabulary

side
angle

Mat Man® Shapes

In the *Mat Man Shapes* book, Mat Man has his usual Mat (a rectangle). Then we give him different shapes. With each shape change, Mat Man does something different. With the circle, he rolls out the door. With the oval, he sits by Humpty Dumpty, and so forth.

Activity

Which Mat Man has an oval body? Which has a diamond body? A square body? Continue the discussion using different shapes.

Look and Learn

Children find the real Mat Man. His body is a Mat. **What shape is the Mat?** Compare square and rectangle. Compare circle and oval. Compare square and diamond.

Color and Draw

Children color the shapes. Demonstrate how to draw a Mat Lady. Children imitate on a separate paper. Give Mat Lady a triangle for a body. When children draw Mat Man, they are ready for other people.

✔ Check

Observe children as they say shape names. When children match correctly, that shows they know shapes. Yet they may forget a few shape names, so use shape names often to remind them.

Support/ELL

Make shapes personal. Fold and cut shapes for children.
Learn to fold paper to make a five-point star with one cut.
Fold paper and cut hearts and diamonds.

More To Learn

These illustrations are from the *Mat Man Shapes* book. If you have this book, read it to your students and try the suggested activities.

Look What We're Learning

Foundation Skills
- Recognize familiar two-dimensional shapes
- Use correct top-to-bottom, left-to-right directionality for letters
- Observe and sort

Oral Language
- Demonstrate active listening by attending to instruction
- Respond to simple questions

Writing
- Hold a crayon with proper grip to write
- Use helping hand to stabilize objects and papers

Sensory Motor
- Use same hand consistently to hold crayons
- Use fingers to hold crayons

Vocabulary

oval
diamond
square
heart
star
rectangle
circle
triangle

Pre-Stroke for V & W

Prepare children for **V** and **W** with this pre-stroke page. The roller coaster slides down and up like **V**.

Activity

The roller coaster slides down and up. The children go for a V ride. What's that in the background? That's a van.

Look and Learn

Roller coaster rides are exciting. Look at the children. They're screaming for the scary fun. Let children pretend they're on the ride too. The roller coaster slides down and up like letter **V**.

Trace and Color Pre-Strokes for V and W

Demonstrate **V** in the air first. When you face children, you point up to top right. **Big line slides down, big line slides up.** Children put their crayons on the ⬂. **Big line slides down, big line slides up. Look, we went on a V ride.**

✔ Check

Observe and wait before you trace **V** in the air. Wait for all to point up to the left. You face the children and point up to your right.

Support/ELL

Make fingers into **V**s. Make **V** with Wood Pieces.

More To Learn

Find and trace **V**s hiding in the structure. Use different colors.

Look What We're Learning

Foundation Skills

- Recognize and use common prepositions in speech
- Sequencing
- Imitate teacher's body movements

Oral Language

- Demonstrate active listening by attending to instruction
- Respond to simple questions
- Learn words linked to content being taught

Sensory Motor

- Use index finger to trace letters in the air
- Notice and attach meaning to visual information
- Move naturally and place body to perform a task

Vocabulary

up
down
roller coaster
van

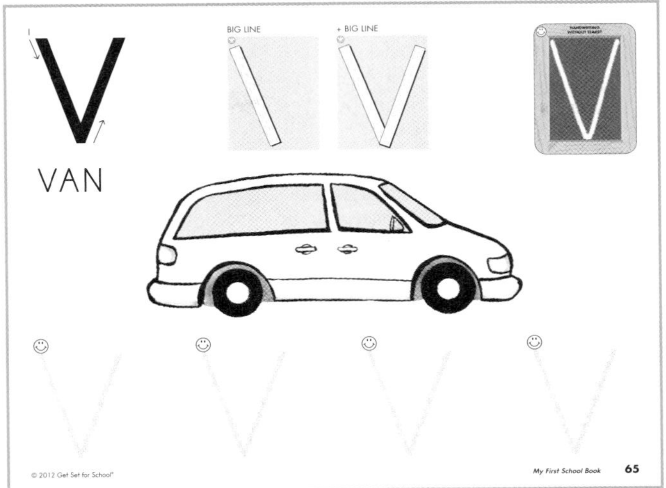

Activity

This is the V page. Do you know V words? V names? V sounds? Have you been in a van?

Look and Learn

Let's find Vs on this page. Look. There's a van. Van starts with V. What do vans do? What color are vans? Show pictures.

Color and Draw

Let's color the van. Show different ways to color. **Draw people in the van.**

Trace and Write V

Finger trace the V at the top of the page. (Say directions.)

Let's write V for van. Put the crayon on the ☺. Big line slides down. Big line slides up.

✔ Check

Check the point of **V**. Help children make a sharp point. Come to a full stop, then turn. **K** is the first letter with a sharp turn. There are more to come!

Support/ELL

Make fingers into **V**s. Make **V** with Wood Pieces.

More To Learn

Teach Air Writing for **V** with *Rock, Rap, Tap & Learn* CD, "Sliding Down to the End of the Alphabet," track 15.

Look What We're Learning

Foundation Skills

- Use correct top-to-bottom, left-to-right directionality for letters
- Sequencing
- Listen to oral directions to attend to a simple task

Oral Language

- Respond to simple questions
- Talk about experiences and observations

Writing

- Hold a crayon with proper grip to write
- Use helping hand to stabilize objects and papers
- Trace capital letters

Sensory Motor

- Use same hand consistently to hold crayons
- Use fingers to hold crayons

Letter W BIG LINE + BIG LINE + BIG LINE + BIG LINE

Activity

This is the W page. Do you know W words? W names? W sounds? A W day of the week? Have you seen a wagon?

Look and Learn

Let's find the Ws. Look. There's a wagon and a wheel. Wagon and wheel start with W. Discuss wagon opposites (in/out, push/pull, on/off, empty/full), riding in a wagon, how wheels work.

Color and Draw

Color the wagon and wheels. You may draw grass or dirt, or maybe a ball in the wagon.

Trace and Write W

Finger trace the W at the top of the page. (Say directions.)

Let's trace W. Put the crayon on the ☺. Big line slides down... and up. Down and up.

✔ Check

Observe children change direction. Avoid rounded turns by teaching them to stop before they turn.

Support/ELL

Show children how to make **V**s with two fingers and put two together at the top to from **W**.

More To Learn

W is for wheels. Count wheels on bikes, tricycles, and cars. **W** is for white and winter. Use swabs to dab white snowflakes on blue paper.

Look What We're Learning

Foundation Skills

- Use correct top-to-bottom, left-to-right directionality for letters
- Sequencing

Oral Language

- Respond to simple questions
- Communicate thoughts with words

Writing

- Hold a crayon with proper grip to write
- Use helping hand to stabilize objects and papers
- Trace capital letters

Sensory Motor

- Use same hand consistently to hold crayons
- Use fingers to hold crayons

Vocabulary

wagon
wheel

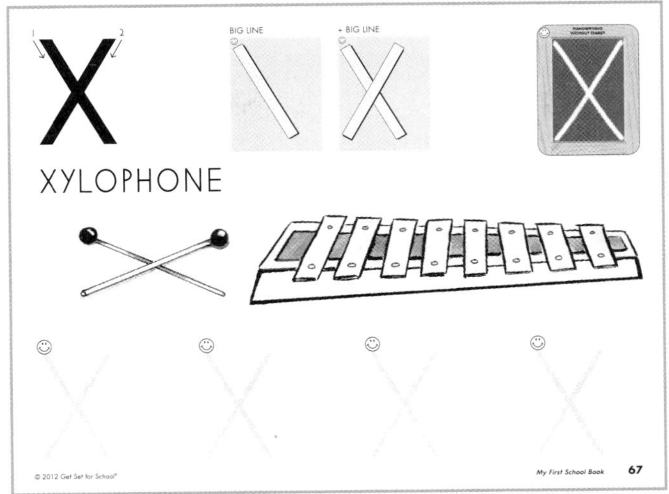

Activity

This is the X page. Do you know X words? X names? X sounds? Have you seen a xylophone?

Look and Learn

Let's find the Xs. Xylophone starts with X, but it doesn't make an X sound. Discuss what a xylophone is and how it is played.

Color and Draw

Color the xylophone. Use different colors for each note.

Trace and Write X

Finger trace the X at the top of the page. (Say directions.)

Let's write X. Put the crayon on the ☺. Big line slides down. Jump to the top of the other big line. Big line slides down.

✔ Check

Observe children as they trace the **X**. Do children start both strokes at the top?

Support/ELL

Use Wood Piece Play activities for diagonals and for **X**.

More To Learn

Play a xylophone. Make **X** with two big lines. Find EXIT signs. Play trains. Make a railroad crossing sign.

Look What We're Learning

Foundation Skills

- Use correct top-to-bottom, left-to-right directionality for letters
- Sequencing
- Listen to oral directions to attend to a simple task

Oral Language

- Respond to simple questions

Writing

- Hold a crayon with proper grip to write
- Use helping hand to stabilize objects and papers
- Trace capital letters

Sensory Motor

- Use same hand consistently to hold crayons
- Use fingers to hold crayons

Vocabulary

xylophone

Letter Y

LITTLE LINE + BIG LINE

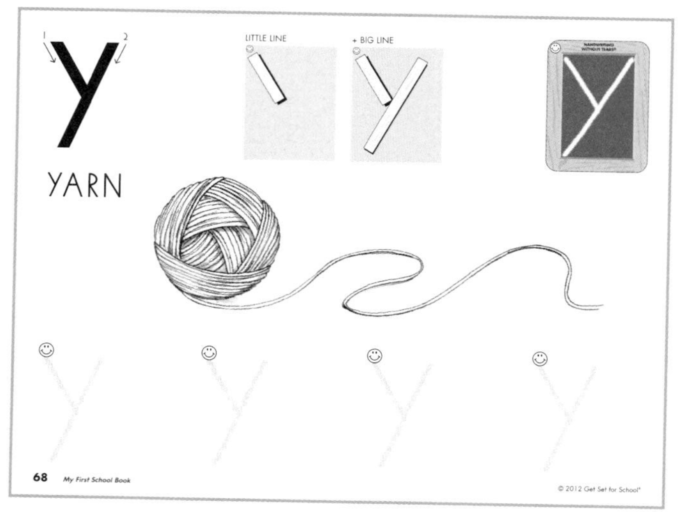

Activity

This is the Y page. Do you know Y words? Y names? Y sounds? Have you seen yarn?

Look and Point

Let's find the Ys. There's yarn. Yarn starts with Y. Discuss the round shape of the ball, and what yarn is used for (knitting hats, scarves, etc.).

Color and Draw

Color the yarn yellow because yellow starts with Y. Draw a longer piece of yarn all around the page.

Trace and Write Y

Finger trace the Y at the top of the page. (Say directions.)

Let's trace Y. Put the crayon on the ☺. Little line slides down to stop. Jump to the top of the big line. Big line slides down.

✔ Check

Observe children as they trace **Y**. Do they stop when the first stroke touches the big line?

Support/ELL

Diagonal strokes can be difficult. Demonstrate in the air. Use the song "Diagonals" from the *Rock, Rap, Tap & Learn* CD, track 5.

More To Learn

Cut little and big pieces of yarn. Dip in glue and glue to make **Y** on a card. Find yellow in the room. Who is wearing yellow today?

Look What We're Learning

Foundation Skills

- Use correct top-to-bottom, left-to-right directionality for letters
- Sequencing
- Listen to oral directions to attend to a simple task

Oral Language

- Respond to simple questions

Writing

- Hold a crayon with proper grip to write
- Use helping hand to stabilize objects and papers
- Trace capital letters

Sensory Motor

- Use same hand consistently to hold crayons
- Use fingers to hold crayons

Vocabulary

yarn
knitting
scarf

Letter Z

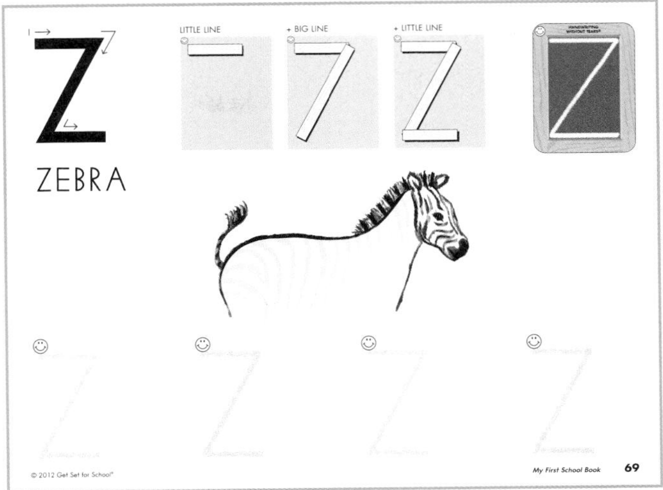

Activity

This is the Z page. Do you know Z words? Z names? Z sounds? Have you seen a zebra?

Look and Learn

Let's find the Zs. There's a zebra. Zebra starts with Z. Discuss what zebras eat, black stripes, four legs, tail, and where they live.

Color and Draw

Color the zebra stripes black. Draw trees or tall grasses.

Trace and Write Z

Finger trace the Z at the top of the page. (Say directions.)

Let's trace Z. Put the crayon on the ☺. Little line across the top. Big line slides down. Little line across.

✔ Check

Do children stop to change direction? This will give them sharp corners.

Support/ELL

Letter **Z** can be reversed. Practice writing letters **Z** by using the Slate chalkboard and Wet-Dry-Try. The starting corner prevents reversals.

More To Learn

Bring in pictures of zebras. Sing a zoo animal version of the song "Animal Legs," track 13, and include a zebra. Make two Big Curves into a huge zero and say zero.

Look What We're Learning

Foundation Skills
- Use correct top-to-bottom, left-to-right directionality for letters
- Sequencing
- Listen to oral directions to attend to a simple task

Oral Language
- Respond to simple questions

Writing
- Hold a crayon with proper grip to write
- Use helping hand to stabilize objects and papers
- Trace capital letters

Sensory Motor
- Use same hand consistently to hold crayons
- Use fingers to hold crayons

Vocabulary

zebra

Alphabet Review

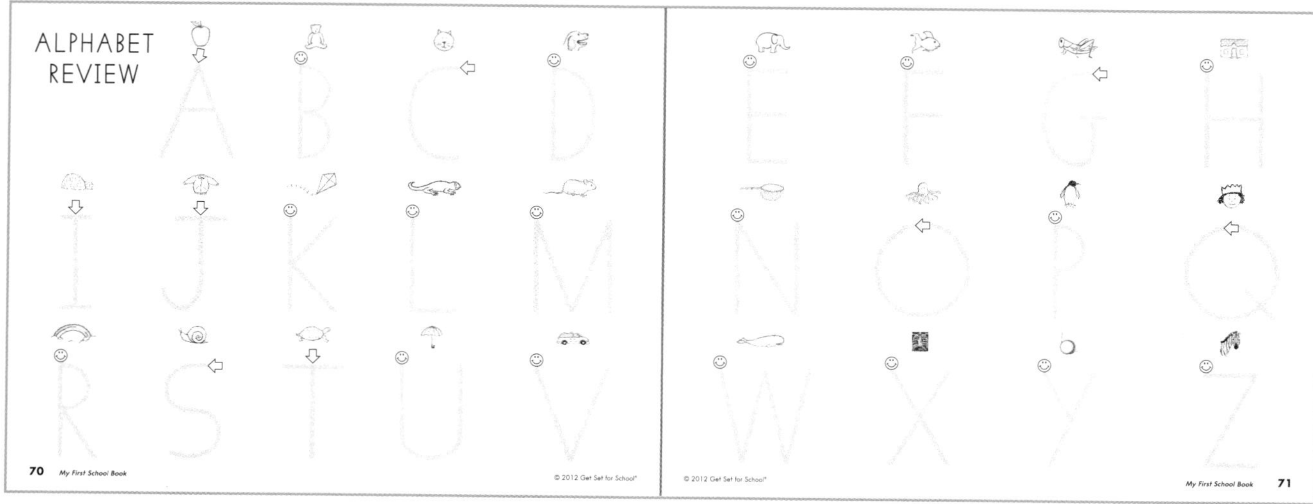

Now your children are ready for alphabetical order. Spend three days on this page. Use a different color to trace beginning letters **A-H**, middle letters **I-Q** and ending letters **R-Z**.

Activity

This is the alphabet! It has letters at the beginning, the middle, and the end.

Look and Learn

"Read" the letters by sections out of order. Read from **I** to **Q**, then **A** to **H**, then **R** to **Z**. Mixing the reading order changes it from rote to real reading. Find random letters and read that letter and the next two.

Trace and Color

Trace the letters after the teacher's demonstration. Use a different color each day.

Day 1 - **A B C D E F G H**

Day 2 - **I J K L M N O P Q**

Day 3 - **R S T U V W X Y Z**

✔ Check

Can children easily name letters out of ABC order?

Support/ELL

Only point to a few letters at a time. Maybe start with letters in a child's name.

More To Learn

Let pairs of children play point and name. One child points, and the other child names. Then they trade places. This builds rapid letter naming, an important skill.

Look What We're Learning

Foundation Skills

- Use correct top-to-bottom, left-to-right directionality for letters
- Listen to oral directions to attend to a simple task

Alphabet Knowledge

- Point to and name capital letters

Writing

- Hold a crayon with proper grip to write
- Use helping hand to stabilize objects and papers
- Trace capital letters

Sensory Motor

- Use same hand consistently to hold crayons
- Use fingers to hold crayons

Vocabulary

alphabet

Children can never get enough good modeling of letters. Line It Up™ gives you an easy way to model for your class. Hang up letters at any time you want to pre-teach a letter (before a workbook page) or review a letter. Because the cards are dry-erase, you can write and erase them repeatedly.

Materials/Setup
- Line It Up Bar*
- Line It Up Letter Cards

Grouping
Whole class

Support/ELL
Allow children to "rainbow write" (trace over with different colors) on the letter. This provides repetition. Be sure to always name the letter and the letter parts.

*For more information about Line It Up, go to **getsetforschool.com**

Activity

1. Choose a letter to model.
2. Invite a child to hang it up on the bar.
3. Discuss the letter.
4. As you model the letter, say the strokes in the letter. **This is an R. It has a big line, little curve, and little line.**
5. Invite children to take turns finger tracing the letter. They may also write the letter in their book.

✔ Check
Observe how children copy or imitate the letter. Are they forming it correctly? Observe crayon grip.

More To Learn
While reviewing letters, see if children can identify when the letter is the first letter of their name.

Look What We're Learning

Foundation Skills
- Sequencing

Alphabet Knowledge
- Point to and name capital letters
- Position capitals right-side up

Writing
- Hold a crayon with proper grip to write
- Use helping hand to stabilize objects and papers
- Trace capital letters

Sensory Motor
- Use index finger to trace letters on cards
- Use same hand consistently to hold crayons
- Use fingers to hold crayons
- Notice and attach meaning to visual information

Help Me Write My Name

For developmental order, teach children's names in all capitals in preschool, then transition to name in title case at the end of preschool. Students won't always write in capitals, but it's the best way for them to start. Explain that there are two ways to write a name: the all capitals way and the capital and lowercase way. Show them they can read their names both ways. They learn to write the all capitals way first. After they learn all capitals, they can also learn the other way. Children will follow your lead.

Materials/Setup

- Capital and Number Practice Strips
- Crayons

Grouping

Individual

Support/ELL

A Click Away — getsetforschool.com/click

Send home some Capital Practice Strips and the Capital Letter Formation charts for parents.

Activity

1. Display names both ways in the room: all capitals and title case.
2. Use the Capital and Number Practice Strips.
3. Put your strip above the child's strip. Demonstrate each letter on your strip and wait for the child to imitate you. Do this letter by letter (see below).

✔ Check

Observe children's crayon grips. Are they holding their crayons correctly?

More To Learn

Write child's name and see if they can identify the letters in their name.

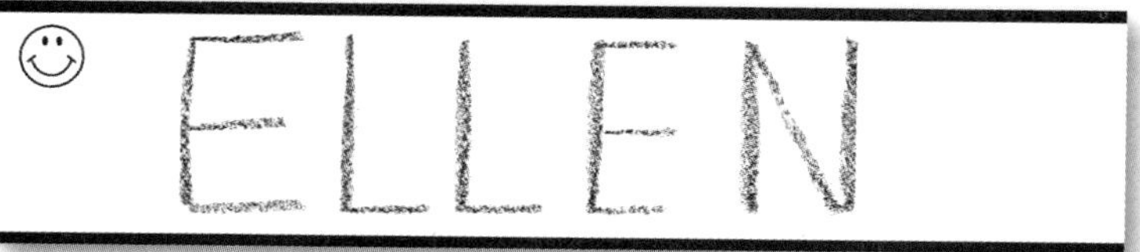

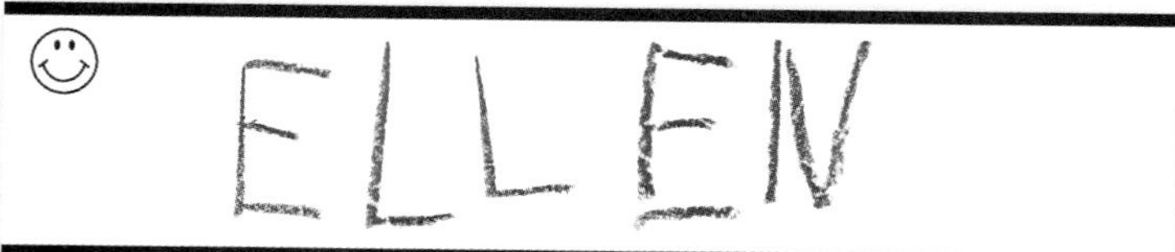

Look What We're Learning

Foundation Skills

- Know name
- Listen to oral directions to attend to a simple task

Writing

- Hold a crayon with proper grip to write
- Use helping hand to stabilize objects and papers
- Understand there is a way to write that conveys meaning

Alphabet Knowledge

- Recognize and name letters in own name
- Position capitals right-side up

Sensory Motor

- Use same hand consistently to hold crayons
- Use fingers to hold crayons
- Notice and attach meaning to visual information

Teaching Name in Title Case

If you have some students who are doing well with their writing and want to write their names in title case, teach them. It is important that they learn the correct formation habits for the letters in the names, but it is also challenging because they aren't getting the benefit of complete lowercase instruction. So, take some extra time to help them understand the size and formation habits for writing the lowercase letters. Use Wet–Dry–Try on the Blackboard with Double Lines to teach these habits effectively.

Materials/Setup

- Blackboard with Double Lines

Grouping

Individual

Support/ELL

Add additional tracing opportunities by allowing child to trace each letter again with a wet index finger. Print a Lowercase Letter Chart and send home to parents.

A Click Away getsetforschool.com/click

Video Lesson

View the video lesson, Writing name using Wet-Dry-Try, at **getsetforschool.com/videos**

Activity

Names

Demonstrate/Imitate: Title Case (Two Blackboards with Double Lines)

1. Write child's name, one letter at a time, with chalk on the Blackboard with Double Lines.
2. After each letter, allow child to trace the letter with a wet sponge. Dry the letter with a small crumbled up paper towel.
3. Continue until all letters are modeled and traced.
4. Allow child to write name with chalk.

Note: This activity helps children learn to write their names on double lines before they transition to paper.

✔ Check

Observe grip. Is the child holding the sponge and chalk correctly?

More To Learn

Write child's name and see if that child can identify the letters in his or her name.

Look What We're Learning

Foundation Skills

- Know name
- Listen to oral directions to attend to a simple task

Writing

- Hold a crayon with proper grip to write
- Use helping hand to stabilize objects and papers
- Understand there is a way to write that conveys meaning

Alphabet Knowledge

- Recognize and name letters in own name
- Position capitals right-side up

Sensory Motor

- Use same hand consistently to hold crayons
- Use fingers to hold crayons
- Notice and attach meaning to visual information

Counting & Numbers

From the time they are two, children are asked how old they are. They hold up fingers and say their ages. Number and math awareness begins even earlier with body awareness and baby games. Parents touch toes and say, "This little piggy went to market... " They play "Patty Cake" and "Where is Thumbkin?" All children discover their bodies, but baby games make it a joy to learn (The Albert Shanker Institute 2009). Children whose parents sing and say nursery rhymes pick up rote counting naturally with "1, 2, tie my shoe... 3, 4, shut the door" and other rhymes. They even get a taste of subtraction with "Five little monkeys jumping on a bed."

Songs, rhymes, and finger plays are an important part of home and school learning (Kenschaft 2006). They help children develop math skills naturally. We teach counting and numbers with music and activities (Cross, Woods, & Schweingruber 2009). For example, with "Animal Legs" (*Sing Along* CD, track 13), a child holds up a toy horse as classmates sing, "Two legs in the front, two legs in the back, the horse has four legs. I know that!" Children also learn as they count and handle everyday objects. You'll find many activities and suggestions in this guide and in the *I Know My Numbers* booklets.

Number writing doesn't begin with paper and pencil. It begins with pre-writing activities. Pre-writing activities teach size, shape, and position concepts. Then children build numbers correctly with Wood Pieces, Roll-A-Dough Letters®, Stamp and See Screen®, and the Slate. We use hands-on number play as preparation for writing.

You demonstrate how to hold the crayon and make the correct strokes. This is the easy, child friendly way to teach children how to write numbers before they go to kindergarten.

Objectives

- Rote count out loud 1-10
- Participate in number songs, rhymes, and finger plays
- Share and take turns during math activities
- Recognize, name, and describe several shapes
- Recognizes and name numerals 1-10
- Use fingers to show how many 1-10
- Count body parts accurately (1 nose, 2 hands, etc.)
- Count objects accurately 1-10
- Counts on from 5-10
- Begin to count by 2s, 5s, 10s
- Understands ordinal numbers, first, second, third, etc.
- Write numerals 1-10

Below is some of the significant research for Counting & Numbers. For additional Counting & Numbers research, see the reference section at the end of this teacher's guide.

The Albert Shanker Institute.2009. *Preschool Curriculum: What's in It for Children and Teachers.* Washington, D.C.: The Albert Shanker Institute. Accessed August 2011. http://www.ashankerinst.org/Downloads/Early%20Childhood%2012-11-08.pdf

Kenschaft, P.C. 2006. *Math Power: How to Help Your Child Love Math, Even If You Don't.* New York, New York: Pi Press.

Cross, C.T., T.A. Woods, and H. Schweingruber, eds. 2009. *Mathematics Learning in Early Childhood: Paths Toward Excellence and Equity.* Washington, D.C.: The National Academies Press.

Wet-Dry-Try on the Slate

It matters which way numbers face. We make it easy for children to learn the right way. Our strategies are visual, auditory, tactile, kinesthetic, and repetitive—but never boring. The little bits of sponge and chalk also build correct grip. Here is how to teach numbers so they will always face the right way.

Numbers on the Slate

The Slate makes it easy to write numbers right-side up and facing correctly. When the ☺ is at the top, the number is right-side up.

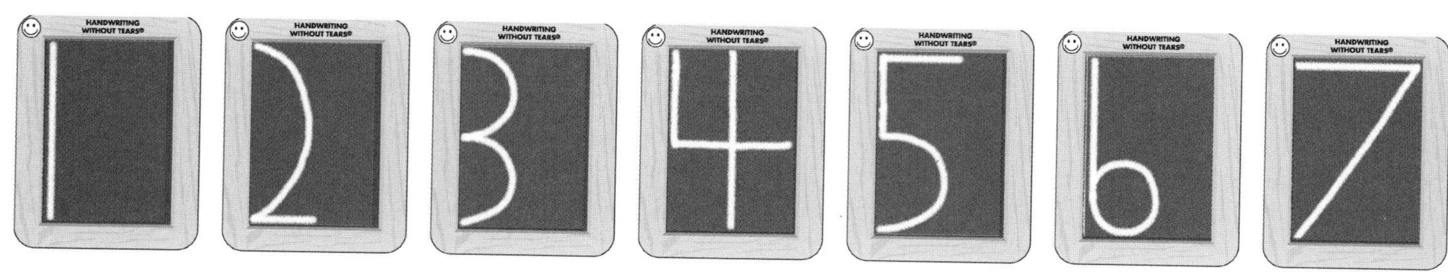

When 1 2 3 4 5 6 7 start at the ☺ in the starting corner, they are always facing correctly.

8 cannot be reversed. It is a symmetrical number.
8 doesn't like corners. 8 doesn't have corners!
8 doesn't start in the starting corner.
8 starts at the top, in the center.

9 is different.
9 has its own corner.
9 starts in the other top corner.
When 9 starts in its corner, 9 faces correctly.

This is a favorite activity because it teaches so many skills. You write a chalk number and teach each step. Children wet the number, dry it, and then try it with chalk. The little bits of sponge and chalk reinforce correct grip.

Materials/Setup

- Slate (1 per child)
- Little Chalk Bits
- Little Sponge Cubes
- Little cups of water
- Paper towels

Grouping

1-5 children

Support/ELL

Say the words for each step slowly. Children join when they can.

Activity

Teacher's Part – Write 4 with chalk

Start in the starting corner ☺.
Little line down. Little line across. Jump to the top. Big line down.

Child's Part – Wet-Dry-Try

Wet 4 with sponge. Say the words with the teacher. Wet 4 with finger, the same way.

Dry 4 with crumbled towel. Say the words.

Try 4 with chalk. Say the words.

✔ Check

Do all children have Slates placed vertically with the ☺ at the top?

More To Learn

Review previously learned numbers **1, 2, 3** with chalk. Demonstrate on one Slate. Children imitate on their Slates. Erase with a tissue.

Teacher's Part

Start in the starting corner
Little line down
Little line across, jump to top
Big line down

Child's Part

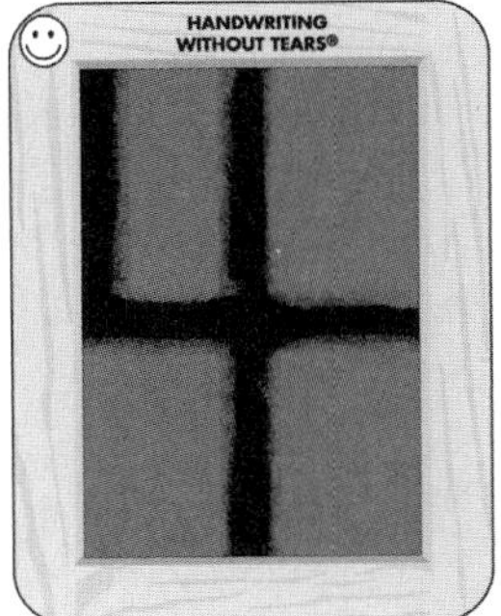

WET: Wet 4 with sponge,
Wet 4 with wet finger,
Say the words

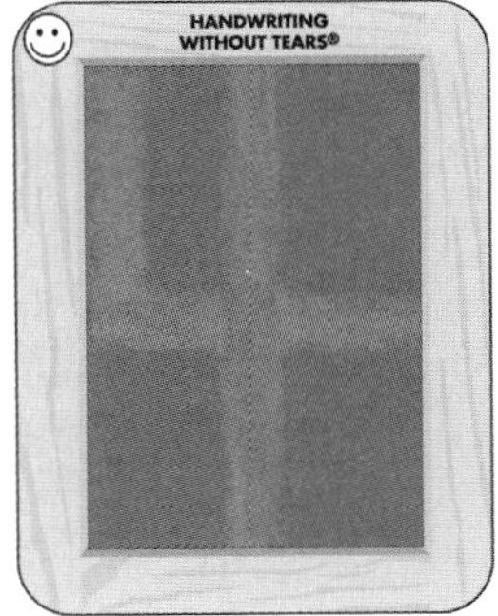

DRY: Dry 4 with towel,
Dry 4 with gentle blow,
Say the words

TRY: Try 4 with chalk,
Say the words

Look What We're Learning

Foundation Skills

- Sequencing
- Listen to oral directions to attend to a simple task

Oral Language

- Repeat teacher's words

Writing

- Use helping hand to stabilize objects and papers

Number & Operations

- Write numerals up to 10

Sensory Motor

- Use same hand consistently to perform skilled tasks
- Use index finger to trace numbers

Social-Emotional

- Interact easily with familiar adults

Vocabulary

Numbers 1-10

Numbers & *Sing Along* CD

This award-winning CD features 25 songs. Here are the tracks that focus on body awareness, numbers, counting, and positions. Some are suggested in lessons, but bring others to your circle time and class.

Materials/Setup
- *Sing Along* CD

Grouping
Whole class

Support/ELL
Bring pictures of birds, farm animals, insects, and spiders for leg counting.

Activity

1. Children gather in a circle.
2. Select song:
   Track 8, "Mat Man" - 1 and 2, by counting on Mat Man and self
   Track 9, "Count on Me" - 1 and 2, by counting on self
   Track10, "Five Fingers Play" - 1 2 3 4 5 fingerplay
   Track 11, "Toe Song" - 5 and 10 by counting toes
   Track 12, "Bird Legs" - 2 by counting bird legs
   Track 13, "Animal Legs" - 4 by counting legs on animals
   Track 14, "The Ant, the Bug & the Bee" - 6 by using fingers for insect legs
   Track 15, "Spiders Love to Party" - 8 by using fingers for spider legs
3. See suggested activities for each song on pages 208-209.

✔ Check

Observe if children are participating. Are they repeating and following directions?

More To Learn

Model numbers on an easel as you play "Number Song," *Rock, Rap, Tap & Learn* CD, track 20. "Number Song" is a great way to introduce children to numbers.

Look What We're Learning

Foundation Skills
- Count up to 10 by rote
- Imitate teacher's body movements
- Listen to and repeat songs and finger plays

Oral Language
- Demonstrate active listening by attending to instruction
- Learn words linked to content being taught

Number & Operations
- Verbally count a set of objects
- Recognize that the last number said is the total

Sensory Motor
- Use large muscle groups to maintain posture/ position and mobility
- Use both side of the body in activities

Vocabulary

Numbers 1-10

Numbers & *Sing, Sound & Count With Me* CD

Music is an important part of our readiness curriculum. Our CDs feature Grammy-winning musicians. As you play songs in the background during free play, you and your children will discover favorites and be ready to use them in activities.

Materials/Setup
- *Sing, Sound, & Count With Me* CD

Grouping
Whole class

Support/ELL
Bring pictures of ants, shapes, and other items that you sing about and show them to children.

Activity

1. Children gather in a circle.
2. Select song:
   Track 2, "The Ants Go Marching" - 1, 2, 3, 4, 5
   Track 5, "Shape Song" - Four basic shapes (triangle, rectangle, square, circle)
   Track 6, "Counting, Counting" - 1, 2, 3, 4, 5
   Track 9, "Counting Candles" – 1, 2, 3, 4, 5
   Track 14, "Counting at the Table" - Count by 1s, 2s, and 5s
   Track 20, "Big Numbers" - One hundred, one thousand, one million or two!
3. See suggested activities for each song on pages 210-211.

✔ Check

Observe if children are participating. Are they demonstrating appropriate gross motor skills?

More To Learn

After singing "Shape Song," track 5, see if children can identify shapes in the room.

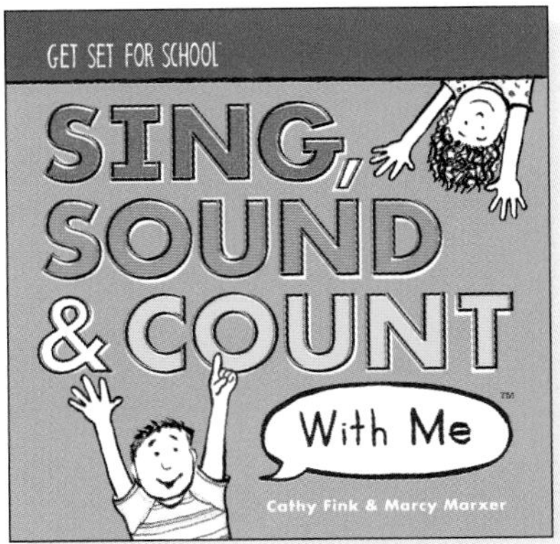

Look What We're Learning

Foundation Skills
- Count up to 10 by rote
- Recognize familiar two-dimensional shapes
- Imitate teacher's body movements
- Listen to and repeat songs and finger plays

Oral Language
- Learn words linked to content being taught

Number & Operations
- Verbally count a set of objects
- Recognize that the last number said is the total

Sensory Motor
- Use large muscle groups to maintain posture/position and mobility
- Use both side of the body in activities

Vocabulary

Numbers 1-10

Count on Me

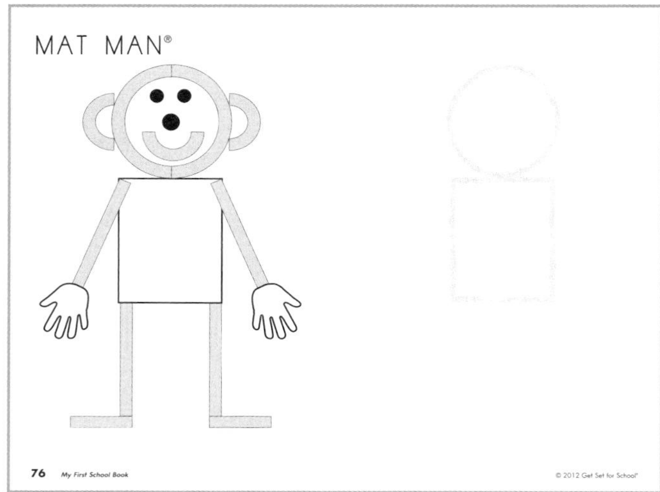

MAT MAN®
76 My First School Book
© 2012 Get Set for School®

Children love to sing about, build, and draw Mat Man. See pages 36-41 of this guide.

Activity

Do you know Mat Man? Do you remember the Mat Man song? See page 36.

Look and Learn

Count on Mat Man. Mat Man has 1....head, 1 nose...,1mouth...,1 body. Mat Man has 2... eyes, 2...ears, 2...arms, 2 ...hands, 2...legs, 2 ...feet

Color and Draw

Color Mat Man's mat and hands blue. Draw a new person. It can be Mat Man or a friend for Mat Man. Encourage children to add clothing, hair, or hats.

✔ Check

Observe if children are able to name body parts. Can they count how many?

Support/ELL

Build Mat Man on the floor again, perhaps before this page. Teach one body part at a time. Consider reviewing terms in a child's native language.

More To Learn

If children know all these body parts, teach them more: eyebrows, necks, elbows, wrists, hips, knees, ankles, heels, etc.

Look What We're Learning

Foundation Skills
- Name parts of the body
- Sequencing

Number & Operations
- Match one-to-one
- Verbally count a set of objects
- Recognize that the last number said is the total

Oral Language
- Demonstrate active listening by attending to instruction

Sensory Motor
- Use same hand consistently to hold crayons
- Use fingers to hold crayons

Social-Emotional
- Demonstrate desire for independence

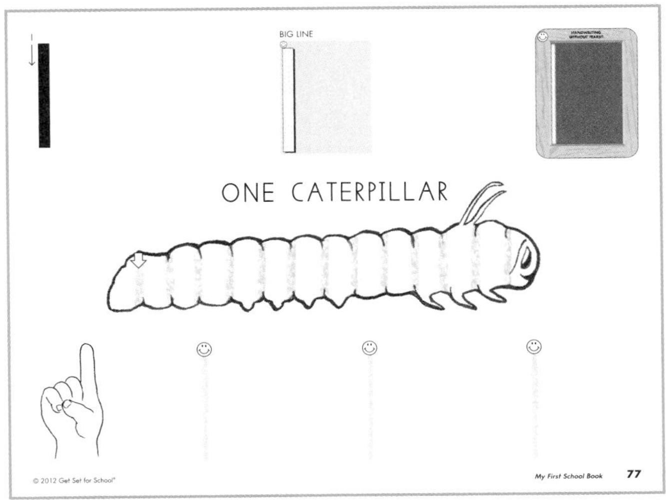

Activity

This is the page for number 1. Point to 1 at the top, 1 on the Mat, and 1 on the Slate. See 1 caterpillar. Find the words, ONE CATERPILLAR.

Count 1 with Bodies

Hold up one finger. Count one on you. Count down the center. You have 1 head, 1 forehead, 1 nose, 1 mouth, 1 chin, 1 neck, 1 chest, 1 belly button.

Count 1 with Objects

Put **1** cup on **1** napkin. Hold **1** crayon in **1** hand. Put **1** block in **1** cup. Screw **1** cap on **1** bottle.

Color and Write

Finger trace the 1 at the top of the page. (Say directions.)
Let's write 1. Put the crayon on the ☺. Big line down. Trace the segments of the caterpillar down. Color the caterpillar.

✔ Check

Observe if children start **1** at the top.

Support/ELL

Review body parts down the center: head, forehead, nose, mouth, chin, neck, chest, belly button.

More To Learn

Talk about firsts: first place, first in line, first grade, first birthday. Use first in a sequence. **First we put on socks, then shoes. First we put on a jacket and then we zip it.**

Look What We're Learning

Foundation Skills
- Use correct top-to-bottom, left-to-right directionality for numbers

Oral Language
- Learn words linked to content being taught

Number & Operations
- Match one-to-one
- Write numerals up to 10

Writing
- Hold a crayon with proper grip to write
- Use helping hand to stabilize objects and papers

Sensory Motor
- Use same hand consistently to hold crayons
- Use fingers to hold crayons

Vocabulary

one
caterpillar

Bird Legs

Quack, quack, peep, peep, cock a doodle do
When we count the legs on birds
We always count 1 2
78
My First School Book
© 2012 Get Set for School®

Birds and people have something in common. Two legs! Children will be counting legs on themselves, and on birds, farm animals, insects, spiders, and octopuses.

Activity

How many legs does the duck have? The chick? The rooster? The ostrich? The crane? The flamingo?

Look and Learn
These birds are different. Look at their necks, heads, beaks, bills, and bodies.

Color and Draw
Watch me make bird legs. Your turn. Now color the birds.

✔ Check

Observe if children can point to and identify the birds.

Support/ELL

Look at books about birds. Have children point to and count the legs on birds.

More To Learn

Use the *Sing Along* CD. Play "Bird Legs," track 12. Show pictures of the real birds as a guide for coloring.

Look What We're Learning

Foundation Skills
- Name parts of the body
- Observe and sort

Number & Operations
- Match one-to-one
- Verbally count a set of objects
- Recognize that the last number said is the total

Writing
- Hold a crayon with proper grip to write
- Use helping hand to stabilize objects and papers

Sensory Motor
- Use same hand consistently to hold crayons
- Use fingers to hold crayons
- Notice and attach meaning to visual information

Vocabulary

two, ostrich, crane, flamingo, bills, beaks, duck, chick

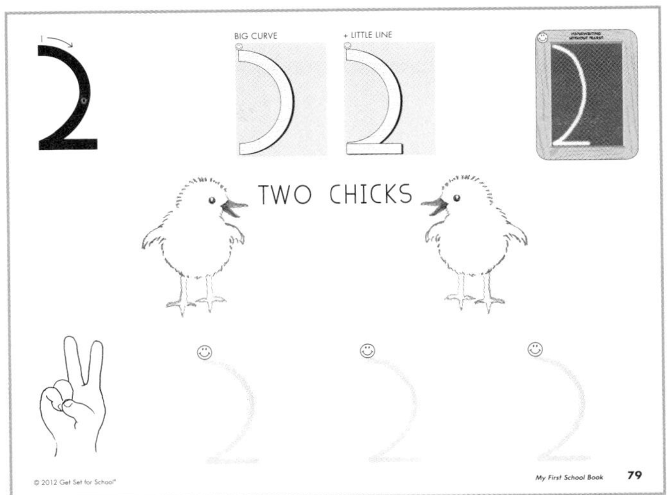

Activity

This is the page for number 2. Point to 2 at the top, 2 on the Mat, and 2 on the Slate. See 2 chicks. Find the words TWO CHICKS. Count the legs on each chick: 1, 2

Count 2 with Bodies

Hold up two fingers. Count two on you. Use 2 pointer fingers. Touch 2 eyes, 2 ears, 2 shoulders. Keep fingers on shoulders and wiggle 2 elbows. Point to 2 legs, 2 knees, 2 ankles, 2 feet.

Count 2 with Objects

Count **2** on clothing: two sleeves, two pant legs, two shoes, two socks, two mittens.

Color and Write

Finger trace the 2 at the top of the page. (Say directions.)
Let's write 2. Put the crayon on the ☺. Big curve, little line across. Trace two legs on each chick. Color two chicks. Color two fingers.

✔ Check

Observe if children start **2** at the top. Do they trace **2** correctly?

Support/ELL

Fold paper in half and cut out a simple paper doll. Unfold and use to teach two body parts: eyes, ears, shoulders, arms, etc.

More To Learn

Introduce "second" with girl-boy lines. Girls are first. Boys are second. Boys stand behind girls. Perhaps children have heard the expression, "Ladies first."

Look What We're Learning

Foundation Skills
- Name body parts
- Sequencing
- Use correct top-to-bottom, left-to-right directionality for numbers

Number & Operations
- Verbally count a set of objects
- Write numerals up to 10

Writing
- Hold a crayon with proper grip to write
- Use helping hand to stabilize objects and papers

Sensory Motor
- Use same hand consistently to hold crayons
- Use fingers to hold crayons

Vocabulary

two
chick

That Would Be Me!

Children love to make believe with this fun song as they swim around the room like fish, fly like butterflies, and pretend to be monkeys.

Materials/Setup
- *Sing, Sound & Count With Me* CD, "That Would Be Me!" track 22

Grouping
Whole class

Support/ELL
Show children pictures of each insect or animal as it is mentioned in the song.

Activity

1. Children stand as a group or sit and take turns acting out the verses in the song.
2. Model movements that are made by butterflies, flowers, fish, and monkeys.
3. Play "That Would Be Me!" track 22 on the *Sing, Sound & Count With Me* CD.
4. Children make motions as the music plays.

✔ Check
Observe gross motor skills and participation in the activity.

More To Learn
Act out other animals and insects. Start by singing, "If I were a ______." Invite a child to finish the sentence. Other children act out the motions.

Look What We're Learning

Foundation Skills
- Imitate teacher's body movements
- Listen to and repeat songs

Comprehension
- Listen to perform a task

Sensory Motor
- Use same hand consistently to hold crayons
- Use fingers to hold crayons
- Use large muscle groups to maintain posture/position and mobility
- Use both sides of body in activities
- Tolerate motion in activities
- Play with body awareness, balance, and regard for people and equipments
- Move naturally and place body to perform tasks

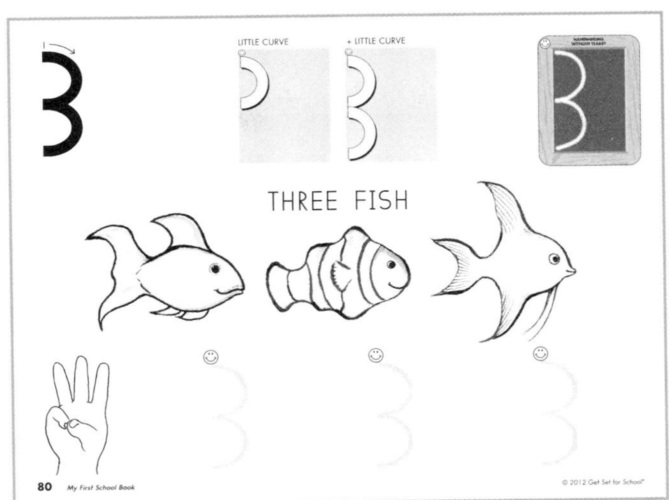

Activity

This is the page for number 3. Point to 3 at the top, 3 on the Mat, and 3 on the Slate. See three fish. Find the words, THREE FISH.

Count 3 with Bodies

Hold up three fingers.

Count 3 with Objects

Count **3** cubes. Build steps with one, then two cubes. Build a triangle with three lines or three straws. Count three sides and three angles.

Color and Write

Finger trace the 3 at the top of the page. (Say directions.)

Let's write 3. Put the crayon on the ☺. Little curve, little curve. Color three fish. Color three fingers.

✔ Check

Observe children's hand skills. Help them hold up three fingers. The thumb holds down the little finger. Help with crayon grip and helping hand.

Support/ELL

Read nursery rhymes and stories with three: *Rub a Dub, Dub, Three Bears, Three Billy Goats Gruff.* Also share with parents.

More To Learn

Give each child something to toss. Do it three times. After each toss say, **That was the first toss. That was the second toss. That was the third toss. All done!**

Look What We're Learning

Foundation Skills
- Sequencing
- Use correct top-to-bottom, left-to-right directionality for numbers

Writing
- Hold a crayon with proper grip to write
- Use helping hand to stabilize objects and papers

Number & Operations
- Write numerals up to 10

Problem Solving
- Use manipulatives to find a solution

Sensory Motor
- Use same hand consistently to hold crayons
- Use fingers to hold crayons

Vocabulary

three
triangle
side
angle
fish

Animal Legs

This delightful activity eases children into being in front of others without the need for public speaking. The child simply shows a toy animal as the class sings. Music and animals help students build poise along with math skills.

Materials/Setup
- *Sing Along* CD, "Animal Legs," track 13
- Animal legs
- Basket or tub
- Four-legged toy animals

Grouping
Whole class

Support/ELL
Notice when a shy child is ready to take a turn. Just watching a few times will help a child build familiarity and ease.

Activity

1. Invite a child to take an animal from the basket. Child stands beside you and shows the animal.
2. You and other children sing:
   We are counting legs, how many will there be?
   (Name) picks a(n) (animal).
   Let's look and see: two legs in the front, two legs in the back.
   The (animal) has four legs, we know that, but only one tail.
3. Another child takes an animal and a turn. Repeat activity just a few times.

✔ Check
Do children know front and back? Can they name animals? Can they count legs?

More To Learn
Learn sounds for the animals in the basket.

Look What We're Learning

Foundation Skills
- Name parts of the body
- Recognize and use common prepositions in speech
- Participate in school routines
- Listen to and repeat songs

Number & Operations
- Recognize that the last number said is the total

Problem Solving
- Use manipulatives to find a solution

Sensory Motor
- Notice and attach meaning to visual information
- Handle play materials without an avoidance response

Social-Emotional
- Take turns with peers

Vocabulary
front
back

Activity

This is the page for number 4. Point to 4 at the top, 4 on the Mat, and 4 on the Slate. See four animals. Find the words, FOUR ANIMALS.

Count 4 with Bodies

Hold up four fingers. Creep on all fours. Count the legs on the horse, cow, lamb, pig.

Count 4 with Objects

Count **4** wheels on a wagon, car, truck, cart. Cut four corners off a card. Count them. Count four corners on a square. Put a bean in each corner. Count the beans! Count legs on chairs and tables.

Color and Write

Finger trace the 4 at the top of the page. (Say directions.)
Let's write 4. Put the crayon on the ☺. Little line down. Little line across. Jump to the top. Big line down. Color four animals. Color four fingers.

✔ Check

Observe if children can count sets of objects up to four.

Support/ELL

Do children know how old they are? Have them practice asking and saying, "How old are you?" "I am four years old (or three, or five)."

More To Learn

In the U.S.A., talk about the Fourth of July. See how fast four boys can line up. Give each boy a number 1, 2, 3 or 4. Say you are first, second, third, fourth. Let girls try next.

Look What We're Learning

Foundation Skills
- Sequencing
- Use correct top-to-bottom, left-to-right directionality for numbers

Writing
- Hold a crayon with proper grip to write
- Use helping hand to stabilize objects and papers

Number & Operations
- Write numerals up to 10

Problem Solving
- Use manipulatives to find a solution

Sensory Motor
- Use same hand consistently to hold crayons
- Use fingers to hold crayons

Vocabulary

four
animals
pig
sheep
horse
cow

Five Finger Play

This is a stand up and have fun finger play. It teaches more than counting. Children learn to start at the top when they go round and round. They start for number 0, shape O, and letter O at the top. Children also learn addition: 5 + 5 = 10.

Materials/Setup

- *Sing Along* CD, "Five Fingers Play," track 10

Grouping

Whole class

Support/ELL

Have children look at the workbook page as they learn the motions.

Activity

1. Play "Five Fingers Play," track 10 from the *Sing Along* CD in the background a few days before the activity to make words familiar.
2. Teach each part by demonstrating first and then doing with children. Use these suggestions:
   - One finger points - Point straight up
   - Two fingers walk - Let fingers walk on other arm
   - Three fingers talk - Have fingers say, "Hello, hello."
   - Four fingers count - Bend each finger down and up from knuckle
   - Five fingers go round and round.

✔ Check

Observe children's fine motor skills. Can they easily hold up the right number of fingers?

More To Learn

Teach children their fingers: pointer, tall man, ring finger, little finger, thumb.

Look What We're Learning

Foundation Skills
- Imitate teacher's body movements
- Participate in school routines
- Listen to oral directions to attend to a simple task
- Listen to and repeat songs and finger plays

Comprehension
- Listen to perform a task

Number & Operations
- Match one-to-one
- Recognize that the last number said is the total

Sensory Motor
- Use same hand consistently to perform skilled tasks
- Move fingers for finger plays
- Tolerate motion in activities

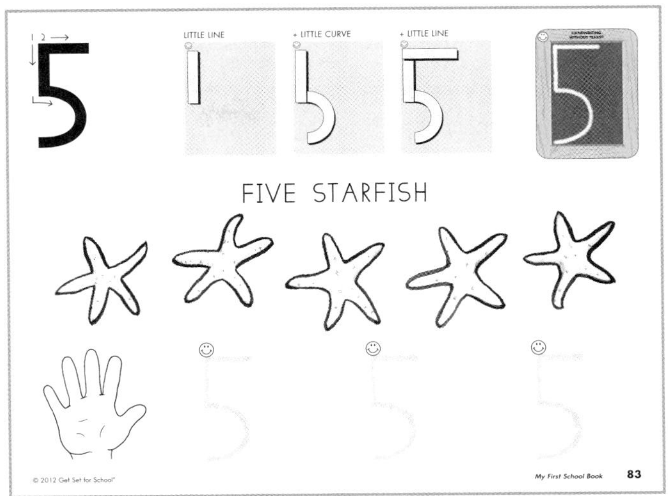

Activity

This is the page for number 5. Point to 5 at the top, 5 on the Mat, and 5 on the Slate. See five starfish. Find the words, FIVE STARFISH. A starfish has 5 arms.

Count 5 with Bodies

Hold up five fingers. Give your friend a high five. Count the arms on a starfish. Count five toes on one foot. Count five toes on the other. One is a big toe and four are little toes.

Count 5 with Objects

Count **5** points on a star. Cut one corner off a square. Now count the sides and corners. There are five sides and five angles now. It's a new shape. It's a pentagon.

Color and Write

Finger trace the 5 at the top of the page. (Say directions.)
Let's write 5. Put the crayon on the ☺. Little line down. Little curve. Jump to the ☺. Little line across. Color five starfish. Color five fingers.

✔ Check

Do children trace **5** correctly? Do they start with a little line down?

Support/ELL

Play *Sing, Sound & Count With Me* CD, "Counting at the Table," track 14.

More To Learn

Teach finger plays with five. **This is the beehive, 1 2 3 4 5, once I caught a fish alive.** Emphasize counting.

Look What We're Learning

Foundation Skills
- Name body parts
- Sequencing
- Use correct top-to-bottom, left-to-right directionality for numbers

Number & Operations
- Verbally count a set of objects
- Write numerals up to 10

Writing
- Hold a crayon with proper grip to write
- Use helping hand to stabilize objects and papers

Sensory Motor
- Use same hand consistently to hold crayons
- Use fingers to hold crayons

Vocabulary

five
pentagon
starfish

Six - 

BIG LINE + LITTLE CURVE AROUND

Activity

This is the page for number 6. Point to 6 at the top, and 6 on the Slate. See six ladybugs. Find the words SIX LADYBUGS. Ladybugs have six legs, so do ants, bugs, and bees.

Count 6 with Fingers

Hold up five fingers on the left hand. Count on by putting up one right hand finger (six).

Count 6 with Objects

Count six cubes. Build steps with one, then two, then three cubes. Put six eggs in a row in an egg carton. There are six eggs (a half dozen), and six empty places.

Color and Write

Finger trace the 6 at the top of the page. (Say directions.)
Let's write 6. Put the crayon on the ☺. Big line down, little curve around. Color the ladybugs red. Trace six legs on each ladybug.

✔ Check

Observe children's crayon grip, helping hand, and seating posture.

Support/ELL

Use Wet-Dry-Try activity to prepare for crayon tracing. If children aren't ready to trace with crayons, then save that activity for later.

More To Learn

Play *Sing, Sound & Count With Me* CD, "Rowboat, Rowboat," track 28. Have children sort items into six piles.

Look What We're Learning

Foundation Skills
- Sequencing
- Use correct top-to-bottom, left-to-right directionality for numbers

Writing
- Hold a crayon with proper grip to write
- Use helping hand to stabilize objects and papers

Number & Operations
- Write numerals up to 10

Problem Solving
- Use manipulatives to find a solution

Sensory Motor
- Use same hand consistently to hold crayons
- Use fingers to hold crayons

Vocabulary

six
ladybug

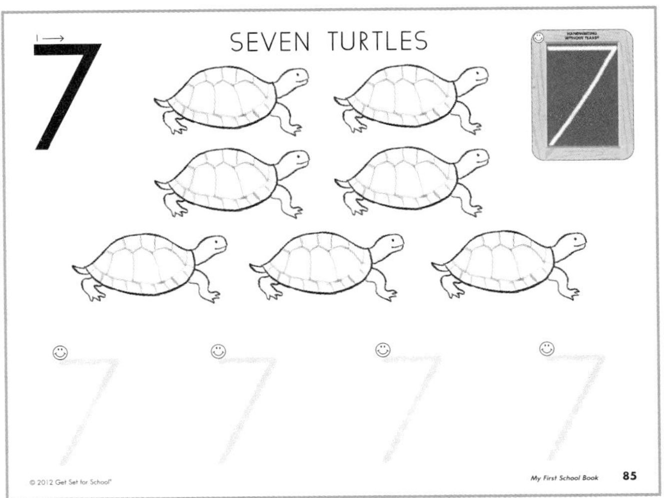

Activity

This is the page for number 7. Point to 7 at the top, and 7 on the Slate. See seven turtles. Find the words SEVEN TURTLES.

Count 7 with Fingers

Hold up five fingers on the left hand. Count on by putting up 2 right hand fingers (six, seven).

Count 7 with Objects

Build a tower with seven cubes. Put seven eggs in an egg carton. See a row of six and one more.

Color and Write

Finger trace the 7 at the top of the page. (Say directions.)
Let's write 7. Put the crayon on the ☺. Little line across, big line slides down.

✔ Check

Observe children as they trace. Do they stop at the end of the little line before they slide down? That habit makes for a nice sharp corner on **7**.

Support/ELL

Put a ☺ on the top left corner of a door. Take **7** for a walk across the top of the door. Then make **7** slide down. Have children Air Trace **7** on the door.

More To Learn

Go on a seven hunt. Talk about seven days in a week.

Look What We're Learning

Foundation Skills
- Sequencing
- Use correct top-to-bottom, left-to-right directionality for numbers

Writing
- Hold a crayon with proper grip to write
- Use helping hand to stabilize objects and papers

Number & Operations
- Write numerals up to 10

Problem Solving
- Use manipulatives to find a solution

Sensory Motor
- Use same hand consistently to hold crayons
- Use fingers to hold crayons

Vocabulary

seven
turtle

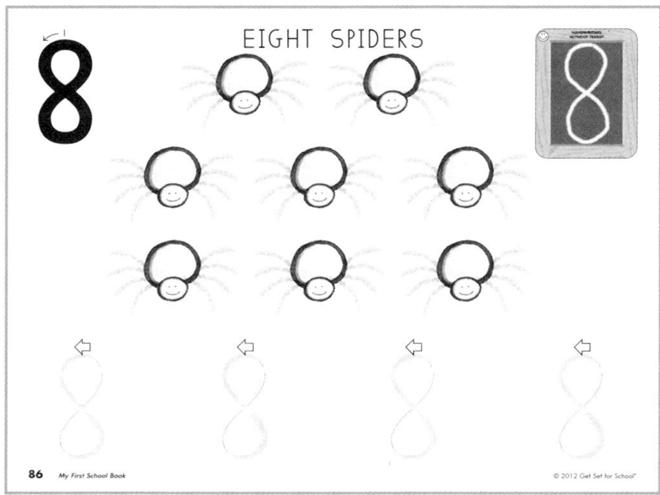

Activity

This is the page for number 8. Point to 8 at the top and 8 on the Slate. See eight spiders. Find the words EIGHT SPIDERS. Spiders have eight legs.

Count 8 with Fingers
Hold up five fingers on the left hand. Count on by putting up three right hand fingers (six, seven, eight).

Count 8 with Objects
Use a toy STOP sign or walk to a real STOP sign. Count the sides. Count the angles. Touch and count eight crayons. Put them in sets of two. Count by twos: 2, 4, 6, 8.

Color and Write
Finger trace the 8 at the top of the page. (Say directions.)
Let's write 8. Put the crayon on ⇦. Begin with the letter S. Back up to the top.
Color eight spiders. Trace eight spider legs on each spider.

✔ Check

Can children trace an **S** before learning **8**?

Support/ELL

Eight is a center starter on the Slate. Help children write **S** on the Slate first. Also teach **8** with a figure **8** car track, or by walking **8** around cones.

More To Learn

Find books about octopuses. Count their legs. Do the same for spiders!

Look What We're Learning

Foundation Skills
- Sequencing
- Use correct top-to-bottom, left-to-right directionality for numbers

Writing
- Hold a crayon with proper grip to write
- Use helping hand to stabilize objects and papers

Number & Operations
- Write numerals up to 10

Problem Solving
- Use manipulatives to find a solution

Sensory Motor
- Use same hand consistently to hold crayons
- Use fingers to hold crayons

Vocabulary

eight
spider

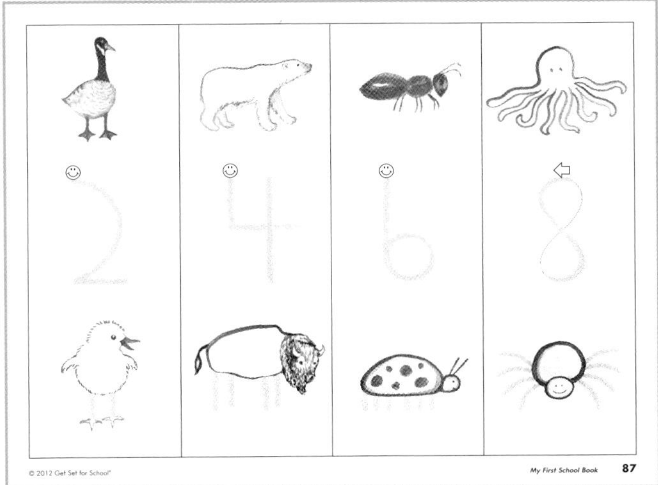

Two, four, six, eight! We're counting legs so don't be late! The chart sorts animals by the number of legs.

Activity

Talk about this page part by part. The first part has a goose, the number **2** and a chick. Why are they together? The goose and the chick have two legs. Continue.

Look and Learn

Talk about categories! The goose and the chick are birds. The bear and the buffalo are mammals. The ant and the ladybug are insects. But the octopus and the spider are in different families.

Color and Write

Lets write 2. Start at the ☺. Big curve, little line across.
Let's write 4. Start at the ☺. Little line down. Little line across. Jump to the top. Big line down.
Let's write 6. Start at the ☺. Big line down, little curve around.
Let's write 8. Start at the ⇦. Begin with the letter S. Back up to the top.
Children color the animals and trace the legs.

✔ Check

Can students count the animals' legs? Ask, **How many legs does the chick have?**

Support/ELL

Use objects to show the concept of 2, 4, 6, 8.

More To Learn

Give the animals shoes! This helps students understand one to one correspondence.

Look What We're Learning

Foundation Skills
- Sequencing
- Use correct top-to-bottom, left-to-right directionality for numbers
- Observe and sort

Writing
- Hold a crayon with proper grip to write
- Use helping hand to stabilize objects and papers

Number & Operations
- Verbally count a set of objects
- Write numerals up to 10

Sensory Motor
- Use same hand consistently to hold crayons
- Use fingers to hold crayons

Vocabulary

two	ant
four	octopus
six	chick
eight	buffalo
goose	ladybug
polar bear	spider

Nine - 9 LITTLE CURVE AROUND + BIG LINE DOWN

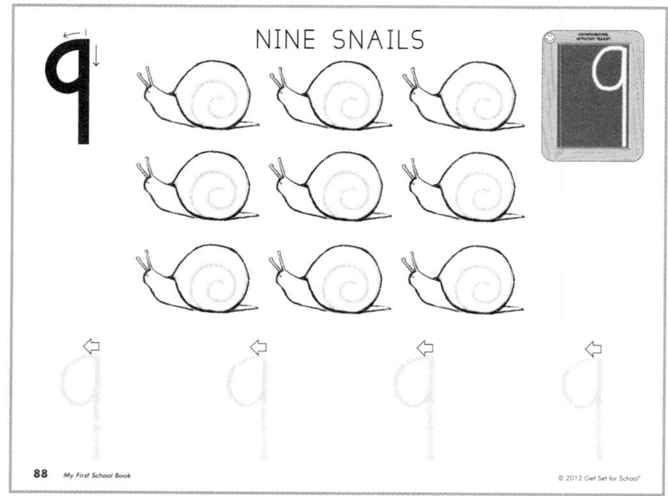

Activity

This is the page for number 9. Point to 9 at the top and 9 on the Slate. See 9 snails. Find the words NINE SNAILS.

Count 9 with Fingers

Hold up left hand for five. Count on by putting up four right-hand fingers: 6, 7, 8, 9.

Count 9 with Objects

Count the snails on the page. Count as if reading a page. Put out three plates. Put three beads on each plate. Take the beads and line them up on the edge of the table. Touch and count each one, starting at the left: 1, 2, 3, 4, 5, 6, 7, 8, 9.

Color and Write

Finger trace the 9 at the top of the page. (Say directions.)

Let's write 9. Put the crayon on the ⇦. Little curve around, big line down. Color nine snails.

✔ Check

Observe how children touch and count the snails. Do they count top to bottom and left to right?

Support/ELL

Nine is the only number that starts in the top right corner of the Slate. Use Wet-Dry-Try.

More To Learn

Ordinal numbers are important and easy to teach. Just say the number with "th." Make a line of 10 children. Say who is first, second, third, fourth, fifth, sixth, seventh, eighth, ninth, tenth.

Look What We're Learning

Foundation Skills
- Sequencing

Writing
- Hold a crayon with proper grip to write
- Use helping hand to stabilize objects and papers

Problem Solving
- Use manipulatives to find a solution

Number & Operations
- Match one-to-one
- Verbally count a set of objects
- Write numerals up to 10

Sensory Motor
- Use same hand consistently to hold crayons
- Use fingers to hold crayons

Vocabulary

nine
snail

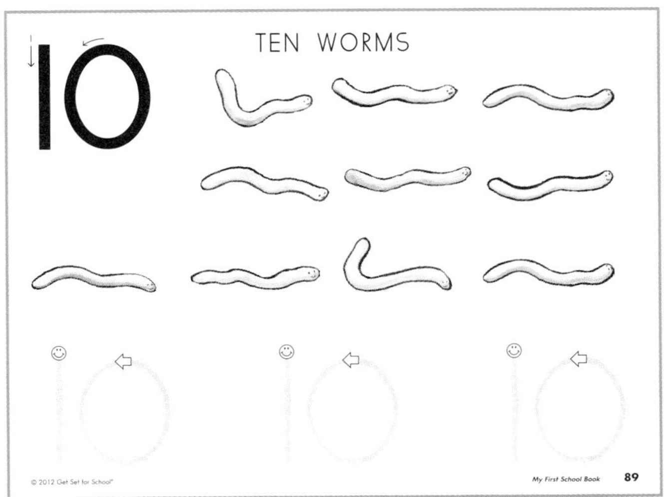

Activity

Point to 10 at the top. See 10 worms. Find the words TEN WORMS.

Count 10 with Fingers and Toes

Hold up left hand for 5. Count on from 5 (6, 7, 8, 9, 10). Count toes by fives. **Five toes here and 5 toes there make 10 toes in all.**

Count 10 with Objects

Count 10 cubes. Make steps with one, then two, then three, then four cubes. Touch and move 10 pennies. Put one by one into a bank, counting as each one is put in.

Color and Write

Finger trace the 10 at the top of the page. (Say directions.)
Let's write 10. First write one. Put the crayon on the ☺. Big line down. Next write zero.
Put the crayon on the ⇦. Big curve, go around. Keep going. Stop at the top. That's 10.

✔ Check

Can children count to 10? Can they trace a **1** and **0** correctly?

Support/ELL

Review numbers with Hop Scotch. Teach children how to play.

More To Learn

Teach children to count by tens. Use the chant "10 Fingers," track 22, *Rock, Rap, Tap, & Learn* CD.

Look What We're Learning

Foundation Skills
- Sequencing
- Use correct top-to-bottom, left-to-right directionality for numbers

Writing
- Hold a crayon with proper grip to write
- Use helping hand to stabilize objects and papers

Number & Operations
- Write numerals up to 10

Problem Solving
- Use manipulatives to find a solution

Sensory Motor
- Use same hand consistently to hold crayons
- Use fingers to hold crayons

Vocabulary

ten
worms

Number Review

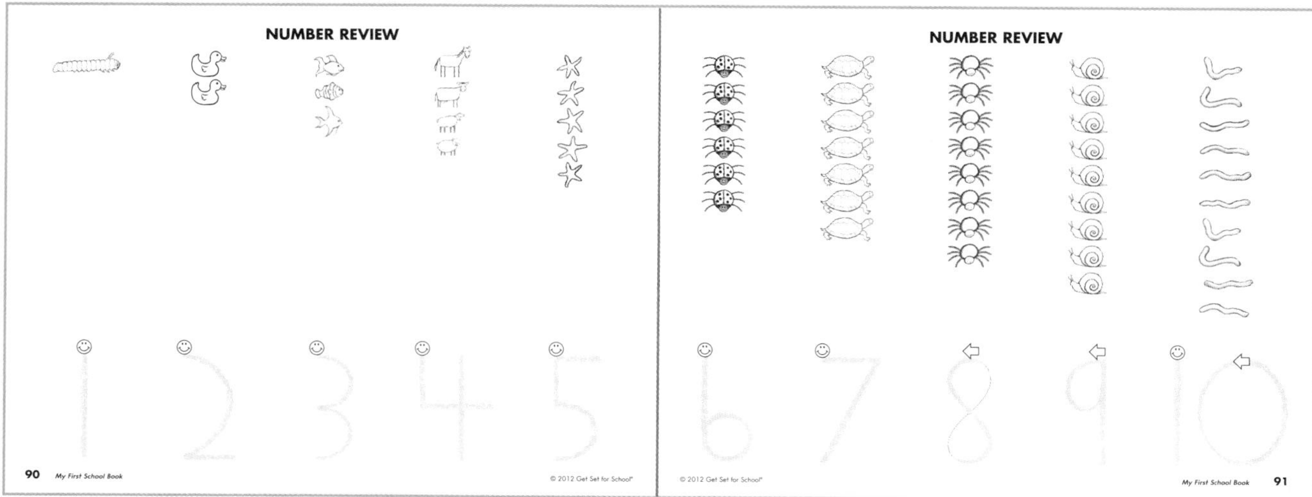

This is a review with something new! Children remember the familiar pictures and numbers. They review counting and number formation. Now there are also pictures in lines to make a chart. Take a few days for this page.

Activity

Children find the words NUMBER REVIEW. Explain the word "review." Repeat means do again. Review means "look again." Look again at pictures and numbers. Where is **6**? What comes after **4**? Continue.

Look and learn

Little pictures show animals. The number of animals matches the number. Let's count the animals to be sure. Count from the top down. Smaller numbers have fewer animals. Bigger numbers have more animals.

Color and Write

Let's write number 1. Watch me first. Your turn. Watch me write 2. Your turn. Color the pictures. Color from the top down.

✔ Check

Point to a number. Can children identify it?

Support/ELL

Encourage "rainbow tracing" going over the numbers with different colors for extra practice.

More To Learn

Play "Name the Number Fast!" See how quickly children can name the number.

Look What We're Learning

Foundation Skills
- Count up to 10 by rote
- Sequencing
- Use correct top-to-bottom, left-to-right directionality for numbers

Writing
- Hold a crayon with proper grip to write
- Use helping hand to stabilize objects and papers

Number & Operations
- Verbally count a set of objects
- Write numerals up to 10

Sensory Motor
- Use same hand consistently to hold crayons
- Use fingers to hold crayons

Vocabulary

before	**ladybug**
after	**turtle**
caterpillar	**spider**
duck	**snail**
fish	**worm**
starfish	

1-2-3 Touch & Flip® Cards

Have you ever heard of muscle memory? That's certain movement patterns that are so automatic they don't require thinking. We want children to know numbers so well that they write them correctly without thinking. When children trace the Touch & Flip tactile number cards, they build stroke visual memory.

Materials/Setup
- 1-2-3 Touch & Flip® Cards (Animal cards–tactile side)

Grouping
Small group 3-4

Support/ELL
Let children who need support watch others first. Extra exposure prepares them.

Video Lesson
View the video lesson, Name, Touch, and Trace with 1-2-3 Touch & Flip Cards, at **getsetforschool.com/videos**

Activity

1. Choose a card from 1-5. Sit at a table. Children stand beside you.
2. Finger trace **3** saying, **little curve, little curve. That's ..3. Your turn!**
3. Children take turns finger tracing the number. Say the words with them as they trace. Waiting children watch others trace.
4. Continue with the remaining numbers. End the activity by turning cards over and counting the animals on each card.

✔ Check
Do children use the correct strokes automatically?

More To Learn
When tracing 1-5, use the 1-5 cards. Have children finger trace number 1 2 3 4 or 5 from memory on the Mat. Start at the ☺.

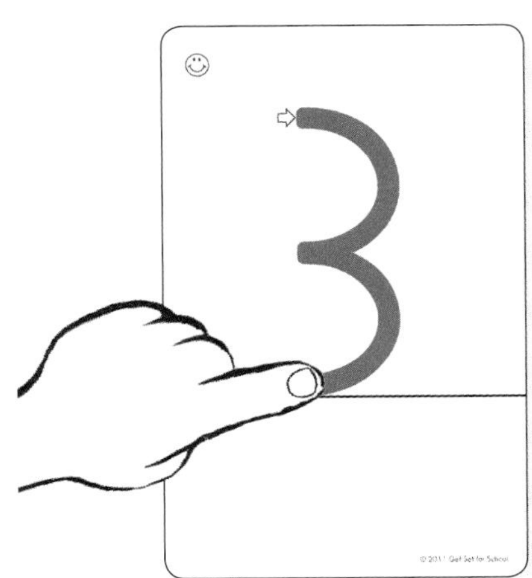

Look What We're Learning

Foundation Skills
- Sequencing

Oral Language
- Repeat teacher's words

Number & Operations
- Verbally count a set of objects
- Recognize that the last number said is the total

Sensory Motor
- Use index finger to trace numbers on cards
- Use same hand consistently to perform skilled tasks
- Perceive the identity of an object by sense of touch

Social-Emotional
- Interact easily with familiar adults

Vocabulary
Numbers 1-10

I Know My Numbers

These are 10 individual booklets, and each child gets the whole set over time. Each child gets all 10 booklets. Start with **1**, and use it at school. After a couple weeks, send it home for children to use at home. Then start **2** and so on. Parents will appreciate the friendly information in every booklet. They'll also enjoy seeing the activities: numbers to trace, pictures to color, simple things to build, and the words for rhymes and finger plays. Share the activities below with parents when you send home the completed booklets.

Go to **getsetforschool.com/click** for a printable copy for parents.

Video Lesson

View the video lesson, Count 9 with *I Know My Numbers*, at **getsetforschool.com/videos**

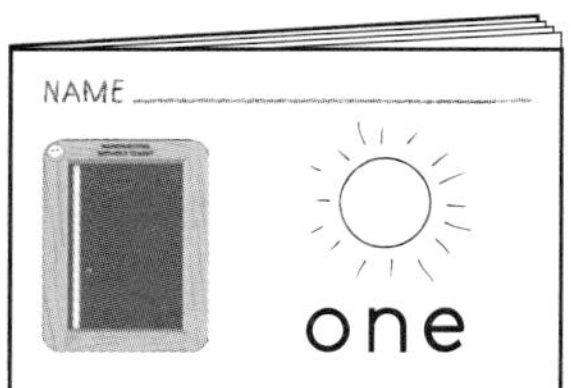

Parents and children explore **1** together as they find the number **1** on signs, elevators, and other locations. They stand on one foot, and count objects one by one. Children practice writing **1**. They talk about **first.** Children color a star and learn, "Star light, star bright, FIRST star I see tonight..." They play with one cap and one cup, putting the cup up and down, and the cap in, out, or on the cup.

Parents and children explore **2**, finding **2** in books and on clocks. They line up shoes and sort socks. Children review **1** and practice writing **2**. They learn "Two Little Ducky Birds" and "One, Two, Tie My Shoe." Parents fold a paper bag and cut out a gingerbread boy with two sides. Children count ants marching two by two.

Parents and children explore **3**, finding **3** on keyboards and buses. They cut sandwiches into triangles and bite off three corners. Children review **1**, **2**, and practice writing **3**. They learn, "Three Little Nickels" rhyme and "Three Little Pigs" story. They find three wheels on a tricycle and three horns on a triceratops. With three cups, they build a pyramid.

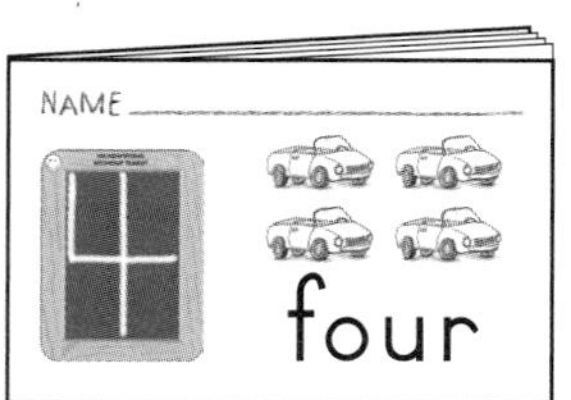

Parents and children explore **4**, looking for furniture with four legs. They fold towels and dishcloths with four corners. Children review **1**, **2**, **3** and practice writing **4**. They learn "Four Currant Buns" and cut four corners off a card. They use four straws to make squares and diamonds.

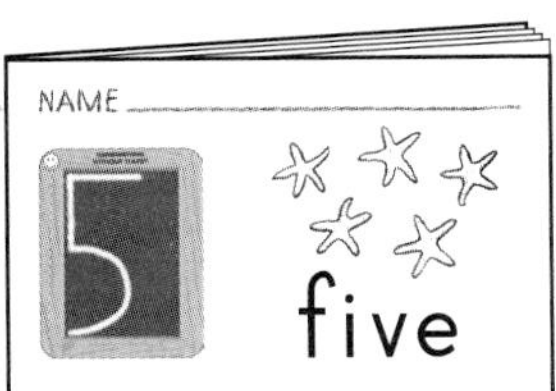

Parents and children explore **5**. They count by fives at the table, taking turns putting hands (5 fingers) on the table 5, 10, 15, 20. They count five toes too. Children review writing **1**, **2**, **3**, **4**, and practice writing **5**. They learn "The Beehive" and "Five Little Ducks." They color and count pentagons.

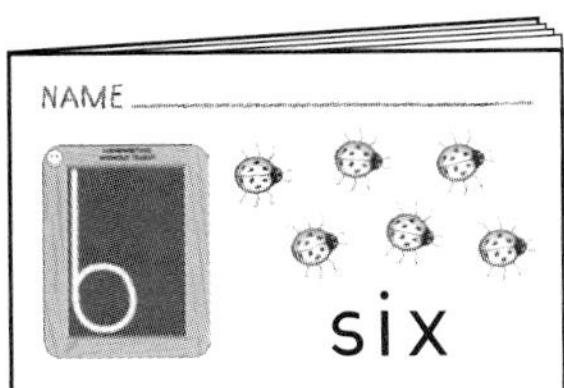

Parents and children explore **6** with three pairs of socks. They count the loose socks by ones, and then put them in pairs counting **2**, **4**, **6**. Children review writing **1-5**, and practice writing **6**. They use an empty egg carton and put in six eggs. They learn the names of six insects. With six cups, they build a pyramid, with three, then two, then one on top.

Parents and children explore **7**. They use a calendar and count the first seven days of each month and say the seven days of the week. Children review **1-6**, and practice writing **7**. Parents put a ☺ on the door. They write flashlight numbers on the door. Children learn "One Potato, Two Potato."

Parents and children explore **8**, finding eight sides on a STOP sign. They review **1-7** and carefully start **8** with Sammy Snake and letter **S**. Children color an octopus with eight long legs. They learn "Little Miss Muffet" and that spiders have eight legs. They even color eight planets and find Earth. They take eight ants marching two by two.

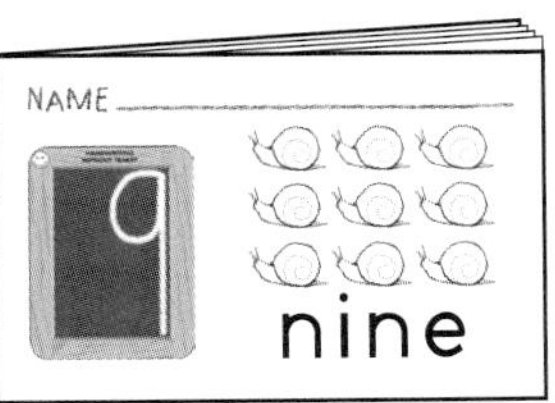

Parents and children explore **9**. They play with nine square crackers and put them in three rows of three to make a big square. Children review **1-8** and practice writing **9**. Parents and Children play Tic-Tac-Toe in the book. Children color nine different fruits, and take nine ants marching three by three.

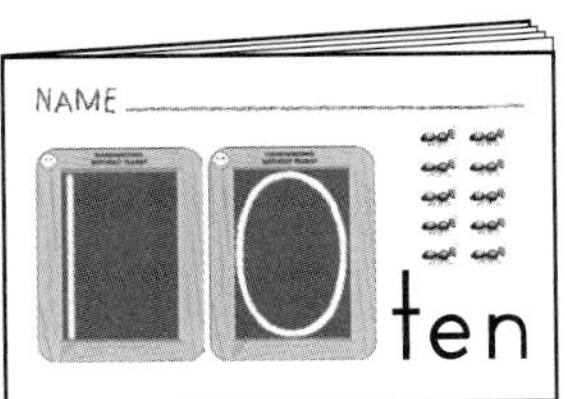

Parents and children explore **10** with fingers and toes. They learn "One, Two, Tie my shoe....up to Nine, Ten, A big fat hen." Children review **1-9** and practice writing **10**. Families put fingers in the air to count by tens. Children build a pyramid with 10 cups: 4, then 3, then 2, and 1. They take 10 ants marching 2 by 2.

Resources

Check Readiness
Readiness & Writing Benchmarks
Sensory Motor Benchmarks
Social-Emotional Benchmarks
Sing Along CD
Sing, Sound & Count with Me CD
Scope & Sequence of Printing
School to Home Connection
- Help Me Hold My Crayon
- Help Me Write My Name
Pre-K Teaching Guidelines
Index
References
Letter Chart

Check Readiness

Use this 1-on-1 informal assessment during the year to evaluate skills and guide your teaching. Share the results with parents. These are key readiness and writing skills expected when children enter kindergarten.

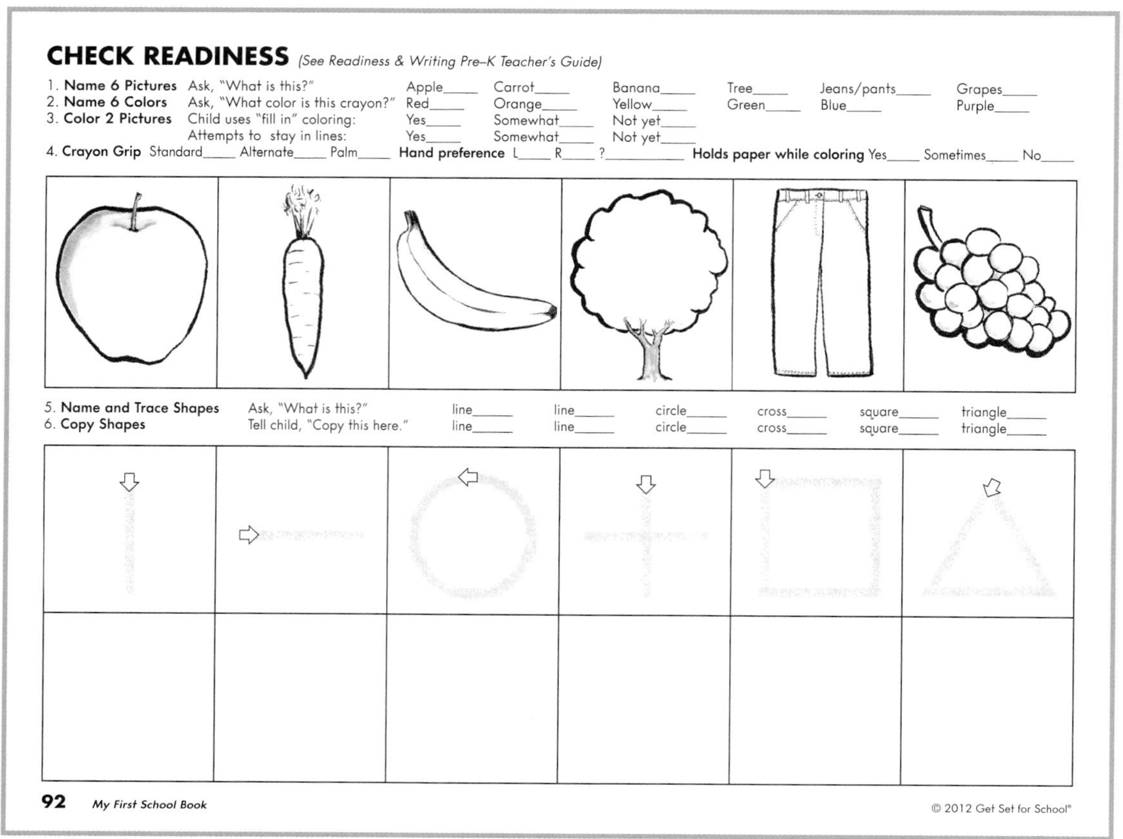

CHECK READINESS *(See Readiness & Writing Pre–K Teacher's Guide)*

1. **Name 6 Pictures** Ask, "What is this?" Apple____ Carrot____ Banana____ Tree____ Jeans/pants____ Grapes____
2. **Name 6 Colors** Ask, "What color is this crayon?" Red____ Orange____ Yellow____ Green____ Blue____ Purple____
3. **Color 2 Pictures** Child uses "fill in" coloring: Yes____ Somewhat____ Not yet____
   Attempts to stay in lines: Yes____ Somewhat____ Not yet____
4. **Crayon Grip** Standard____ Alternate____ Palm____ **Hand preference** L____ R____ ?__________ **Holds paper while coloring** Yes____ Sometimes____ No____

5. **Name and Trace Shapes** Ask, "What is this?" line_____ line_____ circle_____ cross_____ square_____ triangle_____
6. **Copy Shapes** Tell child, "Copy this here." line_____ line_____ circle_____ cross_____ square_____ triangle_____

92 *My First School Book* © 2012 Get Set for School®

General Directions:	Check each correct item. Write in other answers and observations.
1. Name 6 Pictures	Typically, this is easy for English speaking children. When asking a non-verbal child to point, name the pictures in random order.
2. Name 6 Colors	Use crayons with true colors. Ask a child to say the colors as you point.
3. Color 2 Pictures	Let the child choose the pictures to color. Notice how a child picks up and uses crayons. Record this on the next item.
4. Crayon Grip **Hand Preference** **Holds Paper**	See pages 22-29 for information about these skills. Note which hand is used. Mark a "?" if a child changes hands when coloring.
5. Name and Trace Shapes	Children may use other words, for example: one for line, or ball for circle. Simply write a child's words on the page. Tell the child to start on the arrow and trace the shapes.
6. Copy Shapes	As soon as a child finishes tracing each shape, make a dot to show the starting place. This will make you aware of a child's starting tendency.

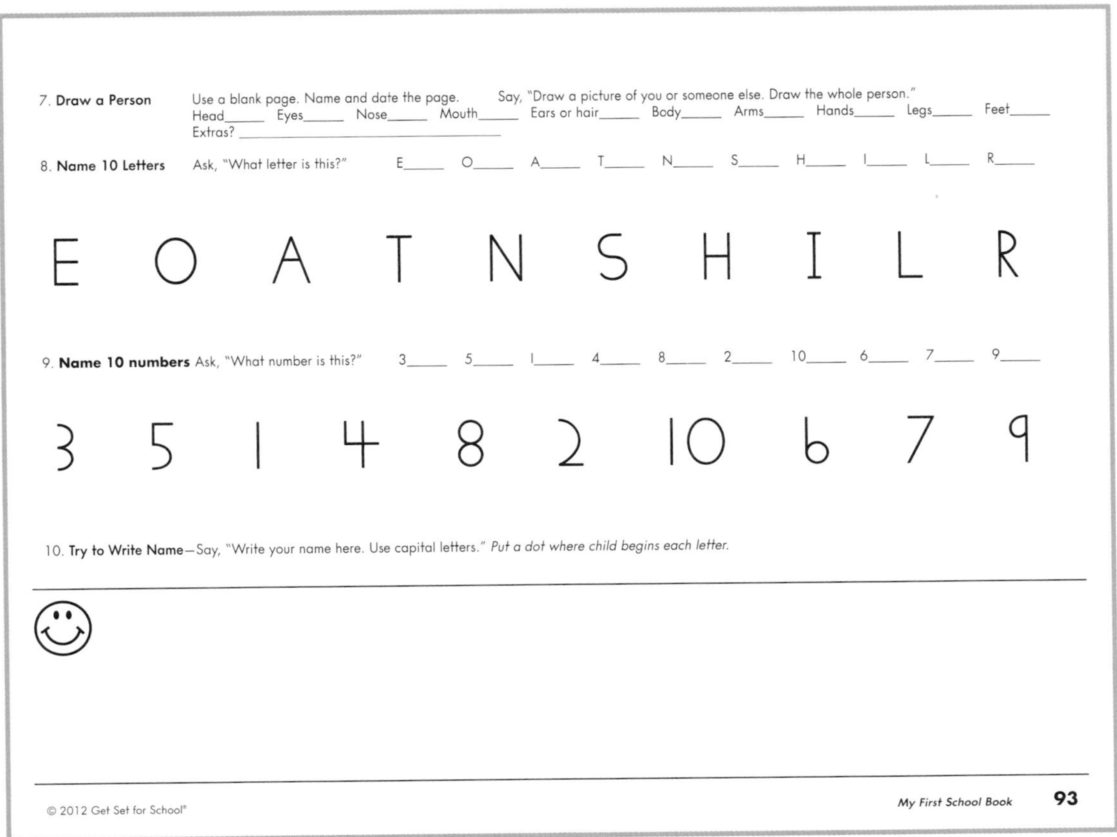

7. **Draw a Person** Use a blank page. Name and date the page. Say, "Draw a picture of you or someone else. Draw the whole person."
Head_____ Eyes_____ Nose_____ Mouth_____ Ears or hair_____ Body_____ Arms_____ Hands_____ Legs_____ Feet_____
Extras? ____________________

8. **Name 10 Letters** Ask, "What letter is this?" E_____ O_____ A_____ T_____ N_____ S_____ H_____ I_____ L_____ R_____

E O A T N S H I L R

9. **Name 10 numbers** Ask, "What number is this?" 3_____ 5_____ 1_____ 4_____ 8_____ 2_____ 10_____ 6_____ 7_____ 9_____

3 5 1 4 8 2 10 6 7 9

10. **Try to Write Name**—Say, "Write your name here. Use capital letters." *Put a dot where child begins each letter.*

☺

© 2012 Get Set for School® *My First School Book* **93**

7. Draw a Person	Name, date, and save these. Check the 10 parts and note any extras.
8. Name 10 Letters	Naming letters out of order shows true recognition. Write in any wrong answers. When asking a non-verbal child to point, say the letters in random order.
9. Name 9 Numbers	Write in any wrong answers. When asking a non-verbal child to point, say the numbers in random order.
10. Try to Write Name	Tell children to start at the ☺. As soon as a child writes a letter, make a dot to show the starting place.

For a printable copy of Check Readiness and other Pre-K assessments visit **getsetforschool.com**

Readiness & Writing Benchmarks

Foundation Skills

- Recognize and identify basic colors
- Count up to 10 by rote
- Say the alphabet by rote
- Recognize familiar two- and three-dimensional shapes
- Name parts of the body
- Draw simple shapes
- Know name
- Exhibit appropriate social skills (e.g., shaking hands)
- Recognize and use common prepositions in speech (e.g., top, middle, over, beside, etc.)
- Participate in school routines
- Use correct top-to-bottom, left- to-right directionality for letters, numbers, and other symbols
- Share with peers and adults
- Imitate teacher's body movements
- Sequencing (e.g., Mat Man, building letters, letter and number formation)
- Listen to oral directions to attend to a simple task
- Observe and sort
- Listen to and repeat songs, poems, nursery rhymes, and finger plays
- Describe self in terms of physical traits and family connections

Language & Literacy Skills

Alphabet Knowledge

- Tell the difference between letters, pictures, and other symbols
- Recognize and name letters in own first and last name
- Position capitals right-side up
- Point to and name capital letters
- Position lowercase letters right-side up
- Point to and name lowercase letters
- Match all capital and lowercase letters

Concepts About Print

- Understand that print can be read and has meaning
- Turn pages from front to back, one at a time
- Follow print from top to bottom and left to right on a page
- Recognize own name in print
- Recognize the names of friends and family in print
- Recognize important signs in our world

Comprehension

- Listen to gain and share information
- Listen to perform a task
- Listen to learn what happened in a story
- Listen to converse with an adult or peer
- Listen to stories, plays, and poems and talk about their meaning
- Identify the main character in a story

Oral Language

- Repeat teacher's words
- Demonstrate active listening by attending to stories and instruction
- Learn words linked to content being taught
- Use new words linked to content being taught
- Ask and respond to simple questions: Who? What? When? Where?
- Listen to follow directions (three to four steps)
- Complete a task by following oral directions (up to three steps)
- Use manners in conversation
- Speak with normal, conversational volume, tone, and inflection
- Communicate thoughts with words
- Communicate feelings with words
- Share opinions and ideas in conversation and discussion
- Talk about experiences and observations
- Speak in complete sentences made up of three or more words
- Use words to describe an object or a person's traits

Writing

- Enjoy writing and engage in writing activities individually or with a group
- Share drawings and writing with others
- Write scribbles, letter-like forms, or actual letters to represent words and ideas
- Hold a crayon with proper grip to write
- Use helping hand to stabilize objects and papers
- Trace capital letters
- Understand there is a way to write that conveys meaning
- Write name
- Write capitals
- Write some lowercase letters

Numbers & Math Skills

Numbers & Operations

- Match one-to-one (up to 5, 10, 15 objects)
- Verbally count a set of objects (up to 15)
- Recognize that the last number said is the total
- Write numerals up to 10
- Share a set of objects evenly with two or three classmates

Geometry

- Identify position or location using in and out
- Identify position or location using before and after
- Identify position or location using top, middle, and bottom
- Identify position or location using above and below, over and under
- Identify position or location using left and right
- Match shapes of same size, shape, and orientation

Algebra

- Sort objects by size
- Sort objects by shape
- Sort objects by function/kind

Measurement & Time

- Sequence events in time

Data Representation & Probability

- Answer questions using organized data

Problem Solving

- Use manipulatives to find a solution

Sensory Motor Benchmarks

Children will naturally engage in discovery and exploration. All you need to do is make materials accessible to interact freely. Some of the best ways to develop sensory motor skills is to engage in activities that promote:

- Movement
- Building and sorting
- Manipulation
- Processing sensations
- Organization

Our activities are hands-on, so children will experience sensory motor learning seamlessly in all that they do. As with social-emotional skills, some children will be better at sensory motor skills than others. In literacy we use finger plays, sing, dance, make actions, color, and trace letters. You will notice our manipulatives have unique features to encourage motor development. For example, children use their index fingers to trace letters with A-B-C Touch & Flip® Cards, and they move cards to position them for use.

What are we teaching?

Our literacy and math activities encourage handedness, fine and gross motor movements, correct crayon grip, tool use, manipulation, motor coordination, motor planning, and body awareness.

How do we do it?

- Use music that encourages movement, finger plays, counting with fingers, clapping, and tapping.
- Set out manipulatives or selected pieces (Sound Around Box™, Touch & Flip Cards) and allow children to discover and explore freely.
- Allow children to hold books, turn pages, and point to letters and pictures.
- Use counters, blocks, and other items that can be counted, stacked, and sorted.
- Model proper tool use and manipulation—children may not always understand ways to manipulate pieces.
- Promote coloring and tracing of letters and numbers.

Sensory Motor Benchmarks

Fine Motor

- Use same hand consistently to hold crayons, toothbrush, utensils, and to perform skilled tasks
- Use fingers to open and close fasteners, hold crayons, scissors, cards, beads, etc.
- Move an object in one hand to position it for use, placement, or release
- Use index finger to trace letters, numbers, shapes, or other objects on cards or in the air
- Move fingers to show age/number and for finger plays

Gross Motor

- Use large muscle groups to maintain posture/position and mobility (e.g., walk, run, hop, skip, jump, climb stairs)

Bilateral Motor Coordination

- Use both sides of the body in activities (e.g., using drumsticks, playing other instruments, dancing)

Visual Motor Control

- Look at hands and use visual cues to guide reaching for, grasping, and moving objects

Body Awareness

- Know where the body is in relation to space
- Use the right amount of pressure to hold and use tools
- Reach across midline to get an object from other side

Movement Perception

- Tolerate motion in activities
- Play with body awareness, balance, and regard for people and equipment

Touch Perception

- Handle play and art materials without an avoidance response
- Perceive the size, shape, or identity of an object by sense of touch

Visual Perception

- Notice and attach meaning to visual information

Motor Planning

- Move naturally and place body to perform task

Social-Emotional Benchmarks

Children in Pre-K have a wide variety of skills. Some may have exceptional motor skills, while others may excel in socialization. Children need practice in all areas of development, which is why many of our activities—although specific to fostering early math, literacy, and writing skills—have social and motor components.

Social-Emotional

We believe that some of the best ways to develop social-emotional wellness in children is to nurture:

- Innovation
- Responsibility
- Teamwork
- Perseverance
- Independence

Today, we have many young English language learners who need reassurance that they are safe and accepted. Depending on their culture, there may be things you notice about the ways children socially engage with their peers. It's important for Pre-K teachers to understand that English language learners may misinterpret gestures and social interactions. For example in some cultures, children may look down when speaking to an adult as a sign of respect. Regardless of their understanding of and ability to speak English, all four-year-olds need guidance and support in building strong social and emotional skills.

What are we teaching?

Our activities are designed to develop self-concept, self-regulation, personal initiative, emotional understanding, and relationships with adults and peers. We want children to have positive self esteem, engage in classroom activities, transition appropriately, take initiative, understand feelings, and take turns sharing and playing with their friends.

How do we do it?

- Model ways to show respect for self, people, things.
- Recognize, name, and respond to feelings. I can tell you are _____ because you are ____.
- Set class rules and teach children to follow them.
- Read stories that introduce children to values. The "Three Little Pigs" teach hard work and hard bricks save the day.
- Teach children how to help each other, for example, work together to lift and carry, to sweep into a dustpan, to say "stop" when someone is hurting, to sit beside a sad friend, and so forth.
- Participate in song, take turns, and share.

Social-Emotional Benchmarks

Self-Concept

- Demonstrate positive self esteem
- Demonstrate self-care skills (e.g., using the bathroom, putting on coats, washing hands, etc.) that are age- and ability-appropriate
- Describe changes in own body

Self-Regulation

- Manage emotions through negotiation and cooperation
- Manage and handle transitions well
- Understand and follow classroom routines
- Participate in clean-up routines with other children
- Treat property with respect

Personal Initiative

- Demonstrate a desire for independence
- Show interest in many different activities

Emotional Understanding

- Name feelings being experienced
- Name emotions displayed by others
- Show empathy to others by offering comfort and help when appropriate

Relationships with Adults

- Interact easily with familiar adults
- Ask for help when needed
- Participate in conflict resolution activities (e.g., puppets acting out scenarios)

Relationships with Peers

- Cooperate with other children
- Participate in imaginary and dramatic play
- Take turns with peers
- Work with others to solve problems

Sing Along CD

Music is a big part of our readiness curriculum. You can use the award winning *Sing Along* CD to teach positional concepts, body parts, and letter formation. Whether you are teaching how to build Mat Man® or how to count animal legs, this CD has all you need to charge up your lessons and catch your students' attention. The lyrics are on the jacket cover of the CD.

You'll like it because . . .

The songs tie into activities in the *Readiness & Writing Pre-K Teacher's Guide* and *My First School Book*. They introduce or reinforce concepts. The songs mention the topic being taught and help children practice the skill. For example, "Crayon Song" teaches children how to position their fingers on a crayon. The "Mat Man" song teaches children how to sequence and build Mat Man. Other songs help Pre-K children develop social-emotional skills, such as smooth transition from one activity to another, recognition of emotions, positive self esteem, or cooperation.

Sing Along CD entices children to sing and move to the music as it teaches important skills. The best way to use the CD is to listen to the songs and read the lyrics on your own. Then play the CD in the background during free play to subtly introduce it to the children. See which songs attract both you and the children. Think about how the skills fit in with your plans. Here are some ideas.

Track	Song	Suggested Activities
1	Where Do You Start Your Letters?	Play a question and answer game with students. Share with parents.
2	Alphabet Song	Sing while pointing to Pre-K Color Wall Cards or pages in their workbook.
3	Alphabet Song (Instrumental)	Sing it on your own.
4	There's a Dog in the School	Here's a chance to say the alphabet from a dog's point of view.
5	Crayon Song	Children enjoy learning that their fingers have important jobs.
6	Magic C	Write Cs and circles in the air.
7	Hello Song	Children learn to look, to smile, and to shake hands.
8	Mat Man	This song helps children build Mat Man® as a group.
9	Count on Me	It's easy to help children count body parts.
10	Five Fingers Play	Children count to 5 with this fun finger play.
11	Toe Song	Children know and love the classic toe play, "This little piggy..."
12	Bird Legs	No matter what they look like or what they do, birds have two.
13	Animal Legs	There are lots of four-legged animals! Learn 4 by counting legs.
14	The Ant, the Bug & the Bee	Learn 6 with insect legs. Don't forget to let children fly like bees.
15	Spiders Love to Party	Party with spiders while learning about 8.
16	Ten Little Fingers	Finger–plays develop fine motor and imitating skills. This is a favorite.
17	My Teacher Draws	Watching the teacher draw prepares children for drawing.
18	Puffy Fluffy	Move to music. Make clouds and rain in the air.
19	Tap, Tap, Tap	Use two big lines to tap. Tap slow or fast, tapping fun lasts!
20	Golden Slippers (Instrumental)	This upbeat instrumental was added for extra practice tapping.
21	Skip to My Lou	Use this song as a gross motor activity.
22	Down on Grandpa's Farm	Sing before taking a field trip to a farm.
23	Peanut Butter and Jelly	Encourage a variety of movements, listening, and following directions.
24	Rain Song	Imitate falling rain motions.
25	Wood Piece Pokey	Move Wood Pieces up, down, and all around.

For a printable list of tracks and suggested activities for all three CDs, go to **getsetforschool.com/click**

Sing, Sound & Count With Me CD

Sing, Sound & Count With Me CD has songs that promote social-emotional skills, listening, and following directions. Although the emphasis is on math and literacy, you can use many of the songs to work on general readiness such as shape recognition, position concepts, basic counting, and other crucial skills.

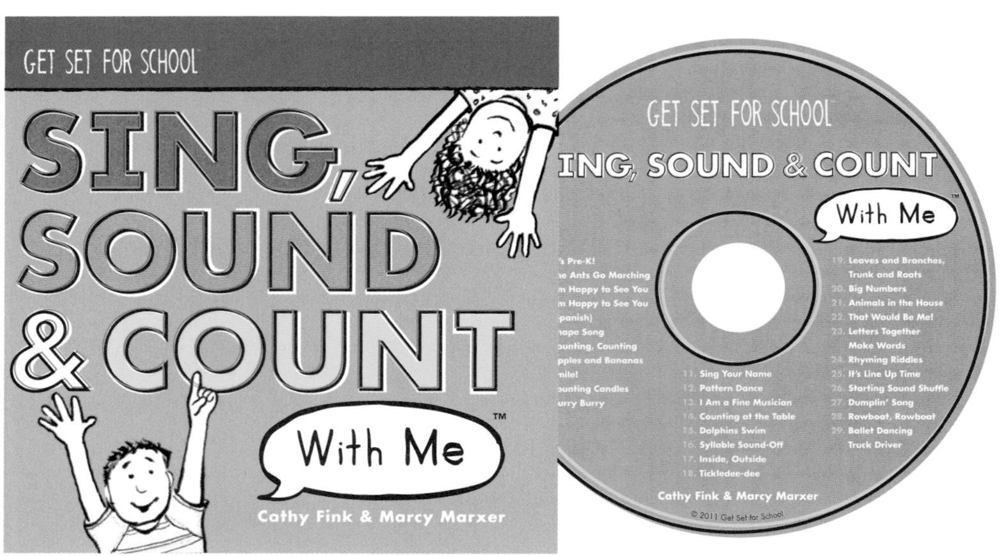

You'll like it because . . .

The songs tie into activities in the *Language & Literacy Pre-K Teacher's Guide* and the *Numbers & Math Pre-K Teacher's Guide*. They introduce or reinforce concepts and mention the topic being taught to help children practice a given skill. For example, "Syllable Sound-Off" teaches children what syllables are and helps them divide lyrics into syllables. Other songs help Pre-K children develop social-emotional skills, such as smooth transition from one activity to another, recognition of emotions, positive self esteem, or cooperation.

Sing, Sound & Count With Me CD entices children to sing and move to the music as it teaches important skills. The best way to use the CD is to listen to the songs and read the lyrics on your own. Then play the CD in the background during free play to subtly introduce it to the children. See which songs attract both you and the children. Think about how the skills fit in with your plans. Here are some ideas to help you along. The readiness and writing activities are in bold.

Track	Song	Suggested Activities
1	**It's Pre-K!**	**Swing bent arms in time. Jump two times and wave hands for chorus.**
2	**The Ants Go Marching**	**March around in groups. Hold up fingers to show numbers.**
3	**I'm Happy to See You**	**Sit in a circle. Tap knees and clap with the beat.**
4	**I'm Happy to See You (Spanish)**	
5	**Shape Song**	**Trace or hold shapes in the air. Show sides and corners.**
6	**Counting, Counting**	**Follow lyrics for movements while counting to 5.**
7	Apples and Bananas	Exaggerate mouth positions for sounds.
8	**Smile!**	**Make facial expressions for each verse.**
9	**Counting Candles**	**Clap to the rhythm. Show fingers while counting.**
10	Hurry Burry	Make motions for each mishap.
11	**Sing Your Name**	**Clap to the rhythm. Clap out the syllables in names.**
12	Pattern Dance	Dance and wave. Then follow lyrics for patterns.
13	I Am a Fine Musician	Motion playing instruments. Clap syllables.
14	**Counting at the Table**	**Follow lyrics for motions, one person at a time.**
15	**Dolphins Swim**	**Swim and dive following lyrics for positions.**
16	Syllable Sound-Off	March around. Clap out syllables.
17	**Inside, Outside**	**Hold index finger in front of mouth for quiet; cup hands around mouth for loud.**
18	**Tickledee-dee**	**Sway to music. Point to child when name is sung.**
19	**Leaves and Branches, Trunk and Roots**	**Wave hands, sweep down arms and body, and pat floor.**
20	**Big Numbers**	**Point to head for know. Shake head never. Act out last line.**
21	Animals in the House	Look around for animals. Motion animals' actions.
22	**That Would Be Me!**	**Make motions for fly, grow, swim, and swing.**
23	Letters Together Make Words	Grasp hands together. Say with cupped hands.
24	Rhyming Riddles	Walk in a circle for chorus. Stand still and nod to beat for riddles.
25	**It's Line Up Time**	**Rhumba into line.**
26	Starting Sound Shuffle	Point to self or children for call and response.
27	Dumplin' Song	Act out question/answer with two groups. Count down with fingers.
28	Rowboat, Rowboat	Have children play the animals and climb into the boat.
29	Ballet Dancing Truck Driver	Create motion for each occupation.

For a printable list of tracks and suggested activities for all three CDs, go to **getsetforschool.com/click**

Scope & Sequence of Printing

The Scope and Sequence of printing defines the content and order of printing instruction. The skills needed for printing develop as early as preschool. Although we do not teach printing formally at the preschool level, we can informally create an environment and encourage activities to help students develop good habits they will need later. We do this by teaching skills in a way that makes learning natural and fun. This Scope and Sequence is provided to show you how learning handwriting is a process. The process begins early. If we all contribute to the process, we can prepare children for amazing handwriting success.

Description

Type of Instruction

Informal/Structured: A variety of activities address the broad range of letter and school readiness skills.

Formal/Structured: Teacher directed activities are presented in a more precise order with specific objectives.

Handwriting Sequence

Pre-Strokes: These are beginning marks that can be random or deliberate.

Shapes: Shapes often are introduced before letters and are a foundation for letter formation skills.

Capitals/Numbers: These use simple shapes and strokes. They have the same size, start, and position.

Lowercase Letters: These are tall, small, and descending symbols with more complex strokes, sizes, starts, and positions.

Stages of Learning

Pre-Instruction Readiness: This is attention, behavior, language, and fine motor skills for beginning writing.

Stage 1–Imitating the Teacher: This is watching someone form a letter first, and then writing the letter.

Stage 2–Copying Printed Models: This is looking at a letter and then writing the letter.

Stage 3–Independent Writing: This is writing without watching someone or even seeing a letter.

Physical Approach

Crayon Use: Crayons prepare children to use pencils. Small crayon use encourages proper grip.

Pencil Use: Proper pencil use is necessary for good handwriting. In kindergarten, children transfer their crayon grip to pencils.

Posture: Good sitting posture promotes good handwriting. This is taught in kindergarten.

Paper Placement: When children are writing sentences and paragraphs, they're ready to angle the paper so they can move the writing hand easily across the page.

Printing Skills

Primary Skills

- Memory: Remember and write dictated letters and numbers.
- Orientation: Face letters and numbers in the correct direction.
- Start: Begin each letter or number correctly.
- Sequence: Make the letter strokes in the correct order.

Secondary Skills

- Placement: Place letters and numbers on the baseline.
- Size: Write in a consistent, grade-appropriate size.
- Spacing: Place letters in words closely, putting space between words.
- Control: Focus on neatness and proportion.

Functional Writing

Letters/Numbers
Words
Sentences
Paragraphs
Writing in All Subjects

SCOPE AND SEQUENCE OF PRINTING				
	Pre-K	**Kindergarten**	**1st Grade**	**2nd Grade**
Type of Instruction				
Informal/Structured	✔			
Formal/Structured		✔	✔	✔
Handwriting Sequence				
Pre-Strokes	✔			
Shapes	✔			
Capitals/Numbers	✔	✔	✔	✔
Lowercase Letters	*See note below	✔	✔	✔
Stages of Learning				
Pre-Instruction Readiness	✔	✔		
Stage 1–Imitating the Teacher	✔	✔	✔	✔
Stage 2–Copying Printed Models		✔	✔	✔
Stage 3–Independent Writing		✔	✔	✔
Physical Approach				
Crayon Use	✔	✔		
Pencil Use		✔	✔	✔
Posture		✔	✔	✔
Paper Placement		✔	✔	✔
Printing Skills				
Primary Skills				
– Memory	✔	✔	✔	✔
– Orientation	✔	✔	✔	✔
– Start	✔	✔	✔	✔
– Sequence	✔	✔	✔	✔
Secondary Skills				
– Placement		✔	✔	✔
– Size		✔	✔	✔
– Spacing		✔	✔	✔
– Control		✔ Emerging	✔	✔
Functional Writing				
Letters/Numbers	✔ Capitals/Numbers	✔	✔	
Words		✔ Short	✔ Short	✔ Long
Sentences		✔ Short	✔ Short	✔ Long
Paragraphs			✔ Short	✔ Long
Writing in All Subjects		✔	✔	✔

*Children in preschool are taught lowercase letter recognition - but not writing. They may be taught the lowercase letters in their names.

School to Home Connection

Research consistently shows that a strong school to home connection helps children build self esteem, curiosity, and motivation to learn new things. Home and school are the two most important places for young children. A successful teacher/family partnership assures children that there are people who care about them and provides a unique perspective about the child. When teachers and families work together, everyone wins.

Here are 10 ways to make a strong school to home connection:

1. Find opportunities to communicate during planned preschool events like teacher/family meetings, conferences, and school visits. Take a few extra steps to communicate through letters, email, and even podcasts.
2. Share important assessment information about a child. Most schools have regular family reports to share key progress details. Use our Get Set for School® Pre-K readiness assessments to help you identify what your children know and can do, and easily share information with families and other educators. You can find them at **getsetforschool.com**
3. Share your curriculum with families. Let them play with some of the products. Tell them about our website, **getsetforschool.com**, so that they can explore the many resources there.
4. Share music with families. Send them home singing songs from our *Sing Along* CD, *Rock, Rap, Tap & Learn* CD, or our *Sing, Sound & Count With Me* CD. If there is a fun song that families sing at home, ask them to share it with you.
5. Reinforce learning at home. Encourage families to do finger plays and read books and nursery rhymes at home. Let them know just how important it is to their child's growth and development. Consider a teacher/family sharing day where family members can learn some of the finger plays and reading strategies for children. For families whose children's first language is not English, encourage them to sing songs and rhymes in their home language.
6. Model language and thinking skills out loud. Children benefit from hearing adults talk and solve problems. They learn vocabulary and critical thinking skills. Families can share thoughts throughout the day. For example: **It looks like it's going to rain outside. I'd better take an umbrella.**
7. Read to children as much as possible. Reading is fun and helps build comprehension and language skills.
8. Share *My First School Book* with families. Send it home when children have completed it. Encourage caregivers to review it with their child and share it with other family members.
9. Help families prepare their children to write. Encourage them to learn proper grip and support their child in holding a crayon correctly. Children love to see their names in print. Help them write their names in block capitals. These are the first and easiest letters to write.
10. Help children recognize letters and notice that print is all around them. Point out signs, logos, and letters wherever you go.

Help Me Hold My Crayon

Even if you're not a teacher and don't hold the pencil correctly yourself, you can still be a very good influence on your child. It's as easy as choosing the correct tools and showing your child how to hold them.

How do I choose the correct writing tools?

- As soon as your child is past age three or the putting-things-in-mouth swallowing stage, give him or her little broken pieces of chalk or crayon and lots of big sheets of paper for loose scribbling/drawing.
- Little pieces of finger food also encourage finger skills.

Why little pieces?

Little pieces promote fingertip control and strength. They encourage the precise pinch that's used for crayons and pencils. Notice how well your child uses his/her fingers with little pieces. There's research to show that starting with small pieces encourages the correct grasp.

What about regular crayons and pencils?

There's nothing wrong with regular crayons and pencils, but you must show your child how to hold and use them properly. Save the pencils for later. Pencils are sharp pointed sticks and are inappropriate for beginners. Fat pencils and crayons are too heavy for little hands.

When should I start?

Start now. Show how to use crayons as soon as your child wants to color.

How do I show my child?

1. Teach your child to name the first three fingers: These are the thumb, the pointer, and the tall man.
2. Move them: Give a thumbs up and wiggle the thumb. Have your child point with the pointer finger, and then put the tall man beside the pointer finger.
3. Make a big open O pinch: This positions the thumb and pointer correctly.

What is the correct grip?

Here's a picture. Notice that there is a choice. Some children like to pinch with the thumb and pointer. That's the tripod (3-pinch with thumb and pointer, pencil rests on tall man). Others like the quadropod (4–pinch with thumb and pointer/tall man together, pencil rests on ring finger).

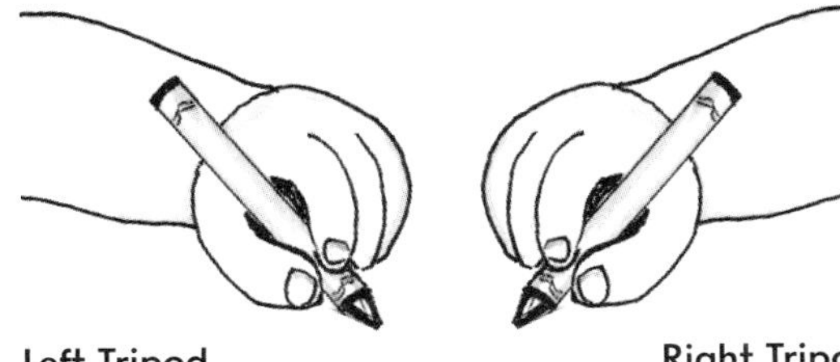

Left Tripod **Right Tripod**

Left Quadropod

Right Quadropod

What else can I do?

1. Pick up and drop! This is a fun way to practice placing the fingers correctly. Help your child pick up the pencil and get all the fingers placed. Then drop it! See if your child can put all the fingers back in the right place again. Repeat activity two or three times.
2. Aim and Scribble. Make tiny stars or spots on paper. Teach your child how to aim the crayon and land on a star to make it shine. Help the crayon hand rest on the paper with the elbow down and the hand touching the paper. Help the helper hand hold the paper. Now just wiggle the fingers to scribble.
3. Show your child how to hold and move the crayon to make different strokes, back and forth, up and down, round and round.

Help Me Write My Name

"That's my name. My name starts with ______." Maybe your child is trying to write or even make letters you can recognize. If so, then it's time to demonstrate how to write a few letters. Here's how:

Copy for Parents

1. Be a good example.
2. Write in all capitals.
3. Start every letter at the top.
4. Teach letters step by step.
5. Write on paper strips, placing a smiley face in the top left corner.

How can I be a good example?

Hold the crayon correctly. Your child will be watching how you form letters and hold the crayon or pencil. Be a good model. You may need to make a special effort to hold the crayon correctly.

Why should I use all capitals?

Capitals are the first letters that children can visually recognize and remember. They are the first letters children can physically write. If they can write their names correctly in capitals, you may introduce lowercase letters.

Does it matter where my student starts?

Yes, it does. English has one basic rule for both reading and writing: read and write from top to bottom, left to right. When you write with a child, always start at the top.

What do I say when I teach the letters?

Always say, "I start at the top." Then describe the part you're making. Say "big" or "little" for size. Say "line" or "curve" for shape. Let's look at **D** as an example: "I start at the top. I make a big line. Now I make a big curve."

What do I use and how do I do this?

Use two strips of paper, one for you and one for the child. Place your strip directly above the child's and demonstrate the first letter in the child's name. Say each step as you make the letter. Be sure the child can see the strokes as you write. (Avoid blocking the child's view with your hand.) Then tell the child to make the letter on his/her paper. Say the steps as the child writes them, encouraging the child to say the steps aloud with you. Continue letter by letter.

To Make Paper strips use a standard sheet of paper. Fold it in half the long way, and then in half again. Cut on folds to make four strips.

Extra Help

If the child struggles to imitate your letter, you may use a gray crayon to pre-write each letter on the child's paper. Do this letter by letter, and let the child crayon-trace over your letter. Make your gray letters progressively lighter and discontinue pre-writing as the child gains ability.

Pre-K Teaching Guidelines

These teaching guidelines are designed to make it easy to plan activities and lessons in your Pre-K classroom. Readiness & Writing activities can be incorporated any time during your school day. Each day is set up with two activities. Some days, the activities will be very quick. If you want more Readiness & Writing, supplement with Favorite Activities. The activity page in this teacher's guide will let you know if it is a small group or whole class activity.

For lessons in *My First School Book,* children should be seated at a table. Our CDs and the Favorite Activities have children moving about the room. The Letter & Number Play Activities are a little quieter and often have children seated.

For the first three weeks, children will participate in Wood Piece Play and social skill activities that will enhance fine and gross motor skills and body awareness. In week four, children start working in *My First School Book,* as you teach grip, colors, shapes, and Letter Play activities.

Writing a name is so important to children that we devoted weeks 7 and 14 to teaching name writing as we reinforce this key developmental milestone. We are committed to the order in which we teach letters – it is the easiest, most successful. But for individual children, we provide extra instruction on the letters in their name because children are motivated and excited about learning these special letters. Focus first on the letters that are easiest.

We continue with coloring and drawing skills as we move into pre-stroke, capital letter, and number teaching pages. Throughout, we offer plenty of opportunities for review and catch up, as well as opportunities for Letter & Number Play and Favorite Activities.

Letter & Number Play provides variety in your teaching as children learn how to form letters. Children can participate on the floor or at a table. Use these activities to introduce letters and to review letters throughout the year. They are listed below in developmental order. **Favorite Activities** engage children in key readiness activities that match their interests. Alternate among activities to keep lessons fun. Repeat these activities throughout the year.

Letter & Number Play

- Capitals with Letter Cards, p. 100
- Capitals with Mat, p. 101
- Roll-A-Dough Letters®, p. 102
- Stamp and See Screen®, p. 103
- A-B-C Touch & Flip® Cards, p. 104
- 1-2-3 Touch & Flip® Cards, p. 195
- Wet-Dry-Try on the Slate, pp. 105, 174-175

Favorite Activities

- Wood Pieces with Music, p. 85
- Build, Sing & Draw Mat Man®, pp. 36-39
- Shake Hands, p. 23
- Sign In Please!, p. 55
- Name of the Day, p. 57
- Music on the CDs, pp. 48-49, 58, 85, 114-115 176-177, 208-211

Numbers are taught starting at week eight, so you can introduce *I Know My Numbers* at that time. Take two weeks to complete each booklet before you send it home. Lowercase letter recognition activities begin at week 20 or sooner, if you choose. There are also two weeks built in near the end of the year for the Check Readiness assessment. You can find additional resources to support your teaching at **getsetforschool.com**.

Pre-K Teaching Guidelines

Notes

Week	Monday	Tuesday
1	**Readiness** Shake Hands, p. 23	**Readiness** Shake Hands, p. 23
	Pre-Writing Wood Pieces with Music, p. 85	*Sing Along* CD "Skip to My Lou"
2	**Readiness** Shake Hands, p. 23	**Alphabet Knowledge** ABC Sing & Point, p. 49
	Counting & Numbers Numbers & *Sing Along* CD, p. 176	**Pre-Writing** Wood Pieces with Music, p. 85
3	**Pre-Writing** Curves & Circles, pp. 92-93	**Drawing** Build, Sing & Draw Mat Man®, pp. 36-39
	Pre-Writing Wood Pieces with Music, p. 85	**Counting & Numbers** "Count On Me," p. 178
4	**Readiness** Teaching Crayon Grip, p. 28	*Sing Along* CD "Where Do You Start Your Letters?," p. 115
	Colors & Coloring Night Sky, p. 67	**Pre-Writing** Capitals with Letter Cards, p. 100
5	**Readiness** Teaching Crayon Grip, p. 28	**Drawing** Build, Sing & Draw Mat Man®, pp. 36-39
	Colors & Coloring Aim & Trace, p. 71	**Colors & Coloring** Red, p. 72
6	**Readiness** Teaching Crayon Grip, p. 28	**Pre-Writing** Stamp and See Screen®, p. 103
	Colors & Coloring Blue, p. 76	**Colors & Coloring** Orange, p. 77
7	**Alphabet Knowledge** Sign In Please!, p. 55	*Sing Along* CD "Where Do You Start Your Letters?," p. 115
	Writing Name, pp. 170-171	**Writing** Name, pp. 170-171
8	**Counting & Numbers** Count on Me, p. 178	*I Know My Numbers* 1 booklet, 2 weeks to complete, p. 196
	Counting & Numbers Wet-Dry-Try for 1, pp. 174-175	**Counting & Numbers** One - 1, p. 179

Wednesday	Thursday	Friday
Pre-Writing Polish, Sort & Trade Wood Pieces, p. 87	**Alphabet Knowledge** ABCs on *Sing Along* CD, p. 48	**Pre-Writing** Wood Pieces in a Bag, p. 88
Pre-Writing Wood Pieces with Music, p. 85	*Sing Along* CD "Ten Little Fingers," p. 26	**Pre-Writing** Wood Pieces with Music, p. 85
Alphabet Knowledge Alphabet Animals on Parade, p. 50	**Prewriting** Wood Pieces in a Box, p. 89	**Pre-Writing** Positions & Body Parts with Wood Pieces, pp. 90-91
Drawing Expressive Easel Art, p. 35	**Counting & Numbers** Numbers & *Sing Along* CD, p. 176	**Pre-Writing** Wood Pieces with Music, p. 85
Pre-Writing Vertical, Horizontal & Diagonal, pp. 94-95	**Alphabet Knowledge** Alphabet Animals on Parade, p. 50	**Pre-Writing** Vertical, Horizontal & Diagonal, pp. 94-95
Pre-Writing Wood Pieces with Music, p. 85	*Sing Along* CD "Where Do You Start Your Letters?," p. 115	**Pre-Writing** Wood Pieces with Music, p. 85
Readiness Teaching Crayon Grip, p. 28	**Pre-Writing** Capitals with the Mat, p. 101	**Readiness** Teaching Crayon Grip, p. 28
Colors & Coloring Twinkle, p. 68	**Colors & Coloring** Fireworks, p. 69	**Colors & Coloring** Aim & Color, p. 70
Alphabet Knowledge Sign In Please!, p. 55	**Pre-Writing** Roll-A-Dough Letters®, p. 102	**Readiness** Teaching Crayon Grip, p. 28
Colors & Coloring Green, p. 73	**Colors & Coloring** Yellow, p. 74	**Colors & Coloring** Purple, p. 75
Readiness Teaching Crayon Grip, p. 28	**Pre-Writing** A-B-C Touch & Flip® Cards, p. 104	**Alphabet Knowledge** Sign In Please!, p. 55
Colors & Coloring Pink, p. 78	**Alphabet Knowledge** ABC Sing & Point, p. 49	**Colors & Coloring** Brown, p. 79
Alphabet Knowledge Name of the Day, p. 57	**Alphabet Knowledge** ABC Sing & Point, p. 49	**Alphabet Knowledge** Wet-Dry-Try on the Slate, p. 105
Writing Name, pp. 170-171	**Writing** Name, pp. 170-171	**Writing** Name, pp. 170-171
Writing Chicks & Ducks, p. 116	**Drawing** Draw in *My Book*, p. 44	Favorite Activity
Counting & Numbers Numbers & *Sing Along* CD, p. 176	**Colors & Coloring** Gray, p. 80	**Colors & Coloring** Black, p. 81

Pre-K Teaching Guidelines

Notes

Week	Monday	Tuesday
9	Favorite Activity	Letter & Number Play
	Writing Bird Legs, p. 117	**Alphabet Knowledge** Capitals on the Edge, p. 52
10	**Counting & Numbers** Wet-Dry-Try for 2, pp. 174-175	*I Know My Numbers* 2 booklet, 2 weeks to complete, p. 196
	Counting & Numbers Bird Legs, p. 180	**Counting & Numbers** Two - 2, p. 181
11	**Counting & Numbers** Numbers & *Sing Along* CD, p. 176	Letter & Number Play for 2 and E
	Counting & Numbers Two - 2, p. 181	**Drawing** Draw in *My Book*, p. 44
12	**Counting & Numbers** Wet-Dry-Try for 3, pp. 174-175	Letter & Number Play for 3 and H
	Counting & Numbers That Would Be Me, p. 182	**Counting & Numbers** Three - 3, p. 183
13	**Counting & Numbers** Wet-Dry-Try for 3, pp. 174-175	Letter & Number Play for 3 and I
	Drawing Build, Sing & Draw Mat Man®, pp. 36-39	**Alphabet Knowledge** Letter & Picture Match, p. 54
14	**Alphabet Knowledge** Sign in Please!, p. 55	**Alphabet Knowledge** Name of the Day, p. 57
	Writing Name, pp. 170-171	**Writing** Name, pp. 170-171
15	Choice Play for 4	Wet-Dry-Try for 4
	Sing Along CD "Animal Legs," p. 184	**Counting & Numbers** Four - 4, p. 185
16	Wet-Dry-Try for 4	Letter Play for 4 and O
	Sing Along CD "Animal Legs," p. 184	**Writing** Pre-Stroke for O, p. 134

Wednesday	Thursday	Friday
Favorite Activity	Letter & Number Play	**Alphabet Knowledge** Name of the Day, p. 57
Writing Shape - Cross, p. 118	**Drawing** Draw in *My Book*, p. 44	**Writing** Letter L, p. 119
Favorite Activity	**Alphabet Knowledge** Three a Day - Capitals to Say, p. 51	**Pre-Writing** Wet-Dry-Try on the Slate for F
Writing Shape – Square, p. 120	Letter Play for F	**Writing** Letter F, p. 121
Letter Play for E Writing, Pre-Stroke for E, p. 122	**Alphabet Knowledge** CAPITALS on the Edge, p. 52	**Writing** Shape– Rectangle, p. 124
Writing Pre-Stroke for E, p.122	**Counting & Numbers** Wet-Dry-Try for 2, pp. 174-175	**Writing** Letter E, p. 123
I Know My Numbers 3 booklet, 2 weeks to complete, p. 196	Letter Play H and T	**Alphabet Knowledge** Name That Capital, p. 53
Writing Draw-Rectangle, p. 124	**Writing** Letter H, p. 125	**Writing** Letter T, p. 126
Sing Along CD "The Ant, the Bug & the Bee"	Letter Play I and U	Favorite Activity
Writing Letter I, p. 127	**Writing** "The Rain Song," p. 128	**Writing** Letter U, p. 129
Alphabet Knowledge ABC Sing & Point, p. 49	**Pre-Writing** Door Tracing, p. 107	Letter Play
Writing Name, pp. 170-171	**Writing** Name, pp. 170-171	**Writing** Name, pp. 170-171
I Know My Numbers 4 booklet, 2 weeks to complete, p. 196	**Writing** Make a Magic C Bunny, p. 130	Letter Play for C
Pre-Writing Door Tracing, p. 107	**Writing** Pre-Stroke for C, p. 132	**Writing** Letter C, p. 133
Alphabet Knowledge Letter & Picture Match, p. 54	Favorite Activity	*Sing, Sound & Count With Me* CD "Shape Song"
Writing Letter O, p. 135	**Drawing** Build, Sing & Draw Mat Man®, pp. 36-39	**Writing** Shape - Circle, p. 136

Pre-K Teaching Guidelines

Notes

Week	Monday	Tuesday
17	*Sing, Sound & Count With Me* CD "Five Fingers Play," p. 186	*I Know My Numbers* 5 booklet, 2 weeks to complete, p. 197
	Counting & Numbers Five - 5, p. 187	Choice Play for 5 and Q
18	Favorite Activity	Letter & Number Play for 5 and S
	Sing Along CD "Five Fingers Play," p. 186	**Writing** Pre-Stroke for S, p. 140
19	*Sing, Sound & Count With Me* CD "Counting, Counting"	*I Know My Numbers* 6 booklet, 2 weeks to complete, p. 197
	Counting & Number Six - 6, p. 188	**Writing** Pre-Stroke for D, P, B, R, p. 144
20	Favorite Activity	Choice Play for 6, D, P, and B
	Wet-Dry-Try for 6	**Alphabet Knowledge** Lowercase Letters on the Edge, p. 56
21	Favorite Activity	Letter Play for R
	Counting & Numbers 1-2-3 Touch & Flip® Cards, p. 195	**Writing** Pre-Stroke for R, p. 148
22	Favorite Activity	*I Know My Numbers* 7 booklet, 2 weeks to complete, p. 197
	Counting & Numbers Seven - 7, p. 189	**Alphabet Knowledge** Lowercase Matching, p. 60
23	Favorite Activity	Choice Letter & Number Play
	Counting & Numbers Wet-Dry-Try for 7, pp. 174-175	**Alphabet Knowledge** Lowercase Letters on the Edge, p. 56
24	**Counting & Numbers** Wet-Dry-Try for 8, pp. 174-175	*I Know My Numbers* 8 booklet, 2 weeks to complete, p. 197
	Counting & Numbers Eight - 8, p. 190	**Counting & Numbers** Legs 2-4-6-8, p. 191

Wednesday	Thursday	Friday
Wet-Dry-Try Q p. 105	Letter Play for Q and G	Favorite Activity
Writing Letter Q, p. 167	**Writing** Pre-Stroke for G, p. 138	**Writing** Letter G, p. 139
Favorite Activity	Letter Play for S and J	Favorite Activity
Writing Letter S, p. 141	**Writing** Pre-Stroke for J, p. 142	**Writing** Letter J, p. 143
Letter Play for D, P, B, and R	**Drawing** *Mat Man Shapes*, p. 41	**Alphabet Knowledge** Capitals on the Edge, p. 52
Writing Letter D, p. 145	**Writing** Letter P, p. 146	**Writing** Letter B, p. 147
Alphabet Knowledge Three a Day-Capitals to Say, p. 51	**Drawing** Draw with Line It Up™, p. 45	**Pre-Writing** Door Tracing, p. 107
Alphabet Knowledge Capital & Lowercase Letters, p. 59	*Rock, Rap, Tap & Learn* CD "Alphabet Boogie" & "Tapping to the ABCs," p. 58	**Counting & Numbers** Numbers & the *Sing, Sound & Count With Me* CD, p. 177
Sing, Sound & Count With Me CD "Counting Candles"	Letter Play for R or K	Favorite Activity
Writing Letter R, p. 149	**Writing** Pre-Stroke for K, p. 150	**Writing** Letter K, p. 151
Letter & Number Play for 7 and A	*Rock, Rap, Tap & Learn* CD Diagonals	Favorite Activity
Writing Pre-Stroke for A, p. 152	**Writing** Letter A, p. 153	**Writing** Shape - Triangle, p. 154
Drawing Draw with Line It Up™, p. 45	Choice Letter Play for M	**Pre-Writing** Door Tracing, p. 107
Writing Shapes - Diamond, p. 155	**Writing** Pre-Stroke for M, p. 156	**Writing** Letter M, p. 157
Letter & Number Play for 8 and N	Favorite Activity	**Drawing** Draw with Line It Up™, p. 45
Writing Pre-Stroke for N, p. 158	**Writing** Letter N, p. 159	**Writing** Shape Review, p. 160

Pre-K Teaching Guidelines

Notes

Week	Monday	Tuesday
25	Letter & Number Play	**Alphabet Knowledge** Three A Day - Capitals to Say, p. 51
	Rock, Rap, Tap & Learn CD "Alphabet Boogie"	**Alphabet Knowledge** Capital-Lowercase Matching, p. 61
26	**Counting and Numbers** Wet-Dry-Try for 9, pp. 174-175	*I Know My Numbers* 9 booklet, 2 weeks to complete, p. 197
	Counting and Numbers Nine - 9, p. 192	**Counting & Numbers** 1-2-3 Touch & Flip® Cards, p. 195
27	**Counting & Numbers** Wet-Dry-Try for 9, pp. 174-175	Letter & Number Play for 9 and/or Y
	Counting & Numbers 1-2-3 Touch & Flip® Cards, p. 195	**Alphabet Knowledge** Name that Capital, p. 53
28	Favorite Activity	*I Know My Numbers* 10 booklet, 2 weeks to complete, p. 197
	Counting & Numbers Ten - 10, p. 193	Favorite Activity
29	*Sing Along* CD "Ten Little Fingers"	Letter & Number Play
	Letter & Number Play	**Counting & Numbers** 1-2-3 Touch & Flip® Cards, p. 195
30	Review Numbers 1-5	Review Letters L F E H T I U
	Favorite Activity	Letter Play
31	Review Numbers 5-10	Review Letters C O Q G S J D P B R
	Favorite Activity	Letter Play
32	Review Letters K A M N V W X Y Z	Favorite Activity
	Letter Play	Letter Play
33-34	Check Readiness	Check Readiness
	Favorite Activity	Favorite Activity
35-36	Letter & Number Play	Letter & Number Play
	Favorite Activity	Favorite Activity

Wednesday	Thursday	Friday
Alphabet Knowledge ABC's on the *Rock, Rap, Tap & Learn* CD	Letter Play for V and W	Favorite Activity
Writing *Mat Man Shapes*, p. 161	**Writing** Pre-stroke V & W, p. 162	**Writing** Letter V, p. 163
Letter & Number Play for 9 and/or V and W	Letter Play for X	*Rock, Rap, Tap & Learn* CD "Sliding Down to the End of the Alphabet"
Writing Letter W, p. 164	**Alphabet Knowledge** Capital & Lowercase Letters, p. 59	**Writing** Letter X, p. 165
Favorite Activity	Letter Play for Y and Z	Favorite Activity
Writing Letter Y, p. 166	**Alphabet Knowledge** Lowercase letters on the Edge, p. 56	**Writing** Letter Z, p. 167
Letter & Number Play	**Writing** Line It Up™, p. 169	Choice Letter & Number Play
Counting & Numbers 1-2-3 Touch & Flip® Cards, p. 195	**Alphabet Knowledge** Name of the Day, p. 57	**Alphabet Knowledge** Capital-Lowercase Matching, p. 61
Alphabet Knowledge Alphabet Review, p. 168	**Writing** Line It Up™, p. 169	**Counting & Numbers** Number Review, p. 194
ABCs on the *Sing Along* CD, p. 46	**Alphabet Knowledge** Capital/Lowercase Matching, p. 61	**Counting & Numbers** Numbers on the *Sing Along* CD, p. 176
Review Numbers 1-5	Review Letters L F E H T I U	Review Numbers 1-5 Review Letters L F E H T I U
Favorite Activity	Letter Play	Favorite Activity
Review Numbers 5-10	Review Letters C O Q G S J D P B R	Review Numbers 5-10
Favorite Activity	Letter Play	Review Letters C O Q G S J D P B R
Review Letters K A M N V W X Y Z	Favorite Activity	Review Letters K A M N V W X Y Z
Letter Play	Letter Play	Letter Play
Check Readiness	Check Readiness	Check Readiness
Favorite Activity	Favorite Activity	Favorite Activity
Letter & Number Play	Letter & Number Play	Letter & Number Play
Favorite Activity	Favorite Activity	Favorite Activity

Index

Index

References

Amundson, S.J. 2001. "Prewriting and Handwriting Skills." *Occupational Therapy for Children,* 4th ed., edited by J. Case-Smith, 545-570. Sydney, Australia: Mosby.

Bailer, Kathleen. 2003. "Developmental Stages of Scribbling." Accessed August 2011. http://www.k-play.com/pdf/The%20Developmental%20Sta.pdf

Boyd, J., W.S. Barnett, E. Bordova, D.J. Leong, and D. Gomby. 2005. "Promoting Children's Social and Emotional Development Through Preschool Education." New Brunswick, NJ: National Institute for Early Education Research.

Cross, C.T., T.A. Woods, and H. Schweingruber, eds. 2009. *Mathematics Learning in Early Childhood: Paths Toward Excellence and Equity.* Washington, D.C.: The National Academies Press.

Gesell, A., H.M. Halverson, H. Thomson, F.L. Ilg, B.M. Castner, L.B. Ames, and C.S. Amatruda. 1940. *The First Five Years of Life: A Guide to the Study of the Preschool Child.* New York: Harper and Brothers.

Kenschaft, P.C. 2006. *Math Power: How to Help Your Child Love Math, Even If You Don't.* New York, NY: Pi Press.

Lust, C.A., and D. K. Donica. 2011. "Effectiveness of a Handwriting Readiness Program in Head Start: A Two-Group Controlled Trial." *American Journal of Occupational Therapy,* 65(5):560-568.

National Association for the Education of Young Children & International Reading Association. 1998. "Learning to Read and Write: Developmentally Appropriate Practices for Young Children." *Young Children,* 53(4):30-46. Accessed August 2011. http://www.naeyc.org/files/naeyc/file/positions/PSREAD98.pdf

National Center for Infants, Toddlers, and Families. 2011. "Learning to Write and Draw." *Zero to Three,* Accessed August 2011. http://www.zerotothree.org/early-care-education/early-language-literacy/writing-and-art-skills.html

Neuman, S.B., and K. Roskos. 2005. "Whatever Happened to Developmentally Appropriate Practice in Early Literacy?" *Young Children,* 60:22-26. Accessed September 2011. http://journal.naeyc.org/btj/200507/02Neuman.pdf

Robertson, Rachel. 2007. "The Meaning of Marks: Understanding and Nurturing Young Children's Writing Development." *Child Care Exchange,* 176:40-44.

Schneck, C.M. & Henderson, A. 1990. "Descriptive Analysis of the Developmental Progression of Grip Position for Pencil and Crayon in Nondysfunctional Children." *American Journal of Occupational Therapy,* 44, 893-900.

Strickland, D.S., and J.A. Schickedanz. 2009. *Learning About Print in Preschool,* 2nd ed. Newark, DE: International Reading Association.

The Albert Shanker Institute. 2009. *Preschool Curriculum: What's in It for Children and Teachers.* Washington, D.C.: The Albert Shanker Institute. Accessed August 2011. http://www.ashankerinst.org/Downloads/Early%20Childhood%2012-11-08.pdf

Yakimishyn, J.E., & J. Magill-Evans. 2002. "Comparisons Among Tools, Surface Orientation, and Pencil Grasp for Children 23 Months of Age." *American Journal of Occupational Therapy,* 56:564-572.

GET SET FOR SCHOOL®
A
Big line
Big line
Little line
B
Big line
Little curve
Little curve
C
Big C curve
D
Big line
Big curve
E
Big line
Little line
Little line
Little line
F
Big line
Little line
Little line
G
Big curve
Little line
Little line
H
Big line
Big line
Little line
I
Big line
Little line
Little line
J
Big line
Turn
Little line
K
Big line
Little line
Little line
L
Big line
Little line
M
Big line
Big line
Big line
Big line
N
Big line
Big line
Big line
O
Big C curve
Keep going
P
Big line
Little curve
Q
Big C curve
Keep going
Little line
R
Big line
Little curve
Little line
S
Little curve
Turn
Little curve
T
Big line
Little line
U
Big line
Turn
Big line
V
Big line
Big line
W
Big line
Big line
Big line
Big line
X
Big line
Big line
Y
Little line
Big line
Z
Little line
Big line
Little line